the Ugly One in the middle

ALEX STAN CAMPBELL

Alexis Broadcasting Company
Niagara Falls, Ontario
and
Niagara Falls, New York

Printed in the United States of America

This book is an autobiography
Events and locations are written to the best of my recollection.
Some names have been changed, and some dialogue is
paraphrased based upon my best memories of the events, the
individuals, and their respective language choices.

First Hardcover Edition March 21, 2014

Cover art created by Peter Farmer, Montréal, Québec
Cover and book design by Tuchi Ramirez
Book layout by Debora Lewis

ISBN 978-0-9936550-1-2

ACKNOWLEDGEMENTS

Dedicated to Martica, without whose constant encouragement and inspiration I would never have finished the book that I began writing before I met her.
Also, dedicated to Ben Jewer. He unwittingly named this book.

Thank you to the following people:
First, Paulette Kinnes, my patient editor, who caught my typos, grammar and punctuation errors, and timeline slip-ups, but most of all, grasped my twisted sense of humor.

Special thanks to author-mentor Annie Wilder for providing the first independent review and who lit a fire of inspiration and motivation under me to finish the book.

Paul Sauvé, whose picky eyes first corrected my grammar and spelling and who laughed in all the right places.
Juan Ramirez, who wisely dissected the manuscript and suggested what to leave in and what to leave out.

Artist Peter Farmer, who created the book cover design and tolerated my indecision.
And, to those who kept asking, "When will we get to read your book?"

Contents

Prologue

My roommate, Cyndi, warned me. "Stan, you are crazy for doing this. You will be kidnapped or murdered or both."

My closest friends declared me insane. I knew that many others before me had been kidnapped, killed, tortured, or simply vanished. The U.S. State Department warned Americans of the danger. Of course I was fearful, but I resolved to take a chance, and just in case one of these unfortunate events occurred, I made a plan. The day before my flight to fear, I bought a one-size-fits-all Will kit at Staples, filled in the blanks, and printed it on my last six sheets of legal paper. I read it over. It was a pathetic document. I really didn't need a Will. I shared an apartment with a former co-worker and platonic friend, Cyndi. I owned a double bed in which I had been sleeping single for the past year; a wicker chest of drawers; and a worn, hideous, blue-pastel floral-design couch that my un-platonic friend Allison had given to me after Goodwill refused to take it. My most valuable asset, an 80-CD set, *The History of Rock 'n' Roll*. At least my kids would have that, even if they didn't recognize Fats Domino or Herman's Hermits.

A space for four witnesses filled the last half of page six. The only place where I knew four people in one bunch was at the radio station, WKLT in Traverse City, Michigan, where I had been axed several months previously after the partnership of *Stan & Dean* blew up in a wall-pounding brawl during a morning show.

ing a friendly firing, I received twelve weeks of severance pay, so I assumed that a farewell visit might be acceptable.

My former co-workers at the station were friendly, probably because they knew that I wasn't sticking around. The station receptionist, Patty, agreed to sign, even though I knew that she hated my guts. She signed the date, Thursday May 24, 2001. I involuntarily attracted a crowd of curious and somewhat amused staff members. The word was out. Stan Campbell had lost his mind...again. They seemed to delight in that assumption.

My ex-boss, Richard, always dressed in his pin-striped executive suit, with glossy, slicked back hair, who had fired me politely several months before, shouted from the conference room, "Stan, you're going *where*?"

I chuckled, only slightly embarrassed and a bit proud.

"You'll never learn will you, Campbell?"

"Yeah, you may be right, Richard."

There was no turning back now. I had the airline tickets, purchased on a maxed-out MasterCard, and my Canadian passport. As instructed, I wore my black double-breasted suit with a pink shirt and a Jerry Garcia tie. My friend Dale drove me to the Cherry Capitol Airport in Traverse City for my day-long flight to another hemisphere.

*   *   *

Hours and almost half a world later, the view from the window in seat F17 added to my mounting panic. Outside, the scene evolved eerily like an alien planet with sheer crimson cliffs to my right towering over us, two to three miles high. Passing under me at about four hundred and fifty miles per hour, a plateau of deep blue emerged with black holes terminating somewhere in infinity.

It was 7:22 p.m. I felt sick, and I felt alone. Richard's words grew louder in my head. I heard his cynical, gleeful laughter all morning on the flight from Traverse City to Miami, and it grew louder on this final leg of my flight. Maybe Richard had it right. Maybe I would never learn. Maybe I was going too far this time, literally. My friends and family were aware that I had a long and infamous history with women, but this time, it was a potential life-threatening venture.

I had exited marriage number four with Susan six months previously. We had been married for a dozen years. The tears on the divorce papers were barely dry. I had promised my counselor that I would not repeat the same mistakes. Yet, in spite of my promises to my counselor and to myself, I was in pursuit of another woman. *Why do I keep doing this? Maybe I should have spent more time chasing my mystery mother, whoever she was. I doubted that my father hung around until the sun came up.*

"This is crazy. I'm going to the most dangerous country on earth, on purpose," I muttered to myself, loud enough for the teenaged kid next to me to avoid me by escaping to the bathroom.

I had read a lot of chilling stories of killings, kidnappings, violence, torture, and the *millionaire ride*. That's when you flag down a taxi, but it's a fake one that takes you out into the country where a few less-than-charming pals strip you of your belongings, and if you're really lucky, you get to live. I would not flag down a taxi in front of the airport. Instead, a woman I had never met had agreed to meet me at the airport and take me to a hotel that she had arranged for me.

What if she took me on a millionaire ride? Hey, I'd fool her. I would show her my Will. She could travel to Michigan for a double bed; my ugly, blue, paisley couch; and my History of Rock 'n' Roll. When she and her amigos realized that all I had was a pile of useless crap, they would hack off my limbs, or worse.

Ahh, this is nuts. Stop thinking like that!

Do you remember the last scenes in the TV show *Touched by an Angel* when the top of Roma Downey's head glowed? I'm relatively sure that that happened to me. In the middle of a full-bore panic at my stupidity and the fact that no matter how much I begged, I knew that the captain would not return to Miami to let me off, at least not without restraints.

I imagined that I heard a disembodied voice say, *it will be all right, my son*, as a yellow radiance encircled my head. Had I really heard that? Did I envision a glow over my head, or maybe it was just the overhead reading lamp? Was it God, my Guardian Angel, Roma Downey, or food poisoning from the American Airlines chicken-salad sandwich?

Whatever or whoever it was conferred on me an uneasy sense of calm. I felt like this adventure was going to be okay, or was that how people felt when they were about to die? I was traveling to Colombia, infamous for drug lords, guerillas, kidnappings, and murder, especially of white-faced gringos like me. Would the kidnappers show me mercy if I showed them my Canadian passport? I was simply a guy from Jamesville West, a wide spot in the road in Cape Breton, Nova Scotia, and this was about to be life-altering event number two of three. Life-altering event number one had almost killed me. Maybe this one would.

My Mouth Organ

"Why do you care about what they think?" my daughter Helen asked me recently when I worried aloud about how people viewed me where I grew up in Jamesville West in Iona parish. If you inquire around that community in the middle of Cape Breton Island, Nova Scotia, you'll likely hear that I was married and divorced six...no...maybe nine times and that I threw my mother into the ditch after my Dad died and then tried to abscond with her money. I had done a drunken *Dukes of Hazzard* flight through the air over a fence on a Saturday night next to the church for the entertainment of folks on their way to Mass on Sunday morning. The parish priest even alleged that I, with a local accomplice, had embezzled money from a parish youth group. I was one bad cat, but they didn't know the half of it.

It's easy to say that you don't care what people think of you. If that was really true, we might do our grocery shopping naked. I did care how they viewed me. These were still my people, sort of. Truthfully, they weren't my people at all, but I'll get to that later.

I had earned some of my infamy. I had married almost as many times as Liz Taylor, if you don't count the times that she married the same guy twice. About the embezzling part...I admit it. I did steal...but not what they alleged.

* * *

I was 6, and I wanted a harmonica, bad! I simply assumed that I could play one. You blow into it and music comes out. My grandfather, John R. Campbell, owned the general store down the hill and across the Canadian National Railway tracks from our house. Grandpa was also the Justice of the Peace, School Superintendent, Postmaster, and big-wig in the Liberal Party.

My grandparents, John R. and Nellie, lived in the back of the store and upstairs above the post office. They sometimes foolishly left me alone in the store to alert them if a customer came in. Sometimes, I was overcome with temptation.

I squeezed my hand under the glass of the candy showcase and snatched a Sweet Marie chocolate bar and then hollered, "I'm going to the toilet, Grandpa!"

I ran out to the two-holer outhouse. I was immune to the stench as I munched through the scrumptious chocolate and nuts bonbon in record time, but afterward my chocolate face gave me away. On more than one occasion I got nabbed with my arm under the glass about to grab a goodie.

The T. Eaton summer catalog was my wish book and my poor-man's Playboy as I perused the bra and panties section. I liked girls a lot. One day I would be with someone who loved me madly. Most of all, I salivated over the harmonicas, mouth organs my father called them. I coveted the Hohner Marine Band Harmonica. It cost a dollar twenty-nine, a lot of money for a 6-year-old kid. I begged my father Roddie for the money.

"Cripes Almighty, what are you going to do with a mouth organ?" he mumbled with his face stuck behind the pages of the *Post-Record* newspaper.

My father was relatively tall, with a creased face and dimpled chin and upper lip. He reminded me of the actor Robert Mitchum. He sounded a bit like Mitchum too but with an unhurried, low-range Cape Breton brogue.

I was unrelenting. He was steadfast. No money. No harmonica.

I hatched a plan. I spent a Saturday afternoon hanging around the John R. Campbell General Dry Goods store helping Grandpa carry boxes of Rinso laundry detergent from the back shop and placing them on the shelves. I knew that eventually he would leave, if only for a few minutes. I would be alone in the store, as long as no customers came by. My grandmother rarely came out to the store.

After an interminable wait, he declared that he had to, as he put it, go do his business. I knew that that did not mean that he was going to meet with the Postmaster General. He directed me to keep an eye on the store and run out and notify him if a customer came in. I waited the appropriate time until I was sure that his pants were at his ankles. I crept around the counter and pulled open the wooden till with the brass handle. Dollar bills were in one row, two dollar bills in another, and round wooden cups held the coppers, nickels, dimes, quarters, and fifty-cent pieces. I studied the layout. Should I take the change or a dollar and some change? My math was fuzzy. I listened for his footsteps. I decided. I clutched a dollar bill, two quarters, and assorted change. I pocketed my booty and slammed the till shut, maybe too loudly. I zipped around the counter, knocking a can of Old Chum chewing tobacco onto the floor. I placed it back on the counter as Grandpa rounded the corner, coming in the front door instead of the usual entrance from the kitchen. That was strange.

I gazed at him with big eyes. He froze. He spoke not a word for a long minute.

Finally, he with his back to me, he said, "Stanley, I think it's time for you to run on home."

Was it my imagination, or had his demeanor changed? I ran up the hill to our unpainted gray salt-box house with dreams of becoming a celebrated mouth organ player and amazing my friends and our pretty next-door neighbor, Faye Gillis. She was four years older than I was, but I loved Faye. I thought I would marry her one day.

I had seen my mother Tena order shirts, long underwear, socks, dishes, a washboard, and salt and pepper shakers from the T. Eaton catalog. She filled out the order form, got a money order at the post office, and sent it along to the T. Eaton Company. I had to skip the money order part because I knew that Grandpa would inquire where I had gotten the money. He was nosy, anyway.

Often, when my mother asked Grandpa, the Postmaster, for a money order for the T. Eaton Company, he queried her. "Does Roddie know that you are ordering this?"

I figured that I should send the cash to the T. Eaton Company. I tore the order form out of the catalog, wrote down Honor Harmonica with the item number, and enclosed it in an envelope. I had been sleeping on a couch in the kitchen, near the wood stove, so I stuck the envelope into a crack in the leather. The next morning, I planned to steal a stamp from my Mom's stationery drawer and place it into a mailbag in Grandpa's post office without him seeing it.

The next morning was a Sunday. No mail. Church instead. Mass flew by in thirty-five minutes. My father liked a rapid Mass. My parents never missed Mass, because the Roman Catholic Church demanded that you attend. However, no rules existed about speed.

"Father Rankin was fast today, in and out in just over a half-hour. That's the way to do it!" Papa beamed on the way home but his mood changed before you could say amen. My father, whom I called Papa as a child, turned and shot me a cold, discomforting glare. He rarely made eye contact when he talked to me, but not that day. There was to be a detour.

"Stanley, we need to stop at Grandpa's."

"Papa, can we go later?"

I knew that something was up and that it probably wasn't good.

"No, come along, Stanley. Grandpa wants to talk to you."

I wanted to pee. When you were in shit with Grandpa, he could make you feel one inch tall with merely a stern stare over his glasses and a stroke of his gray moustache. He was short but bigger than life and radiated authority. He wore a shirt and tie with a pin-striped vest every day of his life, adding to his intimidating reputation.

Off we went down the half-mile hill to Grandpa's place. We didn't go to the store. We went in the kitchen door, where normally-smiling Grandma was not smiling.

She peered at me over her glasses and much too melodiously and sternly greeted me. "Hello, Stanley."

Uncle Arthur, my radio buddy leaned in a doorway, observing my impending doom. Uncle Arthur and I listened late at night by the light of an amber dial to *Boston Blackie*, *The Shadow*, and Joe Louis and Jersey Joe Walcott fight to the finish. No radio today. Papa told me to sit down. Grandpa stood in front of me. I was pretty sure that we were not going to recite the rosary. He observed me for a moment like only mustachioed old men with dark, piercing, eyes can do. I sank, as much as one can, into the hard wooden chair.

He waited and then spoke. "Stanley, tell me the truth, did you take some money from the till in the store yesterday?"

He sure gets right to the point.

"Uh, Grandpa, what till?"

I knew that that was not the reply he was waiting for and that it was not going to go well for me. I desperately wanted to be somewhere else, like maybe in the chicken coop leaping into the air, terrorizing the hens.

My father chimed in. "You know very well what till."

Meanwhile, Uncle Arthur appeared to be mildly amused. I was not. I gawked at him with pitiful eyes that begged, *come on, defend me, you're my friend!*

"Let me ask you again, Stanley, did you take money out of the till in the store?"

I guess Grandpa had to add *in the store* so I couldn't pretend that I didn't know where the store was.

I hated it when my tears appeared, my mouth and chin quivered and then, uncontrollably, a sob burst from somewhere in my throat. I needed to pee. I had been caught with my hand in the till. Grandpa had seen me through the store window as he returned from the outdoor toilet, the wrong way.

The words fell out of my mouth through hiccupping sobs. "I wanted the money to buy a mouth organ."

Grandpa, Grandma, Uncle Arthur, and Papa stood back, hesitated, and then blurted in unison. "A mouth organ?"

Papa weighed in. "What the devil are *you* going to do with a mouth organ?"

He emphasized, *you.*

I was not only humiliated by being caught, I felt insulted. Didn't they think that I just might be able to play a mouth organ? I was mad. My already well-known temper neared the exploding point, but I wisely held it.

Grandpa leaned in closer to my face. "What did you do with the money?"

"In the couch crack."

"Where?"

I explained about the kitchen couch and the crack in the leather. They agreed to wait while I went to fetch it. I ran up the hill to home, glad to be out of the courtroom. I returned and sheepishly handed the envelope over. Then the lecture came. Sternly Grandpa commanded me to never, ever go behind the counter again. I promised and I meant it.

Meanwhile, Mama remained unaware about the whole matter until Papa told her that night.

Her first words were mocking. "A mouth organ? What were *you* going to do with a mouth organ?"

I'd show them some day. I would be famous, and I would have a pretty girl who would love me, and I would get drunk and sing Gaelic songs like our neighbor Angus MacKinnon. But one thing was for sure. I terminated my robbery life. But it would not be the last time that I would be accused of larcenous and licentious behavior.

Boogie Nights

"You'll have to talk loud. Tena is as deaf as a doornail," Aunt Ethel hollered to her friend Olive, as though Olive was the one who was deaf.

At age 6, I didn't fully comprehend deaf doornails, but I learned early that my mother's quiet and indifferent attitude came not from a personality trait but was due to the fact that seldom did she hear what people were saying around her. She was critically hard of hearing as a result of a serious bout with rheumatic fever before I came into her life.

She was pretty and bashful. She wore heavy, thick glasses that she habitually had to push back up on her tiny nose. She regularly stared into space while friends and family around her engaged in conversation.

My mother's hearing acuity seemed to change regularly with her moods. Not long after I learned to say Papa and Mama, it became apparent to me that she frequently heard all the words about the events that my father or I did not want her to hear.

On the other hand, she did hear me ask my best friend Howard, in my room down the hall and around the corner, "Did you get the cigarettes?"

There were times when Mama sat with a pleasant wistful visage and sporadically snickered for no apparent reason. I never understood this. As a younger child, I thought that maybe she heard fairies, angels, or on a good day, the Virgin Mary. Her devotion to the Blessed Virgin was extraordinary. It occurred to me that she and Mary had a lot in common. I assumed that she had to be a virgin, and therefore, holy. I could not imagine my mother in an intimate embrace with my father

To say that my parents were not a loving couple would be a huge understatement. I never once saw them embrace or be intimate with each other. I never heard the words *I love you*, but back then, many kids didn't. They never said it to each other that I know of, and certainly never to me.

I do remember rare moments of affection from my mother. On occasion, my father would sit me in his lap and for fun, rubbed the top of my head with his whiskery chin. I guess that could be viewed as affection.

Christena MacDonald was a slim, classy, and attractive lady in the 1930s from Port Morien, Nova Scotia, when she met my father, Roddie Campbell, from Jamesville West while visiting her best friend, Catherine McClusky, up the road in Ottawa Brook. Tena was 28, with wavy, black hair and snow-white skin. She was cultured, stylish, and shy. My father, rough-edged and unrefined with his table manners, managed to impress her. He had recently graduated from the Nova Scotia Agricultural College and held dreams of being an advanced new-age farmer. He enjoyed more than his share of dark rum and clear moonshine.

After a short courtship, somehow, he convinced the lovely Christena to marry him. Roddie and Tena were joined in holy matrimony in Iona, Nova Scotia, on the 17th of September in 1938.

Two years passed with no babies in sight. Roddie worked the farm, bequeathed to him by his Uncle Angus. Tena helped and took on the role of farmer's wife, though she was a city girl. It was lonely in Jamesville West, forty muddy miles from the steel mill city of Sydney, Nova Scotia. Jamesville West consisted of four houses, including our unpainted gray house on the hill, the O'Donnell's, my grandparents' down the hill across the railroad tracks, and the more well-to-do Campbell's across the hayfield next door.

Tena missed the city and her friends, even though her dearest friend Catherine McClusky lived three miles down the road.

Down the road was a long hike. Roddie and Tena had access to a horse and buggy, but convincing Roddie to hitch up and take Tena to visit her friend was a challenge. In fact, he wasn't that fond of the McCluskys. Little by little, tension developed.

World War II began in earnest, and Roddie's pals, the Murphy boys, were off to take on Adolph Hitler. For reasons unknown to me, Roddie did not volunteer. Instead, Roddie and Tena discussed having a child. Eventually they got together, and I arrived.

My earliest memory is of lying in what I assume was a crib, peeking through bars. At least, I think it was a crib. Jail wasn't going to happen for at least eighteen years.

Not everybody went to fight the Germans, apparently. Sufficient males remained behind to initiate a roaring good *ceilidh* in our kitchen. They sat around the best-smelling and warmest room in the house drinking foul-smelling bull beer, holding hands, and singing Gaelic songs, all the while banging their feet down hard on the cold linoleum floor in time to their music. The party did not include me. Papa carried me off to bed just as the fun commenced. I can still smell my father's breath as he exhaled the rancid stench of bull beer.

Bull beer was unique. We lived forty miles from a liquor store, and besides, booze was expensive. So some local folks made their own beer. They were Scottish and clearly descendants of the people who had invented another repulsive concoction, haggis.

Bull beer is made with molasses, brown sugar, yeast, and of course, water. A few home brewers added potatoes, simply because we had lots of those. Several gallons of this potion were stored in a barrel in the woods, or a barn away from prying old ladies and the Mounties. The sickly brown blend fermented for a week or two, depending upon the date of the next ceilidh. If the amateur brewer was patient, the brown, muddy swill grew potent but tasted like bad cheese. Finally, the beer-maker bottled the potion in jam jars or old liquor bottles, and stored it for the next event. The only thing more putrid was when someone threw up after consuming bull beer. That happened a lot.

The more serious brewer raised the process up to a second dodgier step. It required more technical equipment, namely copper tubing and a boiler. Yes, a still. Moonshine. A few resourceful individuals added bleach to clarify the final explosive drink. No warning labels existed, so a few innocent souls drank it.

The ceilidh volume at our house increased dramatically thanks to a bottle of *shine,* as we called it. Occasionally, the moonshine contributed to a few fistfights.

When the ceilidh took place at our house, my father didn't invite me. But how could a kid sleep with all that singing, roaring, and stomping going on? Then, things grew creepy with the *bochdan* tales. That's when the old-timers told stories of meeting the devil late at night on a shadowy road or having seen a mammoth talking dog with hooves. I heard the stories from my darkened bedroom, and the terrifying tales frightened me to death.

It got worse when my father unexpectedly pounded on the other side of my bedroom wall with his fist and bellowed in a great growling voice, "I'm the boogeyman. Go to sleep!"

That was one more character that freaked me out. The boogeyman! I never saw him, but I had a good idea that he didn't look like James Brown, and if he showed up, it wouldn't be to boogie.

* * *

There were moments and periods of strife in my parents' life. My mom suffered from a nervous condition, which flared up at times.

One summer evening, wild-eyed, she took my hand and whispered, "Hurry, come with me, Stanley, they're after us!"

She pulled me along, running behind her out the door and down through a hayfield and into the woods. I was frightened. I wasn't sure if I should be scared of whoever was chasing us or if I should be afraid of Mama.

Luckily, we were in full view of Grandpa's store, where Papa and the Murphy boys sat outside telling war stories.

Hughie Murphy noticed my mother disappear into the woods with me in tow. "Roddie, where are Tena and Stanley going?"

Immediately, Papa knew.

Papa shouted as he ran, "Help me, we have to catch her."

They sprinted a half-mile up the hill and found both of us cowering in front of an invisible enemy. The Murphy boys, more than my father, reassured Mama that they would protect her. I got the sense that she trusted the Murphy boys more than she trusted my father.

My mother vanished a few days later. No one told me why, but Papa told me that she had simply gone away to Sydney for a while. I was worried and feared for her. A few weeks later she returned, apparently much more tranquil. In fact, she seemed like she was in a different world. A year later, she disappeared again.

My mom loved the city, especially Sydney, a steel mill –city of about thirty-five thousand, forty miles away. She loathed the country, what with having to milk cows, shovel cow shit every morning, feed the pig and chickens, and then bake, make meals, and do the laundry. She carried snow from outdoors in buckets to melt on the coal stove to have enough water to do laundry with a scrub board and a galvanized tub.

I helped her collect the snow and found out that it takes an Everest-sized mountain of snow to fill a washtub with water. To get the stove hot enough to melt the mountain of snow, she carried coal from the frozen coal pile behind the house. I suggested that if she set the coal pile on fire she could melt the snow. She didn't buy into that idea.

My father gave up on his dream farm when he found out that the Canadian National Railway paid a lot more money, and every two weeks. My mother became the full-time farmer. My father claimed that his job as a section foreman on the CNR was hard work, but each time I visited him, I caught him and the section gang sleeping in the railway bunkhouse.

Occasionally, though, on a day when Papa and his gang needed to replace a rail, I got a ride with them on the Speedie, a putt-putt four wheeler for the rails. I loved the joy ride with the wind blowing in my hair, but the thought of a train racing toward us around the next curve worried me. In that case, throw the Speedie into reverse, and go like hell to the next railroad crossing, and yank the rig off the tracks in the nick of time. I reasoned that maybe if his railway life wasn't hard, it was dangerous.

On most days, Papa arrived home at 4:30 p.m. dressed in his Carhartt overalls and striped railway cap, smelling like grease and creosote. On Fridays, he smelled like Governor General rum.

He usually asked as he crossed the threshold, "Tena! Is supper ready?"

It usually was.

He wolfed down his supper, but if something was missing, such as salt, considered a spice in our family, he shouted, "Tena, I need salt."

He expected to be served. Usually, my mother silently complied.

On rare occasions, my mom whirled around, glowered, and presented an option. "Get off your lazy arse and get it yourself!"

That response both shocked and amused me. She so rarely spoke up for herself. When she did, the response was met with a few unintelligible murmurs from Papa. Normally, Mama dutifully waited on him, and only after he had devoured supper did she sit down and eat. Before she took her first bite, Papa fell asleep on the couch.

After my father had had too many hooters of rum one weekend in June of 1948, my mother hit the breaking point. He had been carousing with his friends while working short hours on the railroad. My mom, the demure, once-stylish Tena, had evolved into a milkmaid, pig-slopper, egg-gatherer, cook, bottle-washer, dish washer, and shit-shoveler in the barn. She was exhausted, angry, and fed up, and she missed her friends and her life in Sydney. To my mother, the city of Sydney was the center of the universe.

She found a driver, and quicker than you can say cow shit, she disappeared down the road, but before she left, she took me aside and explained that she had to go away for awhile. I thought that I should wake Papa, who was asleep in the hollow that he had made in the living room couch.

When the realization hit him that she was gone and maybe never coming back, my father ran down the hill with me running behind. I was worried. Who would feed us? Would I be home alone while Papa went to work? Besides, I missed her occasional hugs.

Papa and I strode into the kitchen where Grandma was busy kneading dough on the wooden kitchen table. Then, I witnessed something that I had never seen before. It shocked me to the core. My father cried... bawled openly. Grandpa came in from the store and stopped in the doorway, gazing at Papa disapprovingly. He seemed embarrassed that his son, a grown man, was crying openly.

"Tena left me."

I gradually backed into Grandma's rocking chair by the window and gazed at my grandparents, expecting them to do or say something to make this uncomfortable scene end.

Grandpa was apparently undaunted. "Och, she'll come back, Roddie."

Then Grandpa used a few Gaelic words that I didn't quite grasp but figured that they translated to *knock off the whimpering*!

Grandma was more sympathetic. "Yes, I wouldn't worry. She needs some time with her friends in Sydney. But you would do well to be nicer to her, Roddie."

Grandpa admonished him. "Now stop that crying. It's not good for Stanley to see that."

Papa dried his face and blubbered. "I want her to come home."

Grandma placed her hand on Papa's shoulder. "You might think about getting that bedroom set that she's been wanting. She showed it to me in the Eaton's catalog."

"What bedroom set?"

"For Mercy's sake, do you not listen when she talks to you?"

I knew that he didn't pay any attention when my mother talked to him. He mostly mumbled an acknowledgement that my mother had spoken, but had no idea what she had said.

When she caught him ignoring her, without warning, she shrilled loudly enough to cause crows outside on the fence to fly away. "Roddie! Are you listening to me?"

Papa and I both jumped several inches off our chairs. She got his attention, and mine.

Two weeks later, on a Saturday, four large cardboard boxes consumed all the extra space in the living room. I had been staying with Grandma and Grandpa in my mother's absence, but I got to return to the house with Papa on Saturday afternoon. He wore a clean white shirt and a tie, something I had only seen him wear on Sundays.

His mood was unusually good. I heard a car outside. That was a big deal. Not many cars drove up the rut-filled road to our house. I ran out in time to see a man and a woman step out of the car. The man opened the back door as Papa went out the kitchen door. I spotted Mama! She looked beautiful. I ran to her. Papa spoke to the driver for a moment. Then, Papa turned and faced my mother. It was the first time, maybe the only time, that I had ever seen him hug her. She seemed somewhat happy to be home, but I detected hesitation to go into our house.

Papa directed her to the living room and showed off a bureau with a large oval mirror, two bedside tables, and a chest of drawers. She giggled with enthusiasm. Her giggle was one of her most endearing qualities until the day she died.

It didn't take more than twelve hours for life to return to normal between Roddie and Tena. She spoke, he ignored her. He mumbled. She never heard him. I'm not sure that my mother ever heard my father. He spoke with one of those low-range voices that one can hear through a concrete wall but never understand.

Mama eventually bought a hearing aid. The two-pound black brick had vacuum tubes that required a hydro electric plant to light up. The hearing aid was heavy, but the battery was heavier than the one in my Uncle Arthur's Jeep. It also protruded from her dress like an electric tumor while it squealed and hissed. It had some advantages, though. When my father grumbled incessantly about the damn weather, she shut it off.

I imagined that Mama knew Mary, the Mother of Jesus, personally. After all, my mother was devoted to her.

I overheard my favorite Aunt Ethel describe Mama to my father. "Tena is a saint if ever there was one."

I believed her. As I grew older, I became increasingly exasperated with my father's inability to communicate with Mama, so I attempted to fill the void. Even at age 7, I learned to speak with greater resonance and a pitch higher than my normal speaking voice. It was as if I could cause her to tune in to me. I noticed that she heard me when I spoke that way, and I didn't have to shout.

I also believe that my desire to communicate with my mother in dulcet tones was a portal to a future career. I was blessed with a decent voice, but it was honed by my desire to be heard by a bashful woman who simply giggled instead of saying, *I didn't hear you.*

Talking to my mother and being understood made me feel good. I felt like I was able to do something my father couldn't, make myself understood.

I figured that if it worked with my mother, then maybe it would work with the hens. I liked hens. We had twenty or thirty of them. There were no boys or girls my age nearby, just me and my imaginary friends, and the hens.

One boring days, which was mostly every day, I ran to our henhouse. In the daytime, the hens pecked around the barnyard and were not especially interested in me. However, in the evening, they became a captive audience, all sitting obediently on their roosts in the henhouse.

One evening in late August of 1948, as most of the hens slept, I readied my act. I stood and surveyed my audience. The ones still awake kept a wary eye on me. They weren't prepared for me but, *Heeeere's Stanley!*

I began by telling them stories that I made up, in sort of a primitive Cape Breton improv. I blathered on for what must have been five or ten minutes but noticed that instead of my fine feathered captive friends being captivated, my words apparently lulled the nervous hens to sleep, as they squatted down on their nests.

I felt offended. As an act, I was dying. I needed to liven up that bunch. I leapt into the air with arms flailing while shrieking like a possessed banshee. I elicited an immediate response. Hens, feathers, dust, fleas, and dried hen shit flew everywhere, accompanied by screeching, squawking, and fowl flinging into the walls and each other. The rooster was most upset. I felt fulfilled. I had gotten their attention, damn them.

My act also aroused the attention of our farm-hand, Ronald. From what I remember, Ronald was hired to help out on the farm when my father went to work on the railroad, shortly after my mother stated unequivocally that she would no longer sling cow shit.

Ronald rounded the corner and rushed in through the doorway. He seized me by the collar of my tweed coat and threw me against the wall. I picked myself up off the floor in time for him to grab me again and pull my pants down to my ankles. Ronald took off his leather gloves and used both of them as a weapon to redden my arse. I squirmed loose, pulled up my pants, and ran out crying, promising to never rile the hens again.

I couldn't stop. Show business was in my blood. My hen harassment persisted. Each time I staged my chicken dance in the henhouse, Ronald caught me and whipped my pants down and tanned my arse with apparent glee.

Our gray house on the hill was not large. We didn't have a name for the house style then, but today it would be a salt-box or Cape Cod. It had two bedrooms, a big kitchen with a couch in it, and a parlor that no one ever entered. Well, maybe the parish priest, if he ever came to visit to perform an exorcism on the possessed kid in the house.

Thanks to our under-sized house, Ronald and I had to share a bed. At first, I thought it was fun because he liked to play games in bed by grabbing my *bird*, as he called it.

He chuckled and asked, "What's that?"

I squirmed and answered, "I don't know"

I knew what it was but didn't want to say. I figured that bird was as good a name for it as any. I assumed that that's what everyone called it.

After several months, for no apparent reason, I told my mother that Ronald liked to play with my bird. Her reaction was instantaneous. Her hearing did not fail. Not that time. She stopped shoveling coal into the stove hole and glared at me with that black shovel still in her hand. Her eyes became burning coals.

"Bird? What bird?" she quizzed me, as she stared holes through my head.

I suddenly felt stupid.

"You know...my bird."

"What bird Stanley?" Her voice raised several levels in volume and pitch.

I wished that I had never brought the subject up because Mama's angry tenor convinced me that I had done something wrong. Tears welled up, and my lower lip trembled. I feared that she might whack me on the side of my head with the coal shovel.

"Stanley, what bird are you talking about? Do you mean the hens?"

"No." I knew that she was hoping that it was the hens.

"Stanley, tell me what bird you are talking about?"

I pointed to my pants. "Here."

"Virgin Mary!" Her face grew crimson.

I knew that I never should have mentioned it. She never said *Virgin Mary* like that unless it was something graveyard serious. I guessed that all hell was about to break loose, and I might be the one in the fire.

"Stanley, run down to your Grandpa's and tell him to call your father. He needs to come home, right now."

I sniveled, convinced that I was in shit, until she hugged me and said something softly in Gaelic.

A whole day went by. No one came after me with leather gloves or a coal shovel, and there were no serious lectures. Best of all, no official car showed up to take me away to the reform school. Ronald didn't sleep in my bed any more. In fact, I never saw Ronald after the day that I told Mama about the bird.

Ronald was gone, and my amusement with flying, flinging hens at dusk had died. I liked the hens as friends because no other kids lived within walking distance of me.

I did grace some of the other barnyard animals with my stories, even Angus the pig, but that relationship came to a bloody end one cold morning in October when Donald Murphy showed up at our house. He and Papa went into the carriage house and sharpened a large knife. I followed. I was 8 and apparently old enough to witness a murder.

Donald held the big knife up and proclaimed that it was sharp as a *Gillette* razor blade. He chuckled. Papa and Donald advanced to the pig pen. I followed, far behind. Papa opened the fence. Donald chased Angus around the pen. I did not follow. Donald fell into the stinking mud behind the pig, who squealed...like a pig. Between Papa and Donald, they managed to hold the pig in a corner as Donald pulled his sharp-as-a-Gillette-razor-blade knife across Angus's throat. Blood gushed onto the ground and Donald's hands. The pig's squeal became a horrifying shriek as he ran in circles around the pen with blood spurting from his partially severed neck.

"Papa, is Angus going to die?" I questioned my father, hoping that somehow the pig's injury would heal like my finger had when I cut it with my pocket knife.

Papa ignored my question. I wanted to run away, but my curiosity compelled me to stay.

Five minutes passed before Angus stumbled and then fell down and made a few more feeble attempts to get up. Eventually, he remained still, except for occasional pitiable breaths and a kicking leg.

Donald and Papa dragged him to the front of the carriage house, where they had a three-legged triangle set up with a chain hanging from its center. They tied the chain around Angus's hind legs and hoisted him up in the air so that his head hung down. More blood drained from him. Occasionally, Angus made a pathetic kick, but no one seemed to notice or care as Donald raised his knife and plunged it into the pig's belly and made one long cut all the way to the pig's neck. I was frozen to the ground as his insides fell out while steam rose up in the October chill.

They spent the rest of the day and into the night slicing and dicing. I went to bed late but remained awake for a long time, replaying the day's events. I ran that movie in my mind for weeks and imagined what it felt like hanging upside down on a three-legged triangle.

A month later, Papa came home with a blonde dog that I wanted to call Lassie, like in the comic books, until Papa convinced me that I could not call him Lassie because it was a boy dog. He became Laddie.

Six months later, on the way home from school, I stopped at Grandpa's store. Uncle Arthur met me in the doorway.

"Stanley, Laddie is dead." It was as if he was advising me that my shoelace was undone.

"What?" I couldn't believe what he had said.

"That's right. Laddie is dead. He got hit by a train. He was injured so badly that we had to whack him with a crowbar so he wouldn't suffer."

I stood there and wept as my uncle casually went about stacking boxes on the shelves. Dead pets, dead people, and ghosts were about to dominate my world.

Dead Visitors

Angus the pig, my second favorite fan, was murdered as I watched, and my dog Laddie met his cruel fate at the business end of a crowbar. Most kids lose pets and family members, but not many children have dead people reclining in the living room. My father invited them.

I have a murky memory, from a couple of years earlier, of holding Papa's hand as we visited Neil D. MacKinnon's house to see an old guy sleeping in a gray felt-covered box, suspended on two chairs in the living room. Papa knelt down and made the sign of the cross in front of the man-in-the-box and muttered a few fast prayers. I stood on the end of the kneeler by my father and peered over the edge, as I held the bronze handles and wondered if the man-in-the-box surrounded by satin might wake up at any minute. He didn't. He didn't appear well. His lips seemed to be stuck together, and his face reminded me of the gray putty my father placed around the windows before winter arrived. There was something about the scene that I didn't like, but I did enjoy the cookies and cake that the women in the kitchen handed out with strong tea. The guy in the box didn't have any. He slept through the whole party, at least while we were there. I suspected that maybe he was drunk. He reminded me of Papa on Saturday mornings after too much Governor General rum.

* * *

I awoke to loud knocking combined with muffled sobbing. It was Saturday, July 25, 1953, at 6:00 a.m. I was almost 13. I had been sleeping on the couch in the kitchen. Our door didn't have a lock on it, so the door-pounding was followed by a sudden whirlwind rush into the kitchen by my Uncle Arthur as he wept. Terrified, I shot up straight in bed.

"Roddie! Wake up! Mama's dead!" he blurted between sobs.

Papa was scarcely awake and not quite believing what he had heard. "Arthur, what are you talking about?"

"Mama is dead. She died in her sleep last night."

Papa became unusually composed as he stepped out to meet his hysterical younger brother. I heard Mama jump out of bed, but because she hadn't yet fired up her ten-pound hearing aid, she didn't quite catch what had happened until she saw Papa's lip tremble.

"What's wrong, Roddie?"

"Tena, Mama died last night."

"Mother of God!"

Those three words always stopped me in my tracks and frightened me. She only said that when something awful had just occurred, like a sudden death, or a thunder storm.

* * *

Grandma Nellie received the dubious honor of being one of the first people in Jamesville West to be handled by a funeral home. Her body was picked up and taken to the T.W. Curry Funeral Home in Sydney and returned the next day, dressed up to go away.

It was the first time that I had seen a hearse. I was impressed. A couple of skinny, spooky characters in pin-striped pants, who appeared like they could have been funeral home customers, carried her fancy oak coffin from the black Cadillac into her living room and set it up on an expandable base with wheels with two tall candles at each end. I thought that was neat. No matching kitchen chairs for Grandma.

The creepy pin-striped guys told us to leave the room while they opened the lid in case they had forgotten her at the funeral home. Eventually, they invited us in to gaze at her ashen face and say a few rounds of the rosary.

She stayed there for three days and nights while relatives and visitors that I had never seen before came to pray but mostly to chat and tell funny yarns. It was especially irritating when our local story-teller, Angus Rory, was in the middle of a hilarious tale only to be interrupted by the parish priest saying in a booming voice, *In the Name of the Father, the Son, and the Holy Ghost,* and we had to hit the floor on our knees with one more round of the rosary.

Grandpa was a short, no-nonsense man, tough as nails, but when I saw him break down and cry it shocked me. I also saw him laugh aloud when my Great-Aunt Maude told stories about crazy things that Grandma had done as a young woman. It didn't sound to me like the straight-laced Grandma that I knew.

The stories got zany, and the jokes got funnier as the night wore on. Great-Aunt Maude pulled a chair up to the coffin and rested her elbow on the edge, right next to Grandma's head and had 'em rolling in the aisles! Not me. I was ordered off to bed, but I knew that they would be up all night because the adults somehow knew that a dead body shouldn't be left alone overnight. That was a rule. I wanted Papa to explain why, but he ignored me. I don't think he knew why either. I imagined that shutting off all the lights and leaving dead Grandma in the living room seemed spooky, so it kind of made sense. What if you got up in the middle of the night to go outdoors to the toilet and you forgot that she was there?

*   *   *

Less than a year later, we repeated the whole thing when Grandpa died. Papa alleged that Grandpa died of a broken heart. They did seem to love each other very much. I got that. Grandpa didn't speak to Grandma the boorish way my father talked to my mother. Strange.

My Uncle Arthur took over the John R. Campbell General Dry Goods Store and the post office. We had a fairly good idea where that was going to end up, due to the fact that Uncle Arthur was heavily into anything that had a sub-atomic level of alcohol, including vanilla, lemon, orange, and almond extracts, which he kept in good supply in the store. There was an advantage to consuming those flavorful drinks. He didn't have a problem with halitosis. Even when he barfed, it smelled like oranges.

Some days he was so hammered that he couldn't open the store, which was probably a good thing because he threw up on himself a lot. When customers arrived at the store, they found the door locked, yet they could see him sleeping on the counter. They rapped on the door and windows.

The response was almost immediate. "Fuck off!"

I learned that phrase from my uncle, but I promptly learned that it was not wise to say it to Mama.

"Arthur! Come on, open the door. I need milk and bread for my kids."

"Go fuck yourself! Come back tomorrow. I'm sick."

Uncle Arthur was clearly not schooled in customer relations. As a result, the business went downhill rapidly. Besides learning the f-word from Uncle Arthur, I also learned how to drive a car when I was 13, simply because he was rarely sober enough to keep his car between the telephone poles. I waited eagerly for him to get plastered and develop an urge to go somewhere.

On one of the sober days for Uncle Arthur in mid-summer in 1954, I had nothing else to do but hang out at the store and observe customers and Boston tourists come and go. A black station wagon pulled up out front. Two young guys, dressed to match in black pants and white shirts entered.

"Sir, can you tell us how to get to the Little Narrows Gypsum Plant?" the Elvis look-alike asked Uncle Arthur.

"Yes," Uncle Arthur replied. "Stay on this road for nine miles, and then you keep on for a mile past the ferry wharf. You know someone there?"

"No, we're with the T.W. Curry Funeral Home," the Buddy Holly type said. "There's been an accident, so we have to take the remains to North Sydney."

Uncle Arthur turned to me. "Stanley, you know where the Gypsum Plant is, don't you?"

"Uh, yeah...I know where it is." I was unsure of why Uncle Arthur was asking me.

"Good. Go with them and show them the way. You guys have room for him?"

"Sure, he can sit in the middle," the Elvis guy replied. "We'll drop him off here on the way back."

Buddy Holly placed his hand on my back. "Okay, Stanley buddy, let's go!"

I had serious mixed feelings, although my friends at school might think that this was pretty neat, riding in a hearse, even if it was a black Ford station wagon. On the way to the Little Narrows Gypsum Plant, Elvis told me that a young man had been killed that morning when the truck he had been driving, loaded with twenty tons of gypsum, had careened over an embankment. I became nervous. This could be ugly.

We arrived at the Gypsum Plant and pulled up to a warehouse, in front of open hangar-type doors where a group of men stood. The two undertakers strolled in with me in tow...far behind. A man I recognized as Dr. Ferguson was busy examining a handsome, young man on the floor. Clearly, he was dead. Blood oozed from his ears, mouth, and nose. Dr. Ferguson bent down on one knee and pressed on the man's chest.

The doctor wrote some notes, made a statement to some serious official man, and gave an okay to the undertakers that they could take the body. I suddenly felt important that I was part of the team. I also felt sad for the good-looking young man's mom and dad. I imagined that he had a girlfriend who would cry for him.

The undertaker guys took out a body bag and enclosed the dead man inside and then placed him in the rear of the station wagon. This was obviously just another day at the office for these guys, but for me sitting in the middle, it was not as agreeable. The dead guy's head was right behind me. I spotted holes in the body bag, and I speculated why. Maybe they're there just in case, you know...what if he's not dead? He would need to breathe.

I craned my neck and glanced back momentarily and noticed through one of the holes, an eye, and it was partially open. He stared at me! Shit!

Meanwhile, the Elvis guy drove like a maniac, virtually flying over the rough, crooked dirt road to Jamesville West. As we careened around a curve, he unexpectedly spotted a massive pothole. Elvis Undertaker slammed on the brakes, hard.

I had learned about Newton's Law of Inertia in school. *Every body remains in a state of constant velocity unless acted upon by an external unbalanced force. This means that in the absence of a non-zero net force, the center of mass of a body either remains at rest or moves at a constant velocity.*

The body behind me was no longer at rest. The dead man flew forward at a rather high velocity, crashing into the back of my head. I let out a glass shattering screech. My brand new undertaker friends thought it was hilarious. They chortled all the way back to my Uncle Arthur's store. I wrote off one career that I would not consider for my future.

*   *   *

As I turned 14 and entered high school, girls occupied my thoughts, dreams, and fantasies. I simply dreamed of kissing a girl. I desperately wanted to be desired by a girl. That's all. It was the unleashing of an unrestrained obsession. There were no girls in rural Jamesville West, but there were a few cute girls in high school. Regrettably, I was hopelessly bashful. However, I learned that my timidity could be overcome with a few drinks. Actually, a lot of drinks of anything that contained alcohol. My boozing mentors included my Uncle Arthur, who helped me appreciate the joys of lemon extract or *little ones*, as he called them, and my reclusive Uncle Jim-the-Miner, who offered me my first drink of bull beer, plus some minor sex education, which only confused me.

Getting drunk at 14 was easy. As soon as the first drink hit my stomach, I experienced an instant buzz. I could do anything, dance, sing, walk a tightrope, and most of all, I found the courage to talk to anyone. Hiding my drinking from Mom and Pop wasn't easy, especially when I was anxious to show the rest of the world that I was man enough to drink. But it was a small community, and my drinking got back to them. They didn't seem unusually concerned, outside of a short lecture.

I was a kid, and I did kid stuff, but the growing man in me fixated on girls. I fantasized about Diane, Judy, and especially Sandra Small. Sandra came up to the country from smoky steel-city Sydney in the summer to spend a few weeks with her uncle, who lived two miles down a narrow dirt road from our house. I was enamored with her but too shy to talk to her. We smiled at each other and said hello, and then I slithered off into a corner.

An adorable girl with full lips and a sweet smile, Elizabeth, came up from the city in the summer of '56 with her year-older brother Andy to stay with their Aunt Mary two miles down the road. Andy was my age, and I was alone with no friends to hang out with, so I rode my bike over to their house to goof around on his aunt's farm.

Andy, Elizabeth, and I decided that it would be a good idea to go up and see what was in the abandoned house on the hill behind their aunt's place. Some furniture still remained in the house, so it was a fun place to explore. We found a bedroom upstairs, with a bed still in the room. Elizabeth and I sat on the striped mattress. Andy sat on the floor leaning against the wall. I liked Elizabeth. Of course I liked her. She was a girl, and she had a pulse!

We talked about school, music, boys and girls and sex, something we knew nothing about, but we sure were curious. I don't remember who suggested it, but we got around to the oldest boys and girls game in the world, *you show me yours, and I'll show you mine.*

I wanted to play this game but my bashfulness was a serious issue. However, I knew that it would solve my ignorance of the female anatomy.

The three of us disrobed, bit by bit simultaneously. Elizabeth hesitated. I wished that Andy would go away somewhere.

"You promise not to laugh?" Elizabeth giggled as her cheeks flushed.

Laughing was the *last* thing on my mind!

We both let our underwear drop to the floor. I didn't see Andy's face or anything else about Andy. Who cared? Elizabeth and I stared into each other's eyes and then lowered them to acquire our first lesson in sex education.

One thing was certain. I was visibly excited at the sight of a naked girl, and I began to feel *something* for her. Actually, I felt more than *something*. I wanted to kiss her...and more. Nothing more happened, then.

I didn't see much of Andy after that day of innocent naked revelation. I spent the next five weeks with Elizabeth and ignored Andy. Elizabeth and I romped naked throughout the rest of her summer in the country, in the barn, in the hay, and on a remote section of Jamesville beach. It was my first summer seriously kissing a girl. Mom and Pop didn't see much of me that summer, either, and when I did go home, my lips were bigger than Fats Domino's from kissing Elizabeth. We were in love. At least, we thought we were in love.

Early September came too fast. Elizabeth had to go home to the city. She was still a virgin, and I guess I was too. It was not for lack of both of us trying.

"I love you!" Elizabeth confessed this to me on the day that she left. "Someday we will get married."

"I love you too," I responded in kind but wasn't certain about the marriage part.

Then she made a tearful pledge that I will never forget. "If you don't marry me and you marry someone else, I will become a nun!"

I laughed. She cried. Elizabeth waved out the window of her Mom's car and disappeared in a cloud of Jamesville road dust. I never saw her again. I found out years later that she had kept her promise. Our young summer immaculate romance was a fantasy that I sought to replicate for most of my life.

I was about to become 16, and like most boys my age, I was fixated on girls, but I had one particular girl in mind. I didn't know who she was, but she would haunt me for decades. I saw her in my dreams. Four times, I thought I had found her.

I did have one more passion. I dreamed of being on the radio. The dream began with my Uncle Arthur, before he discovered lemon extract and I discovered girls. He invited me to come up to his room at Grandpa and Grandma's house to listen to his Marconi radio late at night. We sat on his bed against the wall, captivated by *The Shadow, Boston Blackie,* and the Saturday night boxing matches from stations far away. I tried to imagine what kind of world existed behind the glowing dial. It was magic. I was especially fascinated by the announcer.

"I'm going to be the man on the radio," I declared to my mother when I was barely able to reach the radio.

"That's nice," she answered, as she darned my father's woolen socks.

I knew that she didn't believe me. *I'll show her.*

No Shit! I'm Adopted?

The red revolving light flashed in my rear-view mirror. It was the most feared icon of authority in rural Cape Breton, the Royal Canadian Mounted Police, otherwise known as the Mounties. I was with my best friend Howard Campbell, and even though we shared the same last name, we weren't related.

I was three years older than Howard, but we were inseparable in spite of the age difference. We shared a silly, sometimes deranged sense of humor and spent a lot of our time doing impersonations to each other of our neighbors, especially our loveable old neighbor, Philly O'Donnell, next door. *Yogi Bear* and *Snagglepuss* TV cartoons amused us to howling hilarity.

Our neighbors believed that Howard was more than silly. They suspected that he was mentally ill. I saw him as a crazy genius, an early forerunner to *Fonzie* from the *Happy Days* TV show. Howard was lanky and kept an impeccable ducktail in place with *Brylcreem*, when he could afford it. In a failed low-cost experiment, he showed up at school one day with his hair slicked to perfection. At first, my classmates and I assumed that he had bought a new tube of hair goop, until flies began to circle his rancid head. It was butter!

I rolled the driver's window down in my father's '48 Chevrolet. The car had originally been Grandpa's, but when he died it became Pop's. The Mountie bent down and peered in the window at me without saying anything.

"Can I see your license, vehicle registration, and insurance please?"

"Uh...yes. I..." I stammered as I tried to find the papers in the glove compartment.

"Here you go, sir."

He shuffled through the wrinkled papers, as Howard expelled a silent but deadly fart. I wanted to strangle him because my window was the only open window, so I knew that the draft would take the noxious gas in that direction.

"Young man, where is your driver's license?"

He seemed more annoyed. I deduced that it was thanks to Howard's vapors.

I peered up at him with big eyes that I hoped would win me some pity. "I don't have a license, sir."

"I assume that this is your father's car?"

"Yes, sir."

"Does he know that you are driving his car without a driver's license?"

"No, sir."

Howard let another one go, this one audible.

"Don't go anywhere. I am going to my car for a moment."

"Yes, sir."

"Howard, will you put a fucking plug in it! What the hell did you eat, anyway? He probably had to go back to his car for oxygen!"

The brown-coated Mountie returned, and this time he had his Ranger Smith hat on. He handed me a ticket. I noticed that he wisely did not bend down toward my window.

"Give this summons to your father. You will have to go to court in Baddeck and appear before a judge. If you fail to show up, you could go to jail."

"Yes, sir."

After a command to go straight home, the Mountie departed.

"Holy shit, Howard, I have to tell my old man. He's going to hit the roof."

We had taken the car for a joyride while he slept in the hollow in the couch on a Sunday afternoon.

As usual, Pop blamed Howard for the latest problem. That was good for me. Not so good for Howard.

A few weeks later, Pop and I went to the county courthouse in Baddeck. The judge fined me eighteen dollars and fifty cents and gave me a lecture. My father paid the fine, and I picked up a book to study for my driver's test, since I had just celebrated my 16th birthday.

I studied all the rules and filled out a form. The form requested that I send in a birth certificate. I didn't have one. Pop said that he didn't have one and if he didn't, neither did Mom. That struck me as peculiar. It seemed as though they didn't want me to have it.

Aunt Patsy, my Uncle Frank's wife, was sometimes childlike, which suited me fine, since it felt comfortable to talk to her. I mentioned to Aunt Patsy that I had a serious problem because I didn't have a birth certificate. Without blinking, she tossed me the biggest shock of my sixteen years.

"Well, it's probably because you're adopted." She made that earth-shaking declaration so casually that it was as if she had informed me that I had a new zit on my chin.

I stared at her and waited. I expected a *Ha! Ha! Ha! I was kidding*, but it didn't come.

"What? No! Really? You're not serious. Are you? Oh, come on!"

"Yes, of course I'm serious."

"I am? I was...*adopted*? No shit!"

"You didn't know?

"No!"

"Roddie and Tena never told you?"

"No!"

"Yes, you were adopted by Roddie and Tena from an orphanage in Sydney when you were two years old."

We have all seen movies and TV dramas where an older child or an adult finds out that he or she was adopted and they become hysterical, angry, cry, and have a mental breakdown. I didn't. Sure, I was surprised, but that was it...a big surprise.

I don't think I thought about it much after that day, until years later when it became a big deal. I didn't stop to consider whether I had a brother or a sister, and I made no attempt to find out the identity of my birth mother and where and who my father might be. I did ask Mom and Pop about my adoption and who my real parents were. They became defensive when I pressed them for information. They were clearly angry with Aunt Patsy for telling me. My mom became tense and hid in their bedroom for the rest of the day. I didn't care all that much. I merely wanted my driver's license and the freedom to drive and maybe take a girl to the dance on Saturday night, and maybe if I drove her home, we might take our clothes off like Elizabeth and I had.

*   *   *

"Here, come on. Help us out, Stanley!" Jimmy MacKinnon snapped at me. "Give us a hand here, bye. We need to lift him out and onto the floor."

"Are you sure? Do we need to?" I hoped that Jimmy was making a sick joke.

"Come on, Stanley. We don't have all day! You grab his legs, your father can hold him around the middle, and I'll get his head." It was as if Jimmy had done this a dozen times already this morning. I did as ordered. I had Paddy's legs in my arms.

The night before, an hour after we had shut off the TV and had gone to bed, I awoke to hear my father suggesting some bicarbonate for Uncle Paddy's indigestion. Paddy, my mother's half-brother, had been an on-again, off-again boarder at our house for as long as I could remember. He showed up, stayed for a month or two, and then moved in with different relative. He used a cane to get around after a bad fall on black ice one white winter. I was a 16-year-old teenager, and Paddy, being naturally temperamental, didn't like me much.

On more than one occasion, Paddy would lean heavily off to the left on his cane, peer over his twisted wire-rim glasses, and spew sinister harbingers. "By God, Stanley, you'll end up in reform school someday."

When it arrived in our mailbox, he performed his usual daily perusal of the *Halifax Herald* newspaper, which was followed by incessant complaints about the rotten state of the world and how kids like me had a future in maximum security, a mental asylum, or public hanging.

So when he complained late that night that my mother's strawberry jam had given him heartburn, I wanted to yell at him, "Quit complaining, and go to bed, you old fart, so I can go to sleep."

After all, I had to get up and go to school.

Eventually, it became quiet. I fell asleep. Uncle Paddy also fell asleep...forever. The heartburn was a heart attack. Well that was a wild guess. Pop got up early and found Paddy dead on the couch. My father called our old family physician, Dr. Ferguson, twenty miles away in Baddeck. Pop explained Uncle Paddy's symptoms, and that was it. Well, the main symptom at the time was that Uncle Paddy had assumed room temperature. The good doctor was busy. No medical exam, no muss, no fuss. He was indeed dead, and well, it *had* to be a heart attack. For all speed-talking Doctor Ferguson really knew, I could have poisoned him for committing me to reform school.

I wanted to be in school, reform school or even maximum security, rather than play the role of temporary do-it-yourself undertaker's junior assistant.

Not long after my father realized that Uncle Paddy was not holding his breath, he summoned our neighbor Jimmy MacKinnon to the scene. Jimmy was an easy-going, gentle soul, but I always thought he looked a bit like Adolph Hitler, with the same narrow moustache and hair style. On this day Jimmy wasn't doing his usual carpentry jobs or invading Poland, so he agreed to stop along the way at the Saint Columba Church basement and pick up a cheap gray coffin with the felt on the outside and satin innards and bring it to our house on his pickup truck.

Jimmy borrowed my father's razor and shaved Uncle Paddy. Pop found Uncle Paddy's threadbare suit and permanently loaned Paddy his only white shirt and a tie so that he would be dressed for the visitors that were sure to arrive before supper. Jimmy borrowed some of Mom's rouge and powder to give Paddy that healthy, active appearance.

The downright revolting part came when I was commanded to help Jimmy and my father lift him up and place him in the coffin, which was temporarily on the floor in front of our Marconi 21-inch floor-model TV. The strategy was, once we got Patty nice and comfortable, we would move the coffin onto two kitchen chairs in the living room. Mom then complained about being two chairs short.

We arranged him in among the satin folds without too much trouble, but Jimmy noticed a glitch. Paddy sank down out of sight. After all, visitors wouldn't be able to see how great he looked, so on command, we lifted him back out onto the floor. That was the second most revolting thing I had ever had to do. Rigor mortis had apparently set in, so the leg I held felt like a dead tree limb.

We laid Paddy on the cold linoleum to pass the time while we packed as many *Post Record* newspapers and Simpson's and Eaton's catalogs as we could find into the bottom of the coffin. Once again, Jimmy felt the need to snap at me to help. I was a conscientious objector, but I eventually did what I was told. We dropped Paddy in between the silver satin folds once more. It crossed my mind that Uncle Paddy would have reading material. We should have included the *Halifax Herald*.

Visiting time commenced as soon as the call went out and lasted for two and a half days. Few people around this rustic, rural part of Nova Scotia knew him well, but that didn't matter. There wasn't much to do around Jamesville West and Iona, so a wake was an event and a chance to get together with the neighbors and catch up on the latest news, even if you didn't know the guy laid out in the living room.

Through the indigestion, sudden death, and sitting up with the dead, my mother seemed to take the events of the day rather well, as if she had hosted a dead boarder before. She was quite hospitable. She made *the tea* for Jimmy MacKinnon, as she did for everyone else who came to visit. The tea included buttered homemade bread, buttered biscuits, and buttered bonnach followed by lemon pie and strong tea.

Six months later, another casket took up space and two chairs in the living room, when my mom's sister, Aunt Mary, died in Sydney. She was transported to our house for a two day good-bye from people who had never said hello to her.

I had heard that there were places in Africa where elephants went to die. It was kind of like that at our house. A year later we had more felt-covered, satin-lined furniture set up in our living room. It wasn't Belfast or the Belgian Congo, but it seemed like death was a part of my teenage life.

It was 1958, and rock 'n' roll consumed my life. Late at night, after I got into bed, I listened to Elvis, Danny and the Juniors, Chuck Berry, and The Platters with DJ Alan Freed on WABC radio in New York.

During a late night newscast, I heard of a family of six who drowned after driving off a ferry wharf. I imagined what it must be like for the remainder of the family to endure such a shock. Early the next morning, Pop knocked on my bedroom door, something he rarely did. After all, it was summer, and I didn't have to get up for school.

Pop spoke in a serious, hushed tone. "Stanley, I have bad news. Six of Arnold's family drowned last night at the end of the Little Narrows ferry wharf."

Arnold was one of my best friends in my mid-teens. Together, we had smoked, drank beer, flirted with girls, and even stole his older brother Allen's car for a weekend joyride once. I had a crush on Arnold's sister, Francie who also died that night. A few days later, as a pall-bearer, I helped carry Allen's coffin to his grave.

At home, we weren't through with the dead visitors. At least up to this point they had been laid out in the living room, but that was about to change. My bed was waiting.

* * *

"Stanley! Are you paying attention?" Mother Saint Agnes's eyes were fixed on my face.

I had been fantasizing about a different kind of chemistry, between Sally and me, in the next row.

"Yes, Mother."

"Good! Maybe you could come up to the front and show us the formula you worked out at home."

Shit! I had no formula worked out. Elvis had been on TV the night before, and after that, I got sleepy and went to bed.

"Mother, I tried to work it out, but I couldn't get a result."

"Fine, then put your try on the blackboard." That was her favorite line whenever I tried to avoid being singled out.

"Uh...I didn't bring it...because it wasn't worked out."

From the corner of my eye, I could see Sally with her long legs and short plaid skirt smirking. Sally knew. What Sally didn't know was that by then we were rolling around among the dandelions in the field behind my house.

I was in tenth grade and not doing well. I flunked almost everything in high school except algebra and trigonometry. Television was relatively new, and girls wore shorter skirts. I tried hard to be one of the coolest, hippest dudes to hit the scene, except that inside I suspected that my classmates saw me as weird, and I was infuriated by my own timidity.

Math came second to masturbation when I got a long gaze at the mature girls in grades eleven and twelve, with their short skirts, make-up, and self-confident attitudes. No longer was I surrounded by snot-nosed kids smelling of week-old urine in the one-room elementary school at McKinnons Harbour.

Yes, I had had a flirty fling with Norma in ninth grade, but it amounted to love notes carried by willing messengers. We lived miles apart. With my best high school friend Arnold, we walked ten miles in mid-summer to Norma's house in Washabuck, only to be terrified by her intimidating mother. Then without as much as a kiss in return for our blistering feet, we hiked ten miles back home on the shadowy country road at night.

I had no hope of bringing to fruition the immoral thoughts so often forewarned by our teachers, who happened to be nuns. I squeaked by in ninth and tenth grades. I hated and flunked chemistry and biology. Oddly enough, these were the two elements that controlled my life. I dreamed of some sort of chemistry with Melanie with the large boobs. I visualized the real biology that might take place between us, if only I had a chance, but with my bashfulness, it was not to be. At local dances and parties, I got drunk to get brave, but then I was a slob whom *everybody* avoided. I was not aware that a woman had her eye on me.

Dead In My Bed

In the early fifties, my father, after years of prodding, nagging, and pleading from my mother, agreed to build a new house farther down the hill and closer to the road and the railroad tracks. (There is nothing like being closer to the railroad tracks.) With the help of our neighbor, Pius Campbell (not closely related), and carpenter Archie McPhee, we cut the logs from the trees on our property with a crosscut saw and had them sawn into lumber at a local sawmill. Pop let the lumber dry for a few years, until Mom began to pester him.

She and I had a plan for the house. We found a ranch-style bungalow in a book of house plans. Pop didn't like it but reluctantly agreed to build it. Together, we measured and set out the stakes for the foundation.

The day came when the tractor arrived to dig the foundation. Just before Pius Campbell lifted the blade on his tractor, Pop ran around and moved the stakes. He had decided to do his own last-minute house plan. Over several years the house got built by one man and one man alone, Archie McPhee, one of the most opinionated, cantankerous, stubborn carpenters since Saint Joseph. He had built our local mission church almost single handedly without a level or a square.

While working on our house, my father remarked to him once...and only once, "Archie, I don't think I have ever seen you use a square."

"I don't need a square!"

"You don't?"

"No! My eye is square!" He was serious.

Very slowly, over a couple of years, the house was built, but not to my mother's plan, mine, or even to my father's altered plan. No, it was Archie's plan. It reminded me a bit of a barn, with the end peaks of the roof folded down. Nevertheless, we moved in when the house was only partially finished and smelled of fresh wood. It was new, even if it wasn't what we expected. Archie never left. My father invited him to stay without Mom's approval. She cooked for him and did his laundry, even when he didn't want his clothes cleaned.

Archie wasn't exactly a sophisticated gourmet. He lived solely on a diet of uncooked oatmeal mixed with water. He carried the concoction in a half-gallon tobacco can with a wire coat hanger for a handle. That was it. Breakfast, lunch, and dinner. He was finicky, and he got crankier.

My father had priorities. We didn't have running water or even water that wasn't running. We had to carry it in the car in buckets from over a mile away. This meant that we also did not have an indoor bathroom, and frankly, the outdoor one was not a facility in which I cared to take a bath. However, we were one of the first families on our area to have a TV. This meant that we were never lonely with neighbors visiting almost every night to watch *Ed Sullivan, Gunsmoke, and Milton Berle,* as well as *Hockey Night in Canada.*

Archie was not a TV fan, but one night he came out of his room to join us. In the middle of *I Love Lucy,* Archie suddenly, to the astonishment of our TV viewer visitors, dropped to his knees and recited the rosary aloud. We didn't know whether we should join him or crank up the volume on the TV.

Several months later, Archie became ill, vomiting in his room. We tried in vain to convince him to go to a doctor, but he refused, suggesting that whatever he had would be cured by Jesus and Quaker Oats. He got sicker. Then, my father, for whatever reason my mother and I would never grasp, moved Archie into *my* room, into my bed! I was downgraded to the couch in the living room.

We determined that Archie had stomach cancer. The poor man was in excruciating pain. He prayed constantly and so did we. He steadfastly refused to go to a hospital or allow a doctor to visit. It was truly pitiful.

On a Monday in December, at 5:00 in the morning, mercifully, Archie died...in my room...in my bed. I didn't go to school, and it was one day that I desperately *wanted* to go to school...and live there! Pop invited Jimmy MacKinnon for a return engagement as a freelance mortician. My father and Jimmy cleaned Archie up, dressed him in a suit, and set up the gray casket, in our living room, on two chairs for viewing. He lay there for a day and a half.

My mother made the tea for all the visitors who remarked how good Archie looked. In her spare time, Mom cleaned my room, as much as she could. The mattress was stained. She used a can of Glade lilac scent, which combined adequately with the smell of death. Now what? I couldn't sleep on the couch in the living room forever. That's where the coffin was set up like so much pine and satin furniture.

Mom and Pop insisted that I now had to go back and sleep in my own room. I was furious and terrified. My life was evolving into a bad horror movie. I wanted to get drunk and stay drunk. It was my last year in high school. I was determined that as soon as I graduated, or not, I would get out of this bizarre death-house, get a car, get a girlfriend, and be a radio announcer.

Sleeping in my room was making me crazy. The smell never went away. I could still hear Archie's dying moans of pain in my head, and sometimes I swore that he was in the room with me when I went to bed.

I inserted a 100-watt bulb in my bedside lamp and always slept with it on. One night, after Mom and Pop had gone to bed, I scurried into my room and lunged over to turn the light on before Archie's ghost appeared in the darkness. I twisted the switch. Snap! Flash! There was an immediate blinding flash and a pop. I was in the dark and scared shitless! My 100-watt bulb had burned out, and I was left standing in the gloom with eyes the size of dinner plates with the flash still burned into my retinas.

"Fuck!" I ran out of the pitch-black room and smack into the edge of the door.

Pop heard the commotion from his bedroom. "Stanley, what's the matter with you?"

"Nothing." I didn't want to admit that I was petrified and living in a nightmare in my own room.

Under my breath I uttered every swear word that I had learned from Uncle Arthur.

I had a year left at Rankin Memorial High School in Iona, but I knew that night that I had to get the hell out of that house and away from Jamesville West and the cuckoo freelance funeral home. I wanted to quit school and get a job in Toronto or Thunder Bay or anywhere, as long it was not in Jamesville West in our wacky death-house with the one-hole shithouse.

In spite of my father's railway job, we didn't have running water, a heating system other than two oil stoves, and worst of all, no bathroom. I wanted to invite friends from school to spend the night, but I was too embarrassed. We had an outhouse, as my father called it, but I called it what it was, just to irritate Pop, a shithouse! Oh sure. He had promised running water and a bathroom for years. After all, we weren't poor. Our neighbors had caught up with the rest of world, but for some reason, we had not.

Most of all, seeing my mom carry snow into the house to do laundry broke my heart. As a classy lady from the city, I wondered if she ever regretted marrying my father. I doubt that she had envisioned such a life.

I did not care to spend one more winter wading through four-foot snowdrifts in a blinding blizzard at 2:00 in the morning with the raging runs to wipe my arse with a glossy *Macleans Magazine*. I had more and uglier arguments with Pop about why we couldn't have running water like other people outside most third-world countries. Most of all, I wanted this for my long-suffering Mom. For me, I wanted a life with a bathroom and a pretty girl. We would lie naked together at night and plan our future together with a flush toilet.

Until I Need Glasses

During mid-morning break, the high-school principal, a nun, beckoned me to come to her office. She closed the door and invited me to be seated.

"Is everything okay, Stanley?"

"Yes, Mother."

"You're sure?"

"Oh, yes, Mother."

I actually wasn't sure where she was going with that line of questioning. I guessed that maybe she might lecture me because I was getting bad grades, although I didn't see any other kids, especially boys, being ushered into her office. I had a reason to suspect that she might think I was abnormal. I always thought that I was different and appeared odd. My sometimes-friend, Alexander MacLean, had even told me one day that I was weird. That confirmed my own suspicions.

"Stanley, how do you feel about the girls in your class?"

I stared at the floor. "Okay."

"Do they bother you?"

"Bother? Uh, how do you mean bother, Mother?" I was sure I knew what she meant but didn't want to take a chance that I was going down the wrong path to be ambushed later.

Mother Saint Marilyn was, I assumed, about 35 years of age and not all that bad looking...for a nun. She was a nun after all, and the thought never crossed my mind that sex ever crossed her mind. To discuss sex with a nun was enough to make me want to leap out of my skin and slink out the door, but I couldn't. I was trapped. While my buddies smoked outside and checked out Melanie's short skirt and big boobs, I was stuck in the office answering dumb questions.

"Some of the girls wear short skirts and show their legs. Does that excite you, Stanley?"

I squirmed. *How does she know? Oh shit, does it show?*

"Uh, no, Mother. I don't know...uh...I..."

"Tell me, when you go home, do you...masturbate?"

Damn! She knows something. What do I say?"

"It's okay, Stanley, you can tell me. I want to help you."

Ring! The mid-morning break ended. I was literally saved by the bell.

"Uh, Mother, I have to get to my math class." I got up hurriedly, hoping that she would release me from the inquisition.

"Okay, Stanley, let's continue this tomorrow, okay?"

No! It wasn't ok! "Uh, okay, Mother." I escaped out the door.

I was unnerved. *How can I get out of this? I will have to be sick for a week with the flu, or maybe catch something deadly and highly communicable.*

I sat in class for the rest of the day and speculated, why me? What have I been doing that attracted her attention? Maybe she thought that I was a latent sex maniac, destined to rape and pillage if I wasn't stopped before it was too late. What if she discussed this with the parish priest? That's all I needed, to have him breathing down my neck inquiring if I did bad things in the night.

Maybe the confessional wasn't so secret after all. What if he had told her my mortal sins and suggested that she should get me straightened out before I got locked away in an institution where people observe you all day and night to be sure your hands didn't stray down below your belt, except to pee? I tried to think. Did anyone else notice that I might be acting peculiar or had the appearance of a lecherous lunatic? An even more terrifying thought crossed my mind. What if Mother Saint Marilyn contacted my parents! I decided to play along and confess to whatever she thought I was guilty of and pretend to be cured.

For the remainder of the school year, Mother Saint Marilyn regularly invited me to her office during mid-morning breaks. My closest buddies, Vern and Neil, quizzed me about why Mother Saint Marilyn was dragging me into her office so often. They suspected that maybe she had a thing for me. Their suggestion made me want to puke. She was a nun for God's sake!

I tried hard not to gawk at Melanie's milky white legs next to me in class and Judy's growing breasts. As the year progressed, they both seemed to show more and more of them, or maybe it was my imagination. I was torn between fantasizing and pretending that I saw nothing and knew nothing.

Near the end of the year, Judy disappeared. She simply stopped coming to school. A few days before school ended, we heard the news. Judy had given birth to a baby. Now my fantasies grew more vivid. Some guy had done that. He knew those breasts and legs intimately. My visions went into overdrive as Mother Saint Marilyn's questions became more specific.

"Which girl causes you to have an erection?" she inquired, as though she wanted me to explain Newton's Law of Gravity.

I was surprised that she even knew what an erection was. She was a *nun* for God's sake!

I wanted to say all of them but hesitated and blurted out the first name that popped into my head, "Judy."

I picked her because she was gone for good, so there was no danger that Mother Saint Marilyn would tell her.

"Stanley, did you know that masturbation weakens your character?"

I thought it weakened your eyes. I was more concerned about weak eyes. I didn't want to have to wear glasses. I would never have a chance with a girl.

"In other words, Stanley, masturbation is not the answer."

I knew that! She wasn't about to tell me what she thought the answer was.

The sexual inquisition came to an end when one day, a week before graduation, Mother Saint Marilyn floored me with a question that took my eyes off the floor and put them directly into her eyes to see if she was serious.

"Stanley, how much do you know about a woman's sexual organs?"

I swallowed hard. "I, ah...uh...a little."

I had spent a summer romping naked with Elizabeth, but I would only divulge that under Spanish Inquisition-style torture. I knew that she would then send me straight to Father MacDonald for an all-inclusive confession and an Act of Contrition recited aloud for all to hear, and my next summer vacation would be in a monastery.

My head swam, and I felt faint and thought that I might throw up. "No...I...uh..."

Ring!

There *was* a God!

The bell saved me again. Graduation was only days away. Mother Saint Marilyn got busy and I got invisible, except for one last session where she wished me well and repeated that self-gratification affected one's character. I thanked her and left, hoping that that subject would never come up again.

In spite of Mother Saint Marilyn's sex talks and the painful anxiety, I remember her warmly. Maybe I am being naïve, but I like to think that she had my best interests at heart. She might also have sensed that my sexual curiosity and urges were a slightly out of whack, and maybe she saw a glimmer of my future and how it eventually would bring me a ton of turmoil. Sex was becoming my second biggest fixation.

One of the positive tidbits of counsel that Mother Saint Marilyn conferred upon me was that I was apparently a bright kid and that I should apply myself, meaning that I should actually do some homework and stop throwing it all away.

Mother Saint Marilyn was right. I barely squeaked through each year. I rarely completed homework assignments, opting instead for that other obsession, rock 'n' roll, and staying awake until 2:00 a.m. listening to Dick Biondi, Woo-Woo Ginsberg, and Alan Freed on American radio stations like WINS, WABC, WPTR, and WKBW. I dreamed of being a rock 'n' roll DJ in New York, Boston, or Buffalo, but I would have been happy to be on CJCB radio in Sydney, Nova Scotia. I mimicked their style when I was alone. I also attempted to dress hip, like the hot rock 'n' roll singers in the late '50s, such as Bobby Darin, Frankie Avalon, and of course, Elvis.

I was Mister Cool, or so I thought. I practiced longer and harder on my *Silvertone* guitar, but I hated the fact that I was still painfully shy. When possible, I drank to erase the bashfulness, but by the time I was brave enough to sing, dance, or talk to a girl, I couldn't stand up. There was a fine line between losing my inhibitions and losing consciousness. On graduation night, I should have died.

The day before the final day of school, my friends, Norman, Johnny, Jackie, and Kenny and I each contributed five dollars to buy each of us a bottle of wine with which to celebrate our last day of school. We gave the money to Michael Morrison, who knew someone who could legally buy the wine at the liquor store.

The morning of the last day of high school, we party animal guys made a pact to meet in the school furnace room to get and sample our hooch. Unfortunately, I ran into a road block. Mother Saint Marilyn needed to talk to me at the mid-morning break, just when I was supposed to meet the guys for wine-tasting.

"Stanley, can I see you for a moment in my office?"

Oh shit, don't tell me that she wants to talk to me about having sex with myself like she did the last time.

"It will only take a moment."

"Sure, Mother."

She closed the door behind us. She sat on the edge of her desk. I dreaded what I expected her to say.

"Stanley, it's such a shame that you didn't apply yourself this year. I don't know how you are ever going to pass your provincial exams."

"Yes, Mother, I know." I was willing to agree to anything to get to hell out of there.

I figured that the guys were downstairs in the furnace room having a drink, while I was trapped. I hoped that Jackie MacInnis wouldn't piss on the furnace and stink up the school like he had the last year.

"Stanley, I know that we talked about your sexual obsession, but I am worried about your drinking. I have heard stories about you being intoxicated. You will never meet a nice girl someday and get married and have children if you carry on down that road."

I was blindsided by that speech. I thought that she was going to lecture me about the evils of self-gratification.

"Stanley, will you promise me that you will try to stay away from liquor?"

I felt guilty. "Yes, Mother. I will,"

Well I was going to drink wine, not liquor, so technically it wasn't a lie. A part of me knew that she was right, but how the hell was I going to quit the other bad habit if I didn't drink enough to get up the courage to talk to a girl and persuade her to take her clothes off?

"All right, Stanley, you have a good summer. Don't drink and don't abuse yourself, okay?"

I was seriously touched and felt just a bit remorseful when she said, "I'll pray for you."

I left her office thinking for the first time that she actually liked me and seemed to single me out for attention because maybe she saw something that no one else had...good and bad. I left, never knowing her real reasons for all of those closed-door sessions.

My guilt dissipated rapidly as I bolted from her office to the basement just as the bell rang to signal the end of the break. I had missed my chance to take possession of my fine wine. The guys ambled in with stupid grins on their faces. I could tell that they had opened their wine. That was not all that they had opened.

We finished classes at noon, and many said good-bye for the summer, and some who would not be returning said good-bye for good. I was one who was not coming back. I had just completed twelfth grade but had repeat two eleventh grade subjects while in twelfth grade. I wouldn't know the results of final exams until July. If I passed or flunked, I was done.

The world was waiting. I was going to celebrate at the high school dance that night, and maybe I could finally smooth-talk Melanie or Sally into an evening ultimate-intimacy for the first time. Before I went home for the afternoon, I snuck down to the furnace room with Michael, the *wine-pusher*, to retrieve my wine before the janitor locked it up.

"Hey, Michael, who opened my wine?"

"Jesus, Stanley, Johnny Farrell opened it by mistake and took a drink, but then he replaced it with his own. No harm, bye, if you don't mind Johnny's lips bein' on it!"

Then he told me about the spike.

"Stanley, you know that wine doesn't have much kick, so I bought a bottle of alcohol after we got the booze, and we spiked each bottle to give 'er some real kick."

"No shit, Michael! What kind of alcohol?"

"Rubbing alcohol, bye."

I studied Michael's face for a moment to see if he was pulling my leg.

"No shit, Stanley...you'll feel it tonight!"

"Are you sure it's safe?"

"Yeeees, bye, we only mixed in a couple of ounces in each bottle."

I stuffed the bottle under my jacket and hitched a ride home to get dressed for the dance.

Around 8:30 p.m., I arrived at the Legion Hall as the band warmed up. I hid the bottle under a pile of dead branches in the field above the Hall to be retrieved later when courage was called for. I hung around with some of the guys from school and passed judgment on some of the arriving girls. Almost no one had a date. We went single, hoping to change that later.

Around 9:45, I needed a boost of bravery to ask one of the girls to dance. I invited Johnny to accompany me to my wine hideaway. Being polite, I handed it to Johnny to take a drink first. He raised the bottle and took a gulp. His eyes bulged out. He lurched forward and spit it out.

"Jaysus Christ, that tastes like shit! Is that kerosene?"

I scoffed. "Come on Johnny, hand it to me."

I put the bottle to my lips and swallowed hard and swift to avoid the taste.

"Yeeeech!"

Johnny was right. I gagged.

"How can you drink that shit?"

The fiery liquid hit my stomach."Whoooooo!"

I felt a buzz like never before. I instantly felt happy. I took second swig, figuring that if the first one made me feel that good, then the second would send me to heaven.

"Stanley, you're crazy. That stuff will kill you because it has something in it besides wine."

"Yeah, I know."

"You know?"

"Rubbing alcohol," I replied, casually.

"Get out! Are you serious?"

"Yeah."

"For Chrissakes, rubbing alcohol will make you go blind or even kill you."

"I'll just drink enough 'til I need glasses."

"Well, don't offer *me* anymore of that poison. And don't light a match!"

We wandered down to the Legion Hall door as I evolved into a more courageous, better-looking answer to a girl's prayers. I was Elvis.

The band played as I swayed confidently to Mary Collins and asked her to dance. I momentarily forgot that I couldn't dance.

She eyed me and paused. "No, thanks, not right now."

She whispered something to her friend, and they both giggled. My nerve took a nosedive.

I instantly felt the sting of rejection, and the sudden confidence that I had felt earlier crashed like a water-filled condom. My bashful self reappeared. I wasn't Elvis anymore. I was strange Stanley Campbell, with the high sloping forehead and big nose. I made a rapid exit from the Hall, alone this time, and stumbled up to the field to get an additional blast of courage. I slugged down a bigger gulp of the foul liquid, and instead of replacing the bottle under the tree branches, I stuffed it under my charcoal sports coat with the pink flecks in it and weaved back to the hall.

"G'day, Stanley Roddie John R. bye!" It was a raspy voice from the shadows by the Hall door, a familiar face at parties, dances, ceilidhs, and wakes, a man affectionately known as Neil Sticks.

Neil got his nickname Neil Sticks from the crutches on which he walked for most of his life after a bad bout with polio years earlier and three decades before political correctness.

"G'day, Neil, how you doin'?" I answered, now with an air of cockiness.

"Pretty good, Stanley bye. Would you know where a fellow could get a drink?" He stubbed out his cigarette with his good foot.

I proudly handed him the bottle.

"Sure, Neil, have a hooter of this"

Neil took the bottle from my hand, balanced himself on his crutches, tilted the bottle upward, and took a large swig. He lowered it immediately and almost dropped it.

"Jesus, Mary, and Joseph! What the hell is that?"

"Wine," I replied, with a stupid grin.

"Wine my arse! That's rat poison, bye."

I laughed.

"Don't laugh, bye! You drink anymore of that poison, and you'll wake up dead in the morning."

I guffawed and staggered to the other side of the Hall and swallowed an extra mouthful. As I developed more nerve, my walking ability diminished. In fact, Neil Sticks moved straighter than I did. I sauntered into the Hall and approached a few more girls but was sober enough to realize that they wanted to avoid me. I saw two of everybody. I staggered outside to finish the bottle, but when the cool night air hit me, my recollection of any further events dissolved.

I woke up some time in the mid-morning in my bed at home. I didn't know how I had gotten there. My feet rose upward, and my head sank as I rotated in a reverse, rapidly increasing motion...or so it seemed. The bed rotated backward with the foot rising and the head falling faster and faster. I thought I was dying. What had happened the night before? Did my parents know that I was drunk? Were they even here? I didn't know anything. I was paranoid.

The hangover lasted for several days. My throat burned, and my eyesight was blurred.

Days and weeks later I realized how lucky I was to be alive, but conquering my shyness was going to be tough without booze.

The Summer Of My Malcontent

In late July, a letter from the Province of Nova Scotia arrived with the results of my grades eleven and twelve provincial exams. I scanned my grade twelve results to confirm that I had finally graduated from high school. I had...barely. It was official. But wait. Not so fast. I scanned the next document. It was the result of the two grade eleven subjects that I had had to repeat, biology and history. My grade in biology was 23 out of a maximum score of 100. In history, I made it all the way to 43. Shit! I had flunked grade eleven again but passed grade twelve! I could not officially graduate from high school unless I passed those grade eleven subjects. I didn't care. To hell with it! I was done. Life was waiting.

I spent the summer of '59 working for the Nova Scotia Highway Department as a laborer on a new highway through Jamesville West to Iona, a distance of five miles. I went to work at 7:00 each morning suffering from various stages of hangovers.

My hangovers were different. Most drinking people complained of horrific headaches, nausea, and diarrhea after a night of either heavy drinking or consuming brown murky crap, otherwise known as bull beer. No, my hangovers were mental. I was a nervous, psychotic wreck. I had visions of doom. I feared that the world might end at any moment. I didn't trust my own judgment. If I crossed the road, I looked both ways and even though I saw nothing coming, I still was not convinced that a busload of Boston tourists wasn't hurtling down the highway to flatten me.

Ironically, on the job, the boss had me handling sticks of dynamite. Dynamite! I wasn't legally old enough to hold a beer in my hand, yet I was assigned to man-handle a man-sized air drill and bore holes into rock and then drop charges of high explosives down the hole. I somehow got through the summer without losing vital body parts or killing anyone.

My Uncle Arthur, who was dealing with his own hooch demons, when he wasn't driving off the road into the alders, offered advice.

"Why don't you try for a job at the Bank of Montréal in Sydney? I know someone there, and I could put in a word for you."

"A bank? I don't want to work in a bank. I would be bored to friggin' death!"

"Well, the highway job is ending soon, and you're going to need a job."

"Alright, I'll give it a shot, but temporarily until I can get a job at CJCB Radio."

"Okay, I'll call Ronald MacKinnon at the bank and tell him you'll come in."

I was not motivated. I really wanted to go to the esteemed Saint Francis Xavier University in Antigonish, Nova Scotia, and study engineering or science, but I didn't have a high school diploma. I talked to Pop's good friend Jack Small, who was an electronics technician. I knew that I had an aptitude for electronics. I had read *Popular Electronics* since I was a kid. I learned by tinkering with the radio and TV.

I was 14 when we got our first TV. Within the first month, I had unscrewed the rear cover off the TV, removed the chassis, and had it placed upside down on the floor when Pop arrived home from work too early. I had to see how it all worked and actually believed that I could make it work better than the manufacturer had. Mom had already written me off as an electrical madman by that point.

My father's response was predictable. "Cripes Almighty!"

That was his most sinful curse word, although I had already introduced him to the top five profanities of the day.

"What the hell have you done? The TV will never work again! You've ruined it!" He breathed heavily while his face grew the color of boiled beets.

"No, no, it's okay. I can put it together."

"Stanley, you'll never get that back together!"

Mom escaped into the bedroom to avoid the impending explosion.

"I paid four hundred dollars for that TV!"

That was a lot of money in 1954. It could have paid for running water, and maybe even a porcelain toilet.

I began the TV reassembly while Pop complained that I was doing it wrong. In ten minutes, it was done. I pushed the on-button and waited while Pop proclaimed that the TV was done for. For him, losing the TV was a fate worse than a fall hurricane lifting the roof off the house. In fact, as he aged, TV became a priority in his life, while running water, an indoor bathroom, and a furnace came second and third to a satellite dish and a bigger screen. To my suffering Mom, television was meaningless. She pronounced it tele*vision*. Maybe she pronounced it that way because she could see it but rarely heard it.

It took a minute for the TV to warm up, and the usual snowy picture filled the screen. After all, we were forty miles from the TV station. My father remained still. Not another word was spoken about the matter until a few days later when I heard him boasting to our next-door neighbor, Walter MacDougall, that I was a technical genius, but he nervously speculated on how I had learned that stuff. He apparently was proud of me, yet he never told me so. He did worry when I created a timer from an old alarm clock to turn the TV on at 6:00 p.m.

He expressed his fears to Walter. "If he can do that, he could make a time bomb."

Playing with dynamite, drinking, and a girl named Sarah Ann consumed the rest of my summer. I had met her early in the summer at an outdoor wedding reception. My younger zany friend, Howard, and I walked five miles most nights to Ottawa Brook to see Sarah Ann and her sister Wilma. Howard was over six feet tall. He liked Wilma, who was just south of five feet. Sarah Ann became my first steady girlfriend, at least for the summer of '59.

I knew that this was going to be the summer that I would finally get caught up to all my friends and have that first sexual ecstasy with a girl, and since she was my steady girlfriend, we would be doing it every chance we got! Heaven was only a zipper away.

I did have one handicap. I didn't have a car. Pop would not let me have his at night, assuming that I would be drinking, but my drinking took a backseat to Sarah Ann. Sadly, I didn't have a backseat, so we got to be alone at her Uncle Alfie's place when he was at work.

We kissed until my lips hurt while my hands moved farther and farther south, only to be met by her hand which relocated my hand north. I nibbled on her ears, her neck, and tried nibbling down past the equator, but I was again relocated to the northern hemisphere.

This was a bigger challenge than I had expected. I was practicing for radio, so I used my richest tones to swear that I loved her and that she was the only girl in the world for me. She was unmoved.

I tried for the rest of summer. Howard and I brought a jam bottle of bull beer that we had stolen in an effort to ply them with alcohol. That didn't work. They both threw up. Kissing a girl who had just vomited is not an experience I wanted to repeat.

I knew that getting into Sarah Ann's pants was an exercise in futility, especially when she declared, "I really want us to make love, but when we're married."

I thought about it. I was desperate. I bought her an engagement ring. A cheap one. In the meantime, I needed to get a job, and playing with dynamite sticks or working in a bank weren't my ideal career choices. I wanted to be the guy on the radio. Besides, I imagined that girls would drag me into their bedrooms.

I needed moral support, so I asked my friend James Andre MacKinnon to go with me to Sydney to CJCB Radio. It was the only commercial radio in Cape Breton. CJCB played the Top 10 songs on Sundays and country and western music every afternoon. We ascended the stairs to the CJCB studios. I was awestruck. There were knobs and dials, the microphones, the soundproof walls, and even a distinct radio aroma. A guy on the air with headphones rolled back and forth the length of the studio on his chair, and then swung around, turning on his microphone to talk on the air. Oh God! I wanted to do that.

"Can I help you?" A receptionist interrupted my fantasy.

"Uh...yes...I would like to talk to the manager, Mr. Nathanson."

"What did you want to see Mr. Nathanson about?"

"Uh...well, I am interested in a job in radio."

"Well, I'm sure that Mr. Nathanson would be pleased to speak with you, but he is New York until Monday."

"New York? New York *City*?"

"Yes, he is meeting with some broadcast executives in New York."

"Oh...okay. Thanks"

The fact that Mr. Nathanson was influential enough to be traveling to New York *City* to meet with executives intimidated me. I decided to go across the street to CBI Radio, which was in my mind the much lesser of the two radio stations. After all, it belonged to the Canadian Broadcasting Corporation. They played crappy music like opera and classical and aired a lot of news. Nobody listened to that shit, so I figured that it might be a good place to begin my radio career.

It was easy. An elderly lady in a gray suit ushered me into a meeting with a stout, bespectacled guy sporting a tweed jacket and bow tie. He sat in a leather chair and inquired if I had a degree in journalism. I didn't want to admit that I hadn't even graduated from high school.

"You don't have a degree?" He peered over his rimless glasses. "We expect our commentators to have at least a bachelor's degree."

I wanted to tell him that if I had a degree, I wouldn't be sitting in this shithole. He addressed me as though I was five years old.

"All right, well maybe we could give you a minor pronunciation test." He pulled out a long paper from a file cabinet. "There are some foreign place names and other words that I would like you to read aloud for me. Would you go ahead and read them please?"

"Sure!"

There were a few things that I did excel at in school, geography and spelling. I scanned the list. Holy shit! The first word was *Braunschweig*. Was that a place or a sausage? I made my best attempt. The next was *Lyon*, which I pronounced like the king of the jungle. He did not react. He could not curb his impatience when I got to *mischievous*. Like most people, I pronounced it mis-chee'-vee-us, with the accent on the chee.

He yanked the paper from my hand. "Young man, it's mis'-che-vus!"

He put the accent on the *mis*. Apparently that was the Queen's English. Great! I was no fan of the Queen. He curtly informed me that I was not ready for a Canadian Broadcasting Corporation station.

"Who the hell do those CBI assholes think they are?" I griped to James Andre as we marched down Charlotte Street. I was raging. "Screw them! I don't need their big-shot, boring goddamned radio station. Who listens to that shit anyway? Nobody, except a bunch of snooty old ladies."

"You could go back to CJCB and talk to Norris Nathanson, Stanley."

"Nah, I don't think so. I'm going to join the Air Force."

"The Air Force?" James Andre stopped abruptly, causing a lady with a Woolworth's bag to run into him. "Sorry. When did you decide to join the Air Force?"

"Now!" I continued in a breathless, angry rant. "I don't need this shit any more. I can't afford to go to college. Besides, I didn't graduate from high school, so I couldn't get into college, anyway, and I need to find a profession of some kind, maybe a pilot, no wait, I need a degree to be a pilot, well fuck it, I'm doing something, anything to get the hell out of Cape Breton, and I want to marry a nice girl and live in a house with a fucking indoor toilet and lie in bed next to my wife at night. Come on, let's go home!"

I was done. I had worked on the highway, tried out for a job at the bank, found out that being the guy on the radio was too daunting, and my immaculate girlfriend Sarah Ann would not go past heavy breathing. I had lied about lover's nuts and blue balls. I had warned her that I could die from this terminal condition. She said that she was sorry, but she couldn't help. She recommended that I take matters into my own hands. That suggestion stirred up visions of Mother Saint Marilyn. I even cried in a futile attempt to appeal to Sarah Ann's feminine side. She cried along with me.

The summer was over. I had no job, no future, and no sex. I had to get to hell off the island. I searched for the Royal Canadian Air Force Recruiting Centre in the Yellow Pages.

I strolled in and declared, "I want to join the Air Force."

To my amazement, the guy in the blue uniform did not jump from his seat and congratulate me for my wise choice.

Instead, he handed me a stack of forms and a pen. "Fill these out. When you are through, leave them here, and someone will call you."

Well, that was a problem. We didn't have a phone at home. We had never had a phone, even though Alexander Graham Bell had spent the last fifteen years of his life less than twenty miles from our house! We had no phone, no running water, and no indoor bathroom, but we had one hundred and fifty TV channels.

I would have joined the Air Force simply to take a crap on a porcelain toilet without the fear of a deadly snake or poisonous spider nipping at my nuts. I wanted to experience a hot shower. Hey, maybe that was why no girl wanted to feel my skin next to hers.

* * *

I explained to the bored Air Force man that we didn't have a phone at home, but he could call my Uncle Frank down the road, who did have a telephone. Uncle Arthur was across the road, but I couldn't take a chance that he might be drunk and tell the Air Force guy to fuck off.

I filled in all the information and handed the forms to the Air Force recruiter.

He shuffled through the papers and said, "We'll get in touch to let you know if you've been accepted, and if so, you'll have to come in for a complete medical."

I left feeling good about what I had done and caught a bus to Glace Bay to see Sarah Ann to tell her that I was joining the Air Force and that she might never see me again. I might be sent off to war and be killed while being strafed by anti-aircraft fire, even though we weren't at war with anyone. This could be her last chance to make love before I died.

It didn't work. The ring in my wallet was becoming more obvious. Not an engagement ring, but the condom that I had been carrying for the past two years in the event that good fortune would befall me one night in the backseat of my father's '48 Chevy.

Back home in Jamesville West I declared that I was joining the Air Force. My father was thrilled. My mother was not. I think she would have preferred that I get a nice job at the Bank of Montréal or go to work at the Gypsum Plant at Little Narrows, ten miles away. I believe that she was worried that I would go away and never return, now that I knew that I was adopted.

I spent a few weeks watching TV, all one hundred and fifty channels, one hundred of them in French, which none of us understood. I waited for the phone call. My Uncle Frank lived a mile away. If he was at work, his wife Patsy might not tell me for weeks if there was a phone call for me.

I went over to their house. "Any calls for me, Aunt Patsy?"

"Calls for you? Lemme see. Oh, yes, some guy from the Army called."

"The *Army*?"

"Yes, I think it was the Army. A man said that you had to call them."

"Are you sure it was the Army?"

"I don't know. Maybe it was the Navy, something like that. You know, the military."

"Oh, for Christ's sake, let me make a long distance phone call, okay?"

"Go ahead, but don't take too long. Long distance is expensive."

"I know, I know." I dug through the phone book hunting for the Air Force number.

I called Honey, our local phone operator, and asked her to connect me to the Air Force Recruiting Office in Sydney.

"Oh, you're going to join the Air Force are you, Stanley?" Honey inquired.

Honey was a sweet lady, but this time I did not care to engage her in conversation.

"Oh, that's wonderful."

The phone rang on the other end. "Air Force Recruiting Centre"

"Hello, this is Stan Campbell. You called?"

"Who?"

"Alexander S. Campbell, sir, I filled out an application."

"Hold on." He rustled some papers and came back on the line. "Yes, we have your application. You have been approved so far."

"Thank You!" I responded, just a bit too effusively.

"We'll be in touch in four to six months."

"Four to six months? Why?"

"That's the waiting period." The not-so-nice Air Force man interrupted me.

My glee was instantly replaced by disappointment. I didn't want to wait six months. I couldn't. I needed a job, a life, somewhere to go, a girl who would say yes.

"Thank you." I hung up dejected, although I had been accepted.

I held the phone in my hand considering my options, but only for a moment.

I suddenly shot to my feet and ran out the door, shouting, "To hell with the Air Force, I'm joining the Army!"

I caught the CN *Railiner* to Sydney and hired a taxi from the train station to the Army Recruiting Centre. I filled out another stack of forms and then hitched a ride to visit Sarah Ann. I told her that I had changed my mind, that I was joining the Army and that I could be bayoneted in a trench or die in a grenade blast. I reminded her that we were engaged and that we should do it in case we never got to consummate our marriage. She laughed this time. Besides, her mother was scrutinizing me carefully. Mothers know.

I rode the train back to Jamesville West.

Just as I arrived, Aunt Pasty stopped me. "The Army called again."

"You sure it was the Army this time?"

"Yes, of course. The man said that he was calling from the Canadian Army Recruiting Centre in Sydney."

I called Honey again and this time requested the Canadian Army Recruiting Centre.

"Army Recruiting Centre, this is Corporal Collins."

"Hello, Corporal, this is Alexander S. Campbell and I..."

"Right, Mr. Campbell, your application is approved. We are sending you a train ticket to your address in Jamesville West. You need to be in Halifax on January 15th for a complete medical and indoctrination. Basic training begins in Camp Gagetown on February 6th."

"Uh..."

"Is there a problem, Campbell?"

"No...but...I...

"Yes?

"I, well, I want to be in the Signal Corps."

"They will decide that in Halifax after your aptitude tests."

"Uh, what if I don't pass the aptitude test?"

"Well, you will likely go to the infantry or artillery."

I didn't like those options. I needed to learn a profession that I could use when I got out of the Army. There wasn't much demand for shooting off artillery shells as a civilian. I was nervous, but it was a done deal, and I was going for sure.

Sarah Ann would be sorry when I found a gorgeous girl in New Brunswick. One who would be happy to take her clothes off for me, maybe even marry me. This was going to be a whole new life. Besides, the Army had porcelain toilets. I had not yet learned about latrines.

My Two Birthdays

I thought my father was having a heart attack. It was 10:30 at night in mid-January in 1960. We were stuck in a snowdrift on the way to the train station, for my first trip away from home, to join the Army. Pop shoveled hard, too hard, as I kicked the snow from the tires with my feet. He stopped and leaned against the car holding his chest while breathing heavily. His face grew whiter than the snow drifts beneath the car. I was worried. I had to leave while Pop might be seriously ill.

"Are you okay?" I asked.

"Yes, I'm okay. I'm out of breath, that's all." He was clearly struggling.

"Are you sure? You don't look good."

He ignored my question. "Let's get moving, or you'll miss the train."

I wasn't convinced, but I was torn between this new adventure and my concern for Pop. He rocked the car back and forth from low gear to reverse until we freed the car from the deepening snow.

The train was a half hour late but it gave Pop time to catch his breath and recover some color. Nevertheless, I knew that he was not well. I worried about him driving home. The train to Halifax came to a screeching stop as I said good-bye to Pop. I tried to hide my quivering lower lip as I handed the conductor my suitcase and climbed on board.

I wasn't alone on the train. One car was filled with young Army recruits, just like me.

"Holy fuck, man, you should see the broads up in the next car," some guy twice my size but close to my age yelled as he took over the aisle of our sleeper car.

A skinny guy with a terminal case of acne ran down the aisle. "No shit? I'm gonna go check 'em out." I had never heard the word *broads* before. I was too timid and too embarrassed to ask. I suspected that broads might be Army officers. It didn't take me long to realize that I was suddenly out of the woods and out of my league. I was on my way to the big city, Halifax, Nova Scotia. I was a green hayseed from a wide spot in the road.

* * *

A green Army bus picked us up at the train station in Halifax and took us to Windsor Park Army Base. We were assigned rooms, four guys to a room. It was as if all the other guys knew each other, or maybe they weren't as insecure as I was. Already, I felt out of place. I missed the security of Jamesville West and familiar people.

The first morning, those of us who didn't have official birth certificates were ordered to go to downtown Halifax to the Office of Vital Statistics. I had brought along my baptismal certificate, the one that had shocked me four years earlier when I found out that I was adopted. It clearly confirmed my natural mother's name, Cecelia McNeil, but no father was listed.

I pondered my origin. Was I the result of a one night fling in New Waterford, Nova Scotia, where the document indicated that I was born? According to my calculations, I would have been conceived around New Year's Day in 1940. Many thoughts raced through my mind as I sat in the dingy, gray Vital Statistics office studying my baptismal certificate, while waiting for someone to call my name. My birth date was handwritten. September 9th, 1940. Then I noticed something bizarre written on the bottom of my baptismal certificate. My birth was registered on April 6, 1940...five months *before* I was born! How the hell was this possible? Could it be that my mother was homeless, a drunk, or worse.

"Alexander Campbell!" the chubby lady with horn-rimmed glasses yelled out into space, as I sat directly in front of her.

"Here!"

"Here is your certificate of birth," she said, as she pointed out each line with a pencil on the official-looking bond paper. "It shows your place of birth as New Waterford, Nova Scotia, and the date September 13, 1940."

"Thank you. No! Wait a minute. This isn't right. I was born on September 9th. See, it says so right here on my baptismal certificate."

"No, you were born on September 13, 1940.

"That can't be right."

"Sir, we don't make mistakes with this sort of thing. That's what is in the record."

I was bewildered. I had actually been celebrating my birthday on the wrong day...not that anyone had actually celebrated it. I could have had *two* birthday parties in the same year, or one long one from the 9th to the 13th. Now I was convinced that my mother was an alcoholic or on drugs, and who the hell was my father? I tried to imagine where he might be at that moment. Then, I reasoned that 1940 had been the beginning of World War II and that he was probably a sailor, in town for a fun night.

From here on out, I was going to search for my birth mother and find out how and why I came into this world and why she had put me up for adoption. I would get to the bottom of that mystery later.

* * *

At the army base in Windsor Park, after a visit to the john, one with a porcelain toilet, I took a long look at my face in the mirror. I stared back at me. *Who am I? Who do I resemble? Do I look like my mother or my father?* Over the past few years a few friends who were aware that I had been adopted, suggested that I might be Italian or Indian. I joked that my parents were Russian because they named me Alexander Stanislaus, and that my original last name was Smirnoff.

I made myself a promise. *If it takes the rest of my life, I will find out who I am and why I have two birth dates.* I had heard about people who were born again, but I doubted if this was what they meant.

* * *

Over the next few days, I got to know some guys, and we all went through the same routine, forms to fill out, an M-Test (which was the Army's version of an IQ test), and a complete medical. It was the first time that I was naked in a room with a bunch of guys. A corporal marched us into a room where we all got shots for something and then into another room where a doctor stuck his fingers under my balls and told me to cough. Dr. Ferguson back home had never done that.

One smart-ass guy from Newfoundland got sent home on the next train home when he asked the doctor, "Do ya wanna play with my pecker too, bye?"

"Campbell, Alexander!" someone yelled in the barracks hallway.

"Here!" I was getting used to the yelling.

A young lance corporal clicked his hob-nail boots on the concrete floor as he pointed the way. "Come with me."

I obediently marched behind him, not knowing where I was going.

"Step lively, Campbell, we're going to see the shrink."

"The what?"

I didn't want anything shrunk. Shit! I hadn't used it yet.

"A psychiatrist, Campbell. You need to visit the Army shrink."

A wave of anxiety swept over me. *Maybe my sometime-friend, Alexander, in Iona was right when he told me that I was weird. Maybe I do have a screw loose. Maybe the rubbing alcohol melted my brain cells. Maybe the doctor knew from checking my balls that I'm still a virgin. Maybe they don't let virgins into the Army. Shit!*

The psychiatrist reminded me of Jimmy Stewart, with his tweed jacket complete with patches on the arms. He did not wear a uniform, as I expected. He smoked a pipe. I swore that I had seen him in a movie once. He invited me to sit as he introduced himself as Dr. Bonnell. The more I tried to act normal, the more abnormal I felt.

He leaned forward and spoke softly. "Have you ever been in a fight?"

His gentle tone bothered me. Maybe he thought that if he raised his voice, I might come unglued and rip his throat out...or cry.

"Uh, yes a few times."

"Did you win?"

"Sometimes."

"How did it make you feel when you didn't win?"

"I dunno." I couldn't figure where this was going, but then it occurred to me that maybe he thought that I was queer, or somebody did and they had sent me here to find out.

I attempted to act more macho. Then he posed the question that convinced me that either he thought I was a homosexual or that the ball test confirmed that I was a virgin.

He sat back in his squeaky leather chair, making a farting sound. "Do you like girls?"

I didn't hesitate for a millisecond. "Yes, I love them!"

"In the Army, you may have to kill people. How does that make you feel?"

"Okay." *Shit! Was that the right answer?*

If I sounded too enthusiastic, he might assume that I was a latent serial killer.

Then he said something that shocked me. "You know that as a soldier, you are a hired killer."

"Yeah..." I sounded unsure, not knowing how thrilled I should be at the thought of shooting large groups of people.

"All right, that will be all for today, Mr. Campbell."

He dismissed me, as he scribbled something in his notepad.

"Thank you, Doctor." I was glad to be released from this peculiar interrogation.

But what the hell was that thing about, *for today?* I feared that he might move me up to the next level and question me in restraints. I imagined what he wrote on his notepad. *Young man from wide spot in the road in Cape Breton wants to be a soldier. Lunatic virgin. Enjoys shooting large groups of people.*

I raced back to the barracks, speculating about my fate and attempted to learn if the other guys had to go through the same inquisition.

"Hey, MacInnis, did you have to go see a shrink?"

"A psychiatrist?" he guffawed. "No, Campbell, are you kidding?"

"No." I knew I shouldn't have asked.

Too late.

"You had to go see a head doctor, Campbell? Are you a nut case?" MacInnis laughed louder. "Hey Hanson, guess what? They sent Campbell to see a shrink. Ha! Ha! Ha!"

MacInnis rolled around on his bed, still giggling like a girl. I was not amused. I was worried. Maybe the rubbing alcohol from the high school dance had fucked up my brain, or just maybe my famous hot and sometimes violent temper had showed through. Now the whole damn Army knew that I had had to have my head examined. I knew that I should have waited for the Air Force.

February 2, 1960, the day that the army brass would let me know if I had been accepted into the Signal Corps. If not, I would be a boots-on-the-ground infantryman in the Black Watch, complete with kilt and a healthy fear of dying with my boots on and my kilt up. I now wished that I had graduated from high school instead of boozing and fantasizing about being naked in a grassy field with Sally or Sheila. The Signal Corps preferred people with a high school diploma because the training consisted of some heavy math, algebra, and trigonometry. Thankfully, those were my favorite subjects, even if I had flunked almost everything else.

*   *   *

The spiffy sergeant shouted the results to us, one after the other, calling out names in alphabetical order. The letter C came up promptly.

"Recruit Campbell, you are posted immediately to Camp Gagetown, New Brunswick, for ten weeks of intensive basic training with the Royal Canadian Black Watch."

My heart sank. I was going to be in the fucking Black Watch wearing a kilt and running around in the mud with a rifle and a mess-tin full of porridge!

The sergeant went on. "Should you complete your basic training course successfully, you will be posted to the Royal Canadian Signal School at Vimy Barracks in Kingston, Ontario, as Signalman rank to begin your electronics training."

"Thank You, Sergeant."

I was elated. I would be in the Signal Corps. I wanted to go get drunk. I didn't. I was 19 and not old enough to drink. It was something that those of us under 21 bitched about non-stop.

* * *

On Wednesday, February 3, 1960, we, new freshmen recruits, began the journey to Camp Gagetown, New Brunswick, by train from Halifax. We got off the train into the coldest night I had ever experienced, to be met by red-headed Corporal Schlosser, who was colder than Jack Frost.

He was loud and menacing. "Get your asses onto the bus now! What the fuck are you waiting for? Move it!"

He came over to me, his face less than an inch from mine.

I felt his hot breath and saw the vapor from his scream. "What the fuck are you lookin' at, Dopey? Do you like me? Are you queer for me?"

"No, sir!"

"What? I can't hear you!"

"No, sir!"

"Do you see pips on my shoulder? Do you, Recruit?"

I didn't know what pips were, but I figured that the correct response was no.

"No, sir!" My voice cracked as I shouted.

"Are you fucking stupid or just dense? You address an *Officer* as sir. I am Corporal Schlosser. *Corporal* Schlosser! You got that? You see this stripe on my arm, that's Lance Corporal Schlosser. Now get it right. You answer, 'Yes, Corporal'"

"Yes, Corporal!" Tears welled up in my eyes.

I did not want him to see me cry, or he would never get off my ass. I was far from home and the security and politeness I had known all my life. I wanted to be home with my mom. No one had ever spoken to me like that before, especially a stranger.

We were marched into our barracks, which was to be home for the next ten weeks, dumped our bags of personal belongings, and it was lights out.

Had I screwed up this time?

No Fun With Dick And Jane

It was twenty-two degrees below zero Fahrenheit as someone behind me yanked my shorts down to my ankles, exposing my freezing, rapidly diminishing parts to the office windows across the street. I swiftly bent over to pull them up, and as I did, an icy hand grabbed my arse from behind.

"Campbell, are you trying to give the ladies in the paymaster's office a show?" Sergeant Bigger bellowed. "From what I can see, they're not going to be impressed. Now straighten up, and pull your fucking shorts up!"

I couldn't figure out why he was giving me shit when it was the asshole behind me who had yanked my shorts down. I considered for a second the wisdom of complaining, but on second thought, I let it go. Besides, we were standing there, as ordered, in T-shirts, gym shorts, and boots, flash-freezing our arses and other sensitive parts. We needed to do something, or we would be able to donate frozen sperm on the spot!

"Okay, girls, we're going to get you warmed up. We're going for a scenic run."

The short Sergeant Bigger gave us the first official drill instruction for a right turn.

"Squad, right turn!" His high-pitched yell scared the crap out of me.

I smartly spun ninety degrees to the right...face-to-face with tall, skinny, freckle-faced, rooster-headed Recruit Noseworthy from Clarenville, Newfoundland. He had turned left.

Sergeant Bigger, with his swagger stick under his arm, leisurely strolled over to Noseworthy and stared up at him, as we waited for what we all knew would be something out of the ordinary. It was.

"Noseworthy! The *other* fucking right!" We heard the sergeant's echo bounce off the buildings on the other side of the parade square.

Noseworthy spun around one hundred and eighty degrees this time, losing his balance as he twisted.

Sergeant Bigger issued another ear piercing command. "By the right, quiiiiiick march!"

We marched in our disjointed, disorderly, out-of-step new-recruit manner.

"Double time!"

We ran and ran and ran, and ran. I thought my chest might explode. Recruit Robinson fell into a ditch. We kept running. Recruit Donahue fell by the wayside and vomited. I was sure that I would die, but I was not going to go by falling into a ditch or throwing up. The goal was to run ten miles. None of us made it. This was the Army and basic training with the dreaded Black Watch.

Some weaker recruits were sent home early. Noseworthy was one of them. He couldn't march. Most people swing their arms opposite to their leg motion. For some curious reason, his arms swung with his legs. If he put his right foot forward, he also put the right arm forward. He didn't walk down the street like that, but when it came to marching, his coordination got screwed up. It all ended one day after Sergeant Bigger screamed at him one too many times, which caused him to break down and blubber. The next day, he was gone.

Basic training was hell, but it developed my muscles into rocks and sent my testosterone level up past the overflow mark, which was exasperating because I was still a damn virgin. I had no opportunity in the first four weeks to do anything about that situation, simply because we weren't permitted to leave the base.

But the day came when we were allowed to go to downtown Fredericton, a city only thirteen miles away. We were in search of girls. There was one problem. Approximately one hundred thousand other excessively horny soldiers lived on the same base, and they were in pursuit of the same fifty girls who might actually socialize with Army guys. Until we graduated from basic training, we were not allowed to wear civilian clothes. We had no chance with girls. Even after graduating, we still had no opportunity because our buzzed haircuts gave us away.

Four or five guys in my squad were married. They talked about missing their wives, and some even described the joys of snuggling up to a warm and loving female body every night and nights of wild, wall-rattling sex. They described some of the sexy games they played and the rewards that their wives bestowed upon them. This was obviously intended to drive me nuts. It worked. Most of all, I simply wanted a girl in my life to love and to love me. Unlike a lot of guys my age, I wanted to be married. I envisioned us living a life of bliss and maybe later, kids.

One weekend, it seemed like my luck might change. One of my closest buddies, Recruit Dick Hanson, was from nearby Fredericton. He was amicably divorced from his wife Jane. So cordial was their parting that they still slept together on occasion. She invited him over to her apartment one weekend. Dick told her that I needed a date, so Jane lined me up with her friend Sylvia.

Dick and I arrived at the apartment on Saturday evening. Jane introduced me to Sylvia. The deal was made. We were all sleeping there that night. Well, at least Dick was sleeping with Jane. My fate was undetermined. I thought that Sylvia was attractive. She was slightly overweight and wore rimless glasses. She reminded me of a Jehovah Witness lady who had come to our door at home once. She just appeared religious.

After a few bottles of wine, it was time to go to bed.

Before Dick and Jane closed the door to their room, Jane pointed to a door and smiled slyly. "Stan and Sylvia, that's your room. Good night."

Hallelujah! We may have to say our prayers first, but we are sleeping together tonight! I opened the door. She sat on the edge of the bed.

I sat next to her and kissed her. This was it. This was going to be the big night. Wahoo! This was going to be the end of my virginity, and damn, it was about time.

I was nervous. So was she. She removed her glasses and placed them on the night table. I thought that she was pretty even with her glasses on. Oh, this was going to be a night to remember.

"It's late. Maybe we need to go to sleep because you and Dick have to leave early in the morning," she whispered by my face as I held her.

"You're right, maybe we need to go to bed."

In bed was exactly where I wanted us to be.

She smiled sweetly. "We need to shut off the light so I can get undressed."

"Sure. We can both get undressed."

I was euphoric. This was it! My time had finally arrived. I shut off the light. It was dark, except for a street light that blinked on and off.

I heard the rustle of clothes. It was Sylvia slipping out of her dress. I pulled my T-shirt over my head and dropped my pants to the floor and launched myself under the covers. After I got under the covers, I yanked off my Army-issue boxers and threw them on the floor. I was ready! Bliss was just a kiss away!

"Are you already in bed, Stan?"

"Yeah."

"Oh."

"Oh, what?"

"I have to brush my teeth."

I hoped that she wasn't running away. The hallway light burst into the room as I saw her disappear.

I thought that maybe I should go and brush my teeth too, but it was too late. After an interminable wait she momentarily flooded the room with the hallway light again. It grew dark again. I heard the unmistakable sound of fabric on skin. I felt her crawl under the covers on the other side of the bed. It occurred to me that it was an amazing, fantastic thing that this girl, Sylvia, had actually agreed to go to bed with me. I felt accepted. In spite of being an Army trained killer now, able to run ten miles carrying a load of rocks and a rifle, crawl through half a mile of mud under barbed wire, and lob a grenade at the enemy, for the first time this, more than anything, made me feel like a man. Here was a woman who felt comfortable enough to share a bed with me and now, her body.

I reached for her. I kissed her. I slid my arms down her back. She was naked. Oh, joy! After this night, I would be ready to die. We kissed some more until I made it obvious to her how damned excited I was and that we needed to consummate this treasured moment in time.

But then, I felt her move away. "I really like you."

"I like you too." I responded dutifully.

"But..."

"Yes?"

"I can't."

"You can't what?"

"I can't have sex with you."

"What? Why?" I whimpered like the virgin I was.

"I made a promise to God that I would not have sexual relations until I am married."

I felt a bucket of ice cubes drop in my groin. I was silent for a long time.

"Stan?"

"Yes."

"Are you mad at me?"

I wanted to say, *Mad? Yes, I'm fucking mad! I'm a raging bull!* Instead, I wailed. I cried. I begged. I tried to reason with her that God would not be upset with her. Here I was for the second time in my life with a naked girl in my arms, and it went nowhere. I was a 20-year-old virgin. My friends had been laid fifty times over. At least that's what they told me, and some of them were ugly fuckers. What the hell was wrong with *me*?

"No, I'm not mad at you." I lied.

She wasn't convinced. "Yes, you are, aren't you?"

Well, I wasn't really mad. I attempted to understand what was wrong with *me*. How come every guy I knew claimed to have had women rip their clothes off and luxuriate in rowdy, mind-blowing sex all night, except me? No, I was a loser. Women didn't want to be intimate with me, even when we were naked in the same damn bed.

"I'm sorry, I want to save myself for marriage."

"Yeah, sure, I understand." I pouted as I rolled over to face the wall. "Good night, Sylvia."

"Stan, please don't be mad at me. I really like you. You're a nice guy."

"Right."

She caressed my back for a while until she fell asleep. I fell asleep an hour before the sun came up. Sylvia was still sleeping when I awoke an hour later. I sneaked out of bed, got dressed, and went out to the kitchen, where Dick was making coffee.

"Hey, Stan, you horny devil, you got laid last night!" He chuckled wickedly.

"No, I didn't"

"Yeah, sure, you can't fool me, Campbell."

"I'm fucking serious, Dick. I didn't, Goddamn it!"

"Riiiight! You lyin' bastard, you slept with her. Of course you got laid. Hey, you look like you haven't had a minute's sleep."

"Yeah, well, you're right about that, but Dick, I'm telling you that it didn't happen. She told me that she promised God."

This was stupid. Most of my army buddies tried their best to convince the rest of us that they got lucky every night, yet we suspected that they were bullshitting us. Here I was, trying to convince my friend that I had *not* gotten laid, and he wouldn't believe me. If it had been any of the other guys at the base I would never have admitted defeat, but Dick was a friend, and his ex-wife was Sylvia's friend.

Sylvia emerged from our room, rubbed her sleepy eyes, and gave me a long kiss. Dick grinned, further convinced that the sexy deed had been done. I tried for weeks to convince him that I had not made it with Sylvia. He never believed me but wasn't sure why I would deny such a thing. After our night of frustration, I met Sylvia a few times for a movie and drinks. I liked her but knew that there would never be a magic moment with her, at least, not anytime soon.

Graduation day in May for our Pennant Squad 104 was a big day, not simply because the physical and mental grind of basic training was over but because we would be considered soldiers, adults, and most of all, be permitted to wear civilian clothes at night and on weekends. The graduation parade made me feel immensely proud, marching behind a pipe band past the reviewing stand filled with the families of my fellow soldiers. My family was not there.

I was homeward bound the next day for a one-week leave before my transfer to the Royal Canadian Signal Corps Training Centre in Kingston, Ontario. I was not going home without a show. I was a soldier now! I wanted to impress the home folks. The usual army leisure suit wasn't good enough. We had the option of buying the Dress Blues uniform with the white belt and lanyard and patent leather boots. I spent most of my pay and got fitted.

On Sunday morning, I dressed for Mass in my new Dress Blues with the razor-sharp creases, white belt around my thinner waist, and a lanyard and a peak cap. I marched down the aisle straight as a drill sergeant, with my head held high behind my parents to sit in the front row, so I would be seen by all. I was. I was bursting with pride. It was a dramatic change from the guy who had left several months before. A few girls smiled at me after church.

I was in church, but my thoughts were not exactly pure. Could they tell that I was still a virgin? I considered for a moment that if I wore my Dress Blues everywhere maybe I would have a chance. After all, what girl could resist a guy in uniform? Apparently, every girl.

* * *

A large naked guy greeted me at the gate at the Signal Corps School at Vimy Barracks in Kingston, Ontario. It was Mercury the messenger god and the symbol of the Signal Corps. His nickname was *Jimmy*. Vimy Barracks was to be college for the next nine months to study basic electronics. It sure beat basic training.

Our classes began on Monday. I expected to play with top secret electronic equipment. How wrong I was. We were about to spend months learning or re-learning algebra, trigonometry, calculus, and logarithms. I loved it.

My months in Kingston, Ontario, were mostly uneventful. I spent most weekend nights in downtown Kingston, which had been a military city for a few hundred years. On the one hand, it was liberal, thanks to a world-class place of learning, Queens University. On the military side, it was conservative. I tried to meet girls, but my military showed through. The word was out that the only girls who associated with military guys were less than desirable. I didn't care. The older guys warned me that if I was to have a moment of physical bliss with one of those women, I was destined to have many more moments of penicillin shots and agonizing pain while attempting to pee. I contemplated taking the risk. Opportunity knocked.

One night while proceeding to get drunk alone at a red velvet-lined bar on Princess Street, a girl in the booth across the aisle smiled at me. I smiled back. She smiled again. I ordered a double-shot of Jack and Coke courage. She and I smiled, winked, and made dim-witted faces until she strolled over to my table. I wasn't brave enough to go to hers without two more Jacks. I probably would have fallen into her table.

She spoke first. "Hi, how are you?"

"Okay." I was a smooth-talking devil.

"May I sit down?"

"Sure."

"Are you in the Army?"

"Yeah."

"Signal Corps?"

"Yeah."

"Wow, my ex-boyfriend used to be in the Signal Corps, but I caught him with another girl."

"I'm sorry."

"I'd love some company. Can we go someplace more comfortable, after you finish your drink?"

"Uh...yeah sure!" My foggy brain was thinking *this is it!*

"What's your name?"

"Stan. What's yours?"

She hesitated. "Emily."

"Nice name," I responded, for lack of anything better to say.

"Before we go, can you excuse me? I have to go to the girl's room."

She disappeared down a hall. This was it. I might be getting shots in the ass for a few days, but I was willing to gamble. I didn't care if she had the black plague and whooping cough! I wondered where we might go. I gulped down another Jack and Coke and waited for her to return. The waitress hurried to my table while looking back over her shoulder.

"Excuse me, sir?" she whispered. "Are you planning to go somewhere with that girl who was sitting here?"

"Uh...well, yeah, maybe, but why do—?"

"Buddy, if I were you, I'd get my ass out of here. I know her reputation. She is calling a partner who will rob you and maybe beat the crap out of you when she gets you alone."

"Shit!" I threw down ten bucks for my drinks and ran out the front door and down the street, caught a taxi, and told the driver to drive like hell to Vimy Barracks.

My electronics course ended in the spring of 1961. I was 20 and still without a girlfriend, or even a rowdy ten minutes of passion. Several years before I had joined the army, my friend Arnold and I had talked about joining a monastery. Maybe I should have taken it seriously. I was going to end up a monk, anyway! On the bright side, I graduated from the Signal Corps School with excellent test scores. The new big question was where would the Army send me? Everyone got posted somewhere.

The news finally came on a Friday morning. I was being sent to Camp Petawawa, one hundred miles west of Ottawa, but I was being attached to the Canadian Guards, an infantry unit. Infantry? What the hell was I going to do in an infantry battalion? That's what I had wanted to avoid when I joined the Army.

Kill Me, Mama

The Canadian Guards were boots-on-the-ground frontline soldiers in Camp Petawawa. I was nervous, but my fears were put away on the second day when a sergeant showed me my radio shop, where I was to remain available to repair two-way radios and other electronic gear when the Guardsmen brought them in. I learned that I was the only Signal Corps guy in the entire battalion. I figured that there could be a lot of work involved.

I got up most mornings at 7:00, had breakfast, and walked to my shop. I tinkered with the equipment but had no radios to repair. A week went by, and yet, no one come into my shop. I was getting lonely. Did anyone in command know that I was there? Eventually, two guys showed up at my door with a couple of radios to fix. I repaired them in ten minutes. The two Guardsmen weren't happy. I was too fast. They expected some leisure time. They liked my little shop of idleness.

Eventually, I made friends in Camp Petawawa, as my radio shop became a hangout for guys who wanted to get away from the war games and mindless duties. When I realized that no one was checking on me, I cleared off a portion of my workbench to make way for a place to sleep. After I became comfortable with this routine, I began sneaking away in mid-afternoon to go to downtown Pembroke, the nearest city. Taking a bus or a taxi to downtown was not good for my image with girls. I had to change that.

After six months of goofing off, I was due for a vacation. Two days before I left on my two-week leave, I received a letter from Sylvia from New Brunswick. I thought that maybe she had reconsidered and decided that she should have done the deed with me after our night of sleeping double and naked in a single bed.

She told me an unbelievable story. She had married a boxer. It was not a marriage made in heaven. Within days, the marriage had become ugly. She claimed that he beat her unmercifully. She went on to say that she would love to see me if I ever came through that way. I wrote her immediately and told her how sorry I was and that I would gladly stop to visit her when I was passing through New Brunswick.

I was happy to be home in Jamesville West with Mom and Pop and to see some of my old friends, especially Howard, James Andre and Arnold, but I desperately needed a car. After a few days of bumming rides with my friends, I went with my Uncle Arthur to the closest auto dealer, Gordon MacAuley's garage in Baddeck. Between Uncle Arthur and me, we decided on a blue and white two-toned '54 Chevy for nine hundred dollars. My Uncle Arthur co-signed the loan. I drove away proud but with a warning from the salesman.

"You can take it and drive it for the weekend, but it needs a ring job. If you drive it without getting the piston rings replaced, you'll blow the engine. We will do it for you next week."

"Okay. Great! Bye!" I jumped in behind the wheel with Howard as my co-pilot.

"I mean it." The salesman repeated his advice. "You can see by the smoke coming out of the tailpipe that it's burning a lot of oil, and remember, check the oil often."

"Okay, okay."

I drove away with my first car. If I couldn't score girls with this, I would become a monk.

We arrived back in Jamesville, where we celebrated with a few beers and then a few more beers. An inebriated brainwave hit me.

"Hey, let's go to New Brunswick to see Sylvia.

Howard was ready. "Let's go!

I remembered Sylvia's plight with her failed month-old marriage, but I forgot about the serious engine repairs needed by the '54 Chevy. We attempted to leave right away, but Pop figured that we were too smashed, so we put it off until the next morning. I reached for the newly installed phone and called Sylvia.

"Hey, Sylvia, I'm coming to see you tomorrow."

There was a squeal from the other end of the line. "I can't wait to see you!"

I liked that attitude, a lot.

Howard asked me if it was okay to invite his friend, Archie McAdam. Alas, Archie was not the most handsome guy on the block. His eyes bulged out, and one looked to the east while the other one aimed straight ahead. He was also endowed with a gigantic nose. For some reason that Howard and I could not reckon, he always had fine-looking girls hanging off of his arm. Howard and I surmised that he must have had other less obvious attributes going for him.

In spite of an ugly hangover, we left early and neared New Brunswick by mid-afternoon. We had a couple more hours of driving before we got to Sylvia's house. While filling up with gas and oil at a service station outside Fredericton, I called Sylvia from a phone booth. I told her that we were an hour away. She sounded thrilled.

"I checked with my Mom, and she agreed that you boys can spend the night. You can sleep on the couch in the sitting room, and Howard and Archie can sleep on pull-out couch in the sun room, okay?"

"Yeah, sure. That sounds great." I had not considered the sleeping arrangement.

We arrived at Sylvia's house around 5:30 in the afternoon, suppertime for them, and us. Howard, Archie, and I ate like starving dogs. After supper, we were lost for words. Sylvia's mother appeared deadly serious and just a bit scary. The silence was unnerving.

"Sylvia, what do you like to watch on TV?" I had nothing more profound to say.

"We don't watch TV," she said softly, as though someone might overhear her.

"You don't...I mean, you don't watch TV?"

"We don't have a TV. We are not permitted. It's the devil's machine."

"Pardon me?"

Howard glanced at Archie. Archie's right eye looked at Howard. The left eye checked out Sylvia, presumably to determine if she was serious.

"Yes, well, I suppose it can be." I endeavored to be agreeable, seeing as Sylvia's mother was not exactly in a merry mood. It didn't take a psychoanalyst to determine that this visit was not going well.

Sylvia continued, sounding apologetic. "We don't have a radio or a record player. We don't go to dances or movies, either."

It occurred to me that any ideas that I had of fun on the couch were as likely as a meteor strike.

Howard suddenly glanced upward. "Did you hear that?"

"What?" Sylvia and I spoke in unison.

"I thought I heard thunder."

"Thunder?" I didn't get it at first.

I hadn't heard anything.

"Yeah, thunder." He wore a devilish smirk.

It dawned on me that Howard was either desperately trying to change the downhill subject, or more likely it was his attempt at humor, given the subject of music, dancing, and sin. I wanted to kick him in the shins but he was too far away.

Sylvia's Mom returned from the kitchen with a stern suggestion. "I think it's bedtime for all of us."

I checked my watch. It was 8:30. The sun had just gone down. How the hell were we going to sleep this early? I speculated on what would happen if we didn't go to bed. Would Satan come and drag us all to hell? I realized that I had crossed the threshold into a bizarre world.

Howard looked at me with an evil smirk. Meanwhile, Archie's left eye was clearly focused with an expression of terror at Sylvia's mother. I had been drumming my fingers on the table but suddenly stopped, realizing that it might be construed as music. Sylvia gave me a feeble smile, as if to apologize for all of this. Her attitude made me feel only slightly better.

Sylvia's mother came down the stairs with an armload of blankets and pillows and handed them to Sylvia, who made up a bed for me in the living room and for Howard and Archie in the sun room. An interminable period of silence followed. It could have been an hour, or maybe it was fifteen seconds.

I could have sworn that Sylvia's mother levitated up the stairs. "Good night, boys."

It sounded more like a death sentence than have a good night. I tried to imagine what she did for fun. Did she ever laugh out loud, or was that a sin too? Then, I tried to envision how she had conceived her daughter, when my perverted images were broken by Sylvia.

Sylvia placed her lips close my ear. "Good night, Stan."

"Good night, Sylvia. I wish we could be together, alone."

I tried to kiss her, but she pushed me away and pointed up the stairs. I was certain that there was not a chance in hell that I would touch her body that night. If her mother had known what I was fantasizing about, she would have had me sleeping with Satan by breakfast.

Sylvia bounded up the stairs and actually threw me a kiss. I figured that she might be stoned to death for that if she got caught. Howard, Archie, and I stared at each other. I shrugged.

"Okay horny Stanley, now what?" Howard scanned the stairs for the scary woman.

"Go to bed."

"Are you nuts? I can't sleep this early. Can't we go out and get a beer?"

"No! We're stuck here. If we leave now, that's it. I'll never see Sylvia again."

"So what? You're never going to get laid with her, anyway, even if you were Saint Christopher or Saint Jude or whoever that saint of impossible causes is!"

"They don't believe in saints, Howard."

"I'm sure they don't believe in sex, either, so give it up."

"Shut the fuck up!" I whispered too loud. "Now go to bed. We don't have any choice."

"I don't know why the hell I agreed to come with you."

"I know. I'm sorry. I had no idea that they were so...religious."

"Are you ready to go to bed, Archie?" Howard asked Archie's right eye.

"Yes, sweetie. You want the outside of the bed or the wall?"

"Fuck off, Archie!"

"Shut up, both of you! Don't forget to say your prayers."

I crept in the dark to my bed in the living room, undressed down to my boxers, and pulled up the covers over my head. The place was spooky with antiques, or at least old furniture covered with a doilies. Somewhere, what sounded like a grandfather clock ticked. Occasionally, I heard a car pass by on the road out front. Probably some lucky guy on his way to a bar to have a drink and maybe meet up with a couple of fun girls for riotous sex later in a stone quarry somewhere under the New Brunswick quarter moon. I hated him.

Meanwhile, I was trapped in doily-world. If I had been in a convent, I couldn't have had a worse chance of even getting a kiss on the cheek. I had spent forty-six dollars on gas for this misadventure. Oh, and twenty dollars for oil.

Eventually, after what seemed like hours listening to a slow tick-tock, tick-tock, I fell asleep.

"Hey, you awake?" I felt a warm breath at my ear.

"Huh?"

"Shhh!" It was Sylvia. She lifted the covers back and slid in next to me.

"Sylvia!"

"I've been dying to be with you all evening."

"Me too. I mean, I wanted to be with you too."

We kissed like never before. I moved my hands up under her night dress. She wore nothing under it. I was losing my mind with anticipation. At the same time, I was utterly scared stiff (pun intended) that at any moment Sylvia's mother would literally soar down the stairs with a machete and kill us all. My fear wasn't as powerful as my desire to make love to this woman. *Go ahead, kill me, Mama, I will die happy.*

In twenty seconds in my twenty-first year, it finally happened. I had a lot to learn about sex that Mother Saint Marilyn could never teach me. I also had a lot to learn about life and love.

Busted Flat In Miramichi

It was an exciting, delicious, petrifying night with Sylvia in her living room, both of us aware that her mother was upstairs. I was in love. Of course I was. She allowed me to share the ultimate intimacy. I wanted it to go on. Based on my past record of failures, it might never happen again.

There was a detail that I had overlooked. Sylvia was married. Yes, she had been married for just over a month, but she had been viciously assaulted by her new husband. She had wisely left him. He was over six feet tall and a professional boxer. I was glad that I had my best friend Howard around, just in case. Howard was six-foot-four and could handle any takers. He was also never without a comb and *Brylcreem*, so he was ready.

I don't know why Sylvia's mother agreed to allow her daughter travel with us, but she did. Sylvia, Howard, Archie, and I left for Fredericton. It cost me a fortune on my Army pay, but I checked into a cheap hotel. I wanted some alone time with Sylvia without the terrorizing, mind-numbing, impotency-producing fear that her mother caused. After all, I had about seven years of catching up to do.

Howard and Archie were not included in the hotel check-in and didn't want to be. Howard took my car for the evening, aware that I would be busy with Sylvia. I was happy to accommodate him. I didn't expect to come out of our hotel room, not even for food or drink. I threw Howard the keys.

In the middle of our night of passion, and in a moment of temporary insanity, I invited Sylvia to come to Cape Breton with us and meet my Mom and Pop and some friends. By early morning, we were on the road with Howard and Archie in my smoking, choking automobile. With gas and oil refills, it took us six hours. I felt nine feet tall with Sylvia by my side.

I introduced Sylvia to my Mom and Pop as my girlfriend. Mom seemed surprised but was pleased to meet her. They didn't know, and I didn't tell them, that she was married. I did tell a few friends. I wanted them to know that I was with a savvy woman.

We spent several days at home in Jamesville West. Sylvia and I could not share the same room, although I did get caught in her bedroom when my mother got up earlier than usual at 6:30. We received a severe lecture about how we were sinful and dirty. She didn't like Sylvia quite as much after that.

My leave from the Army was almost over, and I had to return to Ontario to Camp Petawawa. I still had not taken care of the needed piston rings, even though my '54 Chevy was burning more and more oil. My father and Uncle Arthur pleaded with me to get it fixed. I figured that I could get it done in Ontario when I got back there.

Howard and Archie accompanied me along with Sylvia back to New Brunswick. This time, they had a mission. Howard and Archie wanted to move to Ontario to find meaningful employment. As we crossed from Nova Scotia into New Brunswick, the smoke from the exhaust grew thicker. We had to stop more often for oil than gas.

"Stan, what's that noise?" Sylvia asked.

"Noise? I don't hear a noise."

"Well, turn down the radio and listen."

I shut the radio off. At first, I didn't hear anything unusual, but then, as I accelerated up the hill, I could hear a distinct, rapid *clack clack clack.*

Howard heard it too. "That's not good. Sounds like the pistons are knocking."

I remembered my father's advice. I was an impatient fool. I was more focused on my newfound sexual adventures than on fixing my car. As we drove on, the knocking grew louder, and the smoke got thicker to the point where people following us wandered all over the road because they couldn't see where they were going. Some people shook their fists at us. The middle finger apparently hadn't been invented yet.

As we drove up a long hill, we noticed that the car was laboring and knocking louder. The black smoke was not only choking and blinding people behind us, it was burning our eyes. As we neared the top of the hill, a loud bang came from the engine as my car lurched to a stop. A truck behind us almost rear-ended us. He laid on his horn. We were stopped on the highway. I had to get off the road. Howard and Archie jumped out and helped push the car backward and off to the side of the road. Howard raised the hood.

"Whoa, you blew a piston. The engine is shot man!"

"No Howard, please don't tell me that."

Sylvia touched my arm. "Stan, what are we going to do now?"

"I don't know. We're screwed!"

I was sorry that I hadn't listened to my father and my uncle and everyone else who had advised me to get the overhaul done. They had even remarked that the car was in great shape and that all it needed was a ring job, which was included in the price of the car. I was the proud owner of a worthless blue and white heap on the side of the road. How was I going to get to Camp Petawawa? Army officers have no sense of humor when it comes to not showing up on time. In wartime, they would shoot you. It's called AWOL.

Sylvia had a suggestion. "Stan, why don't I call my cousin, Kenny? He can tow the car to my place, and he has friends who can fix it."

Lucky for us, we had passed a service station half a mile before. Sylvia and I walked back and called her cousin, Kenny. He was there within an hour. He tied a thick rope to my car, and off we went with my new second-hand car at the end of a tow rope.

My earlier feeling of being nine feet tall shrank to four-foot-nothing.

Kenny towed the car into her driveway, past the house, and to a broken down barn out back. He untied the frayed rope and suggested a place he knew where he could find a rebuilt engine for a couple hundred dollars. I didn't have a couple hundred dollars. I was in Miramichi, New Brunswick, and almost broke. I had only forty-one dollars and change left to somehow make it almost eight hundred miles to Camp Petawawa, Ontario. It was Thursday evening, and I had to report for duty by Monday morning at 0700 hours.

Howard, Archie, and I held a brief meeting. It was too late to hit the road, no matter how we traveled. We decided. We would hitchhike to Ontario. Howard was confident that it would be no problem.

Sylvia made an offer that we couldn't refuse. "You can stay here tonight. I'm sure my Mom will be happy to have you."

"Oh, great. Thank you, Sylvia." I accepted half-heartedly.

I could not imagine her mother being happy with our return visit. In fact, I could not imagine her mother being happy. I was not thrilled at the thought of staying in that house one more night with the dead silence, the spooky atmosphere, and her scary mother. We had no options, other than sleeping in the woods. We were about to be subjected to worse. Jail!

*   *   *

Friday morning, I kissed Sylvia good-bye and promised that I would see her soon. Howard, Archie, and I got on Highway 8 and stuck out our thumbs for the long trip to Ontario. In less than five minutes a pickup truck pulled over. The driver, who bore a striking resemblance to Alfred Hitchcock, told us to jump on the back and he would give us a ride all the way to some place called Bartibog.

"What is your destination, gentlemen?"

"Ontario!"

"You are going the wrong way."

"What?" All three of us harmonized.

"Yes, it's true. You are taking the *long* way up through the north into Matapedia, Québec. You should have been on the Trans Canada Highway. On the map, it is indicated as highway two."

I thought he even sounded like Alfred Hitchcock.

"I told you," Howard said, out of the corner of his mouth.

"Fuck off!" I shot back at Howard under my breath.

The plump driver kept talking as we crawled into the back. "Besides, people around here are rather odd. They don't like to pick up people on the side of the road with their thumbs extended."

He dropped us off at a side road intersection in the middle of nowhere. We said thanks a lot, and he was gone in a cloud of dust, mostly from the bed of his pickup. We stuck out our thumbs again. We waited. Cars passed. Trucks passed. An hour or more went by, and a few people slowed down and then sped up. Finally, one of my favorite cars, a red '56 Ford Fairlane, pulled over.

A guy in a wrinkled suit and an ugly green tie shouted out his passenger window. "Where are you going gentlemen?"

"Ontario!"

"I'm not going that far, but I can take you to Bathurst, that's about fifty miles or so."

We hopped in. I sat in the front. He told us that he had been in the Army years ago, in the Royal Canadian Regiment. His wife had left him six months earlier. He revealed that she had run off with a funeral director. He said that she was always tight with money. Now she could save on her burial, which he hoped was soon.

The ex-Army guy took us to the north side of Bathurst so that we would have a better chance of getting a ride. It didn't help. We stood there for over two hours until another pickup truck pulled over. The driver, a cranky-looking guy with a French accent in a six-day beard, ordered us to get in the back. We did. I guess people felt safer with us in the rear. They could make a sharp left turn and fling us off anytime.

He didn't talk. He didn't ask where we were going. We didn't care. He was going in the right direction, and as long as he kept going, we were okay with that. The ride didn't last long. He pulled onto side of the road and stopped.

"Get off! This is as far as I'm going." Mr. Personality was gone, down a muddy driveway to a farm house.

Howard, Archie, and I took turns sticking our thumbs out. Car after car sped by. Hours passed. Howard figured that maybe people were hesitant about picking three people up. Maybe if there were only two, they might be more inclined to stop. We sent Archie to the woods. He needed to go, anyway. About the time he got his pants down, a Cadillac driven by a white-haired gentleman pulled over a hundred feet ahead of us.

"Archie, come on! Hurry up! We got a ride!" Howard yelled toward the woods.

Archie was somewhere behind a clump of bushes. "Wait a minute, I'm takin' a dump!"

"Well, wipe your arse and let's go! He's waiting"

"Jesus Christ, I can't find any leaves or moss. What kind of fucking woods do they have here in New Brunswick, anyway?"

"Archie! Let's go!" Howard and I screamed in unison.

The white-haired Caddy driver became impatient. "Are you guys coming or not?"

"Okay, we're coming." We ran toward the car.

Just as we reached the car, I turned to observe Archie emerging from the woods, pulling his pants over his hips and zipping up. I heard a spray of gravel. The white-haired Caddy driver had spotted Archie from his rear view mirror. He left us standing in more dust. Howard launched a barrage of swear words at Archie while I cursed the Caddy man.

"You had to take a shit *now* didn't you, you cross-eyed fuck-head! Goddammit, you caused us to miss a ride."

"Well, I'm fucking sorry that I had to take a crap, Howie. Unlike you, I'm not full of shit!"

"Knock it off, you two. Let's try to appear like we're not escapees from the home for the criminally insane. Hopefully, we can get a ride before dark."

We waited for two more hours before a car finally slowed down. It was a young couple. They almost came to a stop but then suddenly sped off. Howard pulled me aside and quietly suggested that he thought he knew why no one was stopping.

"Archie."

"Archie?"

"Yeah, Archie! They get a gander at Archie with his buggy eyes, one peering straight ahead and the other looking east and his huge beak in between. Would *you* pick him up?"

"Great! So what are we supposed to do, kill him and throw his body in the woods?"

"No, maybe you could lend him your sunglasses and your Army cap. It will cover his eyes, and his nose won't stick out so far."

"Howard, you're nuts!"

I walked away, but then I got an idea. I picked up my duffel bag and ran to the woods.

"Oh great! Now *you're* going to take a shit?" Archie scoffed. "Good luck trying to find something soft to wipe your arse, soldier boy!

I returned from the forest a few minutes later dressed in my Signal Corps uniform. It was wrinkled and would never pass inspection, but this wasn't Camp Petawawa.

Howard was impressed. "Hey! Brilliant idea!"

"Yeah, who can't pick up a man in uniform?"

Howard pointed up the highway. "Here's your chance to prove it. Get out there."

A green '60 Dodge Dart darted by. Then a pickup truck flew by with a guy on the passenger side who yelled something at us.

"Maybe you should have saluted." Howard smirked.

"You're a real fucking comedian, Howie." He hated being called Howie.

A dozen or so cars, trucks, 18-wheelers, and busses passed us before a Ford Ranchero braked suddenly and stopped about four hundred feet down the road. We ran. As we got to him, the asshole sped away. We were growing angry, not to mention hungry. Finally, a Chevy station wagon cruised to a stop. We piled in. At least we were inside this time. The driver wasn't talkative. He did inquire where we were going. When we told him that we were trying to get to Ontario, he said that he was going to Ontario too...next month. For now he could take us to Dalhousie, New Brunswick. We were thrilled. That was a big ride.

The quiet guy dropped us off in downtown Dalhousie. It was late summer, and dusk came early in these northern parts. We needed a place to spend the night. Earlier, we each had a sandwich and coffee in a Mom and Pop restaurant. Our next challenge was to find a place to sleep. As we strolled through town on Victoria Street, Howard spotted a vacant house. We scanned our surroundings to be sure that no one was observing as we sprinted around the rear. We tried the back door. It was locked. Archie pushed up on a window. He crawled in.

"Come on guys, it's not bad. There's no furniture, but it might be okay for the night."

I glanced over my shoulder. "Are you sure, Archie?"

"Yeah, hurry up before someone sees us."

Howard and I crawled in. It smelled like old potatoes. We checked out the whole house. It was getting chilly, so we figured that it might be warmer upstairs. We were exhausted. We stretched out on the floor and used some of our packed clothes as a mattress. We slept. Not a sound baby-sleep but a fitful on and off sleep. Old newspapers littered the floor. By 6:00 in the morning, we had covered ourselves with all the papers to ward off the frost. This was no camping trip. I could have had my car. If only. If only I had paid attention. Father knows best.

It was Saturday morning and we had only traveled one hundred miles on the first day. I had seven hundred to go. I grew more worried about making it back to the Army in time. I would be in serious shit if I was late. We had to get moving and get out on the highway. We waited for a ride all morning yet no one even seemed to notice us. I was running low on money, and it was getting colder and began to rain.

Finally, a creepy character stopped in a noisy, early '50-something station wagon. If Archie was scary, this guy was even more frightening. He had a speech impediment combined with a French accent and spit when he talked. The inside of the station wagon smelled like hen shit. I remembered that stink from my childhood, when I entertained the hens.

Howard found humor in almost everything. The problem was that when he started laughing, he couldn't stop. When Scary Guy asked a question, I had to politely ask him to repeat it. He didn't say it slower, just louder, and spit farther. I had no idea what he was saying, but I could hear Howard behind me trying to suppress his snorting. The longer the drive and the one-way conversation lasted, the louder Howard snorted. At one point, I thought I heard him crying. I was afraid that Scary Guy might whip out a large knife and kill us all if Howard didn't quit. I whipped around and glared at Howard with a face that said, *shut the fuck up!*

We arrived in Campbellton, New Brunswick. Scary Guy pulled over, shut the engine off, got out, and walked away, leaving us sitting in the car. He left the keys in the ignition. We tried to guess what he was doing or where he went. Did he go to get cigarettes? Did he stop for a beer? Was there a time bomb in the car? We exited the car and waited for half an hour. He didn't return, so we began walking with our thumbs out...again.

We stood on the side of the highway on the outskirts of Campbellton all afternoon. Not one vehicle even altered their speed to check us out. In fact, a few blew their horns. The message was, *Get to hell off the road!* It was Saturday evening, and we had scored only one ride all day, from a nut case who had abandoned his car. We toyed with the idea of taking his car. We walked back into town. We were cold, hungry, and we were broke. We had spent the last of our money at noon on burgers and fries at a roadside canteen. The sun was setting, and we had no place to stay. We had to get out of that town.

Walking down Roseberry Street, we spotted a classy new Lincoln parked with the windows rolled down. At first, we were simply impressed. We peeked inside. The keys were in the ignition.

"This could be an easy way out of town," Howard mumbled to no one in particular.

Archie spit on the sidewalk. "I would do almost anything to get out of here. I hate this fucking toilet town."

I had a vision. "We could be way down the road really fast with this rig."

I saw no one nearby. No one spoke.

I recalled my Uncle Paddy, who had predicted that I would end up in prison some day. "On the other hand, we could spend the next ten years in Dorchester Penitentiary."

"You know what?" Howard's face brightened. "I heard that if you ask, the cops will let you stay in jail for the night."

That sounded good to me. "Well, I'm desperate for a decent night's sleep, and I could sleep anywhere except on a hard wooden floor under old newspapers."

"Okay, let's call the cops," Howard said.

I laughed. "I like that better than your last idea."

We found a payphone, looked up the number for the Campbellton police, I inserted a dime and called. Someone with a brusque voice answered. I explained that we had been hitchhiking and were cold and tired and wanted to know if we could stay in his jail.

"You want to spend the night in our Crowbar Hotel?"

"Yes, if we can."

"All right. We don't provide a taxi service or room service, though. If you want to stay here, you have to get here on your own."

"Okay, we can do that," I said, not knowing how far away it was.

After a mile and a half hike, we checked into a cell at the city jail. We were advised that the cell door had to be locked. We were technically incarcerated until morning. This was my first time voluntarily in jail.

The last time I had been in a jail cell was in Watertown, New York. It was a year earlier. It wasn't voluntary. I had been plastered drunk and disorderly on State Street while running in and out of bars yelling at customers. In a blinding instant, two burley cops seized my arms and wrenched them up to my shoulder blades and threw me into their police car so violently that it bruised my arms, ripped my shirt, and caused a rather large knot on my forehead. I spent the night in a drunk-tank, but eventually they moved me a cell by myself for the protection of the other prisoners! Truthfully, they likely would have killed me because I insisted on insulting President Kennedy, just to piss them off.

Before Archie, Howard, and I left the Campbellton jail, we were informed that we had to pay for our lodging by sweeping up and wiping down the sink and toilet. That pissed Howard off, so before we left, he swiped a package of *Export A* cigarettes from the sergeant's desk. We spent most of Sunday morning on the road. One older man, who spoke no English, picked us up and took us fourteen miles to Matapedia, Québec. We were broke, hungry, and angry, blaming each other for our situation but mostly me for not taking care of the car.

Sunday afternoon, we made a difficult roadside decision. We had to turn around. We were in Québec. To us, we might as well have been in northern Uzbekistan. It appeared that no one wanted to pick us up. As we walked down the highway in the reverse direction, I spotted a large Catholic Church. Churches are big in Québec, even in rural areas. It was Sunday. Maybe we should visit. We strolled up to the rectory door and knocked. No one responded. We knocked again. Eventually, a disheveled middle-aged priest came to the door.

"Yes? Can I help you?"

He glared at Archie. Archie didn't take his left eye off of the priest.

I pleaded with him. "Father, we have been on the road for several days trying to get a ride to Ontario. We have run out of money, and we're hung—"

"What do you want *me* to do?"

I was startled. The kindly old priest back in Iona never talked like that, even if he had accused me of stealing.

I stammered, "Well, uh, I was hoping that we might get something to eat here or borrow a few dollars to buy some food, Father."

Okay, I knew we weren't really asking to borrow money and pay it back. I just thought that *borrow* sounded more polite. Priests had always intimidated me, ever since I was an altar boy, especially after I got in shit for snickering at my buddy Gordie Andrew during communion.

"No!"

"No?" I was stunned.

This was the Roman Catholic Church. I had attended church since I was a child. I had priests in my family. My family had many friends who were priests. My Aunt Helena was a nun. In an instant, my reverence and respect for the Catholic Church was dashed. I was furious. What hypocrites!

"Father, you can't even spare a dollar?" I pleaded, as my eyes filled with tears, not of sadness or pity but purple anger.

He exhaled with obvious frustration that someone dare interrupt his sleep or whatever he might have been doing that had ruffled his hair. "Just a minute."

It was obvious that he wanted us gone. He reached into his pocket, thumbed through a stack of fives and tens, probably from the morning collection, and came up with a dollar bill. He handed it to us and closed the door without a word.

As angry as we were at this treatment, we found the nearest grocery store and bought a pound of baloney and a loaf of bread. We sat on the side of the road and dined on the most delicious meal in recent memory.

It was late Sunday. Soon, I would officially be in trouble with the Army. We had given up. We began hitch hiking eastward. We got lucky and got a ride with a trucker all the way to Bathurst squeezed together in the cab. We called the police again, this time in Bathurst. They allowed us to stay in jail for a night. I warned Howard to not steal any more cigarettes, especially from these cops. They were Mounties and I had heard that the Mounties always got their man. Almost a decade later, I would get a Mountie's woman.

With three more rides, we arrived in Fredericton, where I parted company with Howard and Archie. They thumbed more rides home to Cape Breton with a plan to get some money together and take the train to Ontario. Meanwhile, I checked into the local Army detachment to tell them that I was technically AWOL. I told the detachment sergeant the truth. He was not sympathetic. I requested an advance on my next pay to get train fare to Ottawa and the bus fare from there to Camp Petawawa.

The train left from Fredericton Junction at 7:30 p.m. I had a few hours to relax, so I called Sylvia. We met at a park and talked about our future. We lay under a tree and went as far as legally possible in daylight in a city park, before I had to say my second good-bye to her in a week.

Somersault

I was met at the station in Camp Petawawa by the military police, officially known as the Provost Corps. I was detained, which is a nicer word than arrested, for being AWOL. I slept in a cell, which was marginally better than an abandoned house under newspapers. The next morning, a nasty military policeman marched me in front of the captain to receive my sentence, which was confinement to barracks for a month. It didn't matter much. I was broke, anyway.

After saving money by going nowhere, I bought a '54 Ford for four hundred dollars from an Infantry Guardsman. It was ugly but it had wheels and a motor, and it didn't burn a quart of oil every ten miles. The tires were so bald that the canvas innards showed through. I didn't care. It was transportation.

The first weekend that I was finally free to go downtown and troll for girls, in my new clunker car, I came down with tonsillitis. It wasn't the first time, but this time it was so bad that I couldn't swallow water. I went to sick bay.

The doctor was blunt. "Those devils have to come out, soldier."

"Now?" I mumbled, while he still held my tongue down with a popsicle stick.

"Well, not this minute, but we will have to ship you off to Rockland Military Hospital in Ottawa to have them yanked out."

I had never been in a hospital in my life. I realized that I was a chicken soldier. Needles, scalpels, and the smell of hospitals made me sick and terrified.

The next morning as I peered up from an operating table, someone with a surgical mask said, "Okay, I would like you to count backwards from ten to one."

"Ten..."

I was released a few days later and given two weeks sick leave. It was the chance to try out my new old '54 Ford. It was unquestionably a chance, because my tires were thinner than condoms. Regardless, I decided to drive 250 miles to Toronto to see my old Iona school buddy, Jamie. Jamie and I weren't best buddies, but we did get drunk together one afternoon in high school. Jamie had always had a severe case of acne and wore glasses that seemed to sit way out on the bridge of his nose. He lived with his brother, Bruce, in the west end of Toronto off Queen Street.

I spent a night with Jamie and Bruce drinking until our lights went out. I do remember a visit from the ugliest woman I had seen to date. I'm sure I didn't sleep with her or do anything else with her. In spite of a raging hangover, Jamie and I went to Mass the next morning and then joined Jamie's German friend, Joe Kruger. Joe, being a patriotic German, owned a Volkswagen Bug.

After Mass, Jamie suggested that since it was a perfect, sunny autumn day, we should go to see Niagara Falls, slightly over an hour away. Joe and I agreed.

We took the Queen Elizabeth Way, with Joe behind the wheel, Jamie in the passenger seat, and me in the back. Fresh from Holy Communion, we talked about our two favorite topics, getting laid and drinking. We seemed to be going faster and faster. A '56 Ford Fairlane passed us, pulled in front of us, and slowed down. Joe switched lanes and passed him. The Fairlane guy with a flattop haircut passed us again and slowed down to a crawl in front of us. Joe passed him one more time, this time going faster. The game continued at an increasing speed until we rounded an unusually sharp curve in the QEW freeway in Burlington, halfway to Niagara Falls.

The VW's rear right wheel slid into the gravel on the shoulder of the road. Almost instantly, although it seemed in slow motion, we spun around and hurtled down the freeway backward, until the rear end hit a ditch. We flipped over...and over. On the first roll, I saw Jamie and Joe in the front. Then, I didn't. They were gone. We rolled again, seemingly end over end. Shattered glass flew everywhere. Then, the oddest thing happened. It seemed like the world went into super-slow motion. I serenely thought about how Mom and Pop would feel when they heard that I had died. It was surreal. No panic, no fear, only concern for them. The car tumbled over one more time. I felt like a ping-pong ball in a tin can.

The car came to rest on its roof. I heard some tinkling noises and the sound of shards of glass falling around me. I looked around. I realized that the car was upside down and that I was still alive. I saw a hole in the bottom, where the windshield used to be. I crawled out on my belly as I heard voices and some people screaming. I stood up bit by bit and staggered a couple of steps until a lady reached out to me.

"Oh, my God, are you okay?"

I didn't answer because I didn't know.

She reached for my arm.

"Here, let me help you. Let me take you to the hospital."

"No...I'm okay" I searched the grassy area for Jamie and Joe.

"No, you're not." She wore a pitiful expression.

She had tears in her eyes. It was then that I felt something warm and wet running down my face. Apparently, I had a piece of windshield glass sticking out of my head.

"Where's Jamie? Where is Joe?" I began to panic.

Then, I spotted them. Jamie sat on the ground and Joe lay there, but they were both moving, thank God.

Ambulances arrived, while the angel lady drove me to the hospital emergency room nearby in Burlington. Jamie and Joe arrived shortly afterward in an ambulance. Joe had a broken leg and cuts and bruises. Jamie had a broken collarbone and head injuries. I had nothing broken, but a nurse cut my hair off and removed all my clothes. She might have been attractive, but for once, sex didn't cross my mind. She picked glass from my ass and pulled shards from my forehead.

That evening, all three of us were bandaged up for the return to Toronto with Jamie's brother Bruce, who came to pick us up. We stopped to see the VW on the way. It was no more than three feet high. People stood around and were amazed how anyone could have walked away from such an accident. Apparently God had plans for us. He did for me.

The next night Jamie and I were in pain, so what better way to feel better than to go for a few beers at a local dive, Dan's Tavern, in the roughest section of Queen Street West in Toronto. We thought that Dan sounded like a typical Cape Breton name, so it felt familiar. Until we found out that Dan was Chinese.

We ordered a couple of beers and talked about our near-death experience. While we talked, I couldn't help but notice a cute girl in the booth across the aisle. She was with a couple and an ugly guy with Elvis hair and a fresh scar over his left eye. I assumed that he was the pretty girl's boyfriend.

I glanced at her. She gave me a come-hither smile. I questioned what the hell she was thinking flirting with a guy with his head in a bandage and covered with Band-Aids and Mercurochrome. Did she think that maybe I had just gotten back from the war? Jamie looked worse, with his arm in a sling and his head bandaged as well. Maybe she thought that we were extras in a Zombie movie.

Scarface snarled at me. "What da fuck are you lookin' at, asshole?"

"Nothing." I wasn't in the mood for more trouble. I even smiled at him, which probably wasn't wise under the circumstances.

"Hey shithead, are you checkin' out my girlfriend?

"No, no man, I just happened to look in her direction. Sorry."

His girlfriend seemed to be enjoying the exchange and kept smiling at me while her meathead boyfriend got even more riled up.

Jamie chimed in. "No, it's true, no one was looking at your girl."

That did not help.

"Who da fuck is talkin' to *you*, four-eyes?" Scarface bellowed.

"Maybe we should leave." Jamie made a timely and wise suggestion.

Alas, too late.

Scarface rose up out of his seat. I suspected that he didn't want to dance. His buddy got up and left with his girlfriend, obviously not wanting any part of the carnage that was likely to take place. I got up. Jamie stood and backed down the aisle, hanging onto the coat racks with his one good arm.

Scarface threw a punch, and I ducked for the most part, although he grazed my ear. He grabbed my sore arms and spun me around onto my back on the seat in the booth, smashing a coat rack off the edge of the booth. A Chinese man, presumably Dan the owner, screamed at us to get out. Believe me, I wanted to get out. Scarface leaned over me to pummel my face.

There is a weapon well known to people who grew up in Cape Breton lovingly referred to as *Cape Breton Boxing Gloves*. The rest of us simply call them, boots. When all else fails, kick. I was wearing my Army boots with the steel hobnails in the soles. As Scarface reached over me to land a punch, I kicked him squarely in the balls with my right boot. He screamed and was thrown off his plan for a second, which was enough time to kick him with both feet and knock him off of me onto the floor.

Not being a fan of boxing or wrestling in bars or anywhere else, I ran for the rear exit, not knowing if he was behind me or not. I raced through the kitchen, where I knocked over a short Chinese guy hovering over a hot stove. I sprinted down an alley, which turned out to be a dead end. I imagined that Scarface was right behind me, likely with a large gun or a machete. He wasn't. I ran in the opposite direction and around to the front of the restaurant, where the police had arrived. Jamie was already talking to them, suggesting that he was a customer who had simply strolled in and had seen the whole thing.

The cops took Scarface away but only because Chinese Dan explained that the big, ugly guy had started it. His girlfriend cursed at me as they put her in the police car. I smiled and threw her a kiss. She had seemed to like me a few minutes earlier.

Jamie and I limped down the street towards to his apartment, where his brother was busy entertaining the second ugliest woman I had seen to date. I went to bed that night dreaming of the perfect girl that I could settle down with. We would cuddle under the covers and make love until the sun came up. I needed to find her.

*   *   *

In Camp Petawawa, I got paid for doing nothing. The infantry guys had no idea what *Sparky* from the Signal Corps was supposed to be doing, and the less they knew the better. Occasionally someone asked me to fix a two-way radio or their TV. The tough part was trying to feign activity when they were around. Trying to pretend I was busy was harder than working.

New Year's Eve arrived, and I had plans to party all night in downtown Pembroke, but the platoon sergeant had different ideas. A nosy officer got wind of the fact that I had nothing to do except goof off downtown most afternoons. He arranged for me to man the office in our barracks on New Year's Eve. There was no way to get out of it.

Skinny Kenny Johnson, from across the hall, asked me if he could borrow my car...my decaying '54 Ford. I hesitated because I had no insurance, and I doubted that he had a license.

"Sure, go ahead, but *please* be careful." I begged him. "I have no insurance, and even if I did, I'm not sure that you'd be covered."

"No problem, Stan. I'm not going to be drinking 'cause I'm going over to Fort Coulonge, Québec, to see a girl that I met last weekend."

I figured that that was bullshit. A lot of Army guys went to Fort Coulonge because the drinking age was lower. I had been there one night during the summer and got blasted doing the twist down to the floor and split the arse out of my pants. I didn't go back. I figured that Skinny Kenny would be okay. I freely admit that I am not the best judge of character. I handed him the keys and got ready for my sober New Year's Eve duty. I was in bed by 12:15.

The PA system echoed down the hall at 7:00 in the morning on New Year's Day. "Signalman Campbell, please come to the orderly's office for an important phone call!"

My first thought was that my father had suffered another heart attack. I raced down the hall while pulling on my gym shorts.

"Hello..."

"Stan, it's me, Kenny. I got a problem, man."

"Shit! What's the matter, Kenny? Did the car crap out on you?"

"No...not exactly. I had a bit of...an accident."

"Fuck! Is anybody dead?" I thought about not having insurance and suddenly got sick to my stomach.

"No...not really."

"*Not really?* What the fuck is that supposed to mean? Somebody is *partly* dead? Just tell me Goddammit! What happened?"

"Well, Stan, you know that steep hill going down into the village in Fort Coulonge?"

"Yes..." I sat down.

I already didn't like where this was going. Downhill.

"Right. Well, you know how that street ends in a T? You gotta go left or right, right?"

"Yeah, yeah. Go on."

"Well, the car's brakes crapped out on the hill, and I kept going through the stop sign at the end and...uh...into an old lady's living room across the street."

"No! No! Is the old lady okay?

"I think so. She was in bed upstairs. I woke her up."

"Oh, no shit, Kenny! You woke her up? Yeah, I fucking guess a car crashing into your coffee table would wake you up too! Thank God she's not dead.

"Yeah, I guess you're right."

"You're fucking right I'm right.

"I'm sorry, Stan."

"So, Kenny, listen carefully. You with me?"

"Yeah, okay. I'll get it fixed, Stan and I'll—."

"Never mind fucking fixing it! I don't give shit about that. The car is yours. Get the registration from the glove box and fill it out on the back where you transfer ownership and date it, I dunno...like four weeks ago. I don't own that car. It's yours. You got that?"

"Uh...okay...but—"

"But *what* Kenny?" I was furious, and I was fearful.

"But...the car is a write-off...it's smashed to hell."

"I don't give a shit if you got nothing left but the fucking dimmer switch! The wreck is yours. You hear me? Tow it, set it on fire, push it into the river, I don't give a rat's ass. Just fill out the fucking registration *now!* It's your problem. Good-bye!"

"But—"

I slammed the phone down as I caught the duty orderly trying to suppress a smirk.

"You laugh, asshole, and I'll wrap this fucking phone cord in a knot around your nuts!"

I hoped that I had heard the last of Skinny Kenny and my car. I had paid four hundred bucks for that damn car!

The following weekend I caught a bus to downtown Pembroke to go car shopping. I fell in love with a white 1956 Oldsmobile Starfire convertible. Somehow, some foolish finance company agreed to approve a loan. I drove it back to the base with the top down, even though it was mid-January. For January it was mild...just above freezing. I used every penny I had for the down payment. Gas was a luxury.

One of my best buddies on the base was Corporal Cliff Lawson. He liked me and I liked him. We regularly hid out in my shop and swapped stories. One day, in early summer, Cliff informed me that his niece, Chelsea, had come to visit him from Toronto. He described her as a stunning blonde. In fact, she was a part-time model in Toronto. He was obviously a proud uncle.

He figured that since I was nice guy, in his estimation, and since she didn't know anyone her age in Pembroke, and since I had a hot white convertible, he should introduce us, and maybe I could take her to a movie or something. I liked the *or something* part. Regrettably, I was broke.

On Friday evening, I borrowed ten dollars for gas and drove to Corporal Cliff's place. He introduced me to Chelsea. She was indeed gorgeous! I stammered a hello. She regarded me as though I had showed up to unplug the toilet. I was intimidated but choked out a suggestion.

"Chelsea, would you like me to show you around downtown Pembroke?" I didn't exactly exude an air of self assuredness.

"Sure," she replied, obviously unmoved by such a generous offer.

She clearly didn't give a shit about tiny Pembroke but had nothing better to do than go for a ride with this clod who had just fallen off the turnip truck.

I played the gentleman and held the door for her. I had seen suave men do that in the movies. It was a superb summer evening, and I couldn't wait until all the guys from the base, hanging out on the main Pembroke drag, saw me cruising in my long white convertible with a dazzling blonde with her hair flowing in the breeze.

I still had my ten dollars. As we neared downtown, I glanced at the gas gauge. Shit! It was almost on empty. I needed to stop and get five dollars worth of gas somewhere and then pray that she didn't want me to drive her to Ottawa or Hollywood.

"Nice evening, isn't it?" I was grasping for anything to talk about.

"Yeah." She twisted the rear-view mirror to check her make-up.

"Yeah, it sure is." My self-confidence was also running on empty.

We turned onto Pembroke Street. There they were! Guys from the Army base were on the street, strolling and trolling for girls. I had mine. There I was, Stan Campbell, cruising in a white Olds convertible, unhurriedly, down the main drag for all to see, with the most impressive girl east of Toronto. A few of the guys recognized me. I was Mr. Cool. One of the guys whistled. A few yelled something unintelligible. I was bursting!

Then, my world ended. The car jerked to a complete stop in the middle of the street. The guy behind me blew his horn, which attracted everyone's attention.

"Stan, what's wrong with your car?" Chelsea's chill was evident.

"Uh...ah...I think we're out of gas."

She rolled her eyes and sank down in the seat. "Oh, my God, this is sooo embarrassing."

She was embarrassed? We were stopped in the middle of the street, as a couple of guys we had passed caught up to us.

"Hey, Campbell, what's the problem? You're blocking traffic," someone yelled.

"I think I ran out of gas."

I heard laughter and then the worst cut of all.

"Campbell, you can afford a swanky car, but now you can't afford to put gas in it!"

Somebody behind us shouted, "Hey, do you need us to push you down the street to the Esso station?"

"Yes, please." I tried to sound in control.

Three guys and then four more pushed my Oldsmobile Starfire convertible down the main street, accompanied by catcalls and guffaws. They pushed me up to the pumps. One guy on the passenger side flirted with Chelsea. It was the first time that I saw her smile. I wanted to run him over with the car. Sadly, I didn't have any gas.

To avoid further embarrassment, I quietly made my request to the gas station attendant. "Five dollars worth, please."

Meanwhile, Chelsea hopped out of the car. "I'm going inside to call Uncle Cliff. Thanks for the ride."

"But, I can drive you home as soon as I get gas," I shouted after her.

"No thanks, Uncle Cliff will pick me up. Bye."

I took a side street back to the base and rapidly downed a half-dozen twenty-five cent draught beers at the wet canteen and tried to figure how I could get out of Camp Petawawa and maybe, out of the Army. I dreamed of Nova Scotia.

Marry Me, Sis

Diane came into my life after I humiliated Chelsea, the uppity model. Diane was cute and lived in Pembroke, twenty minutes away. I spent the rest of the summer of '62 trying to talk her out of her clothes, but neither begging nor crying moved her, even though she said that she loved me. I told her that I loved her too, but that didn't work, either. She did promise me that I would have a life of sexual bliss if we got married. Where had I heard that before? I was desperate and considered it, if only to feel her naked body next to mine, but destiny intervened.

On Monday morning, August 20, 1962, I was summoned to the platoon office.

Sergeant Samson handed me a letter, and before I read it, said, "Congratulations Campbell, you requested a posting to Nova Scotia. Well, you got it!"

I was elated. The Army was sending me home to Nova Scotia, to Halifax, where I would be a technician at a transmitter site, outside the city at Hammonds Plains. I didn't even have to wear a uniform there, and I would be working with civilians.

Two weeks later, I was tooling down Highway 17 on my way to Nova Scotia in my Olds ragtop with the top down, my box of personal crap in the trunk, and the Shirelles *Soldier Boy* blasting on the radio. I was excited. I could go home to see Mom and Pop and my friends back in Jamesville West almost every week if I wanted to.

Before I left, I told my Canadian Guards buddy, Fred Boyd from down the hall, that I would see him in Halifax. He was originally from Halifax, and I knew that he would be home for two weeks leave when I got there. He gave me his phone number and address. We could have a few beers together. It was a meeting that would alter my life.

I checked into the Army base at Windsor Park in Halifax. It brought back memories. It was where I had signed up for the Army, two years earlier. On Monday, I would meet Sergeant Powers and travel out to the transmitter site in Hammonds Plains.

In the meantime, I ran down to the payphone in the lobby to call Fred. He gave me directions to his house in suburban Fairview. We agreed to meet the next day, Saturday. Compared to huge Camp Petawawa and the strict dress codes and over-abundance of military brass, my accommodations were more like a hotel, but they were lonely. There were few people around, and those who were remained aloof with personal lives outside the military.

On Saturday afternoon, with directions in hand, I put the top down on my Olds Starfire and drove down Bayer's Road and up the hill to Adelaide Avenue in Fairview. People were outside enjoying the last warm days of summer. I pulled into the Boyd driveway with *Palisades Park* booming from the radio. Fred sat on the long steps that led up to the kitchen.

"Hey, Stan, how you doin'? Man, nice car. Whatta bomb!" he said, as he stepped back to admire it.

"Thanks, Fred." I tried to sound humble.

I was proud of my car and pleased that he was impressed. If only girls had been as impressed.

We talked about the drive from Camp Petawawa, Ontario, and the posting and what I would be doing and how lucky I was to work so close to home.

A slender girl came down the stairs as Fred and I talked.

"Fred, who's that?"

"Oh, that's my sister. Hey, Sis, come here."

I sat up. "Your sister?"

"Yeah, we all call her Sis, even her friends do, but her real name is Deanna. Hey Sis, this is Stan, a buddy from Camp Petawawa. He's been posted to Halifax. Stan, meet Sis."

"Hi, Sis, how are you?" I tried to sound confident.

"Hi." She giggled and looked away. "I'm fine, thanks."

It was obvious that she was young and shy. I figured maybe 15 or 16. Too young. Too bad.

Fred sat in the car, so I took him for a spin around the neighborhood. I could burn rubber and happily demonstrated.

"Hey, what are you doing tonight, Stan?"

"I don't know. I have nothing planned. Probably go back to Windsor Park to watch TV."

"My girlfriend and I are going to the drive-in tonight. I can ask Sis if she would like to come along. What do you think?"

"Your sister? Sure, if she's okay with it."

"Let's head up to the house to see what she has planned."

"Fred, may I ask, how old is Sis?"

"Stan, she turned 17 last month."

*   *   *

We left for the drive-in at 7:30 in Fred's car. Sis was quiet and so was I. After all, this was Fred's sister, so I wasn't about to get touchy-feely, although we were in the backseat.

The movie *The Absent Minded Professor* was almost a year old. I had seen it in Pembroke with Diane. I missed Diane. She cried when I left, and I had promised her that I would come back. I liked her, but I knew that I would never return.

Near the end of the movie, Sis and I got closer. I slipped my arm around her shoulder. As the credits rolled and Fred tried to maneuver from the theatre lot, I kissed her. Then I kissed her harder. We stopped at an A&W on the way home, and before we all got out of Fred's car, I asked her if I could see her the next night. She giggled and said okay.

I put the top up and drove back to Windsor Park. I felt good. I was happy that I was in Nova Scotia in an Army job that I loved and maybe had found a new girlfriend the first weekend. Sure she was young, but I was only 21.

Sis's mother had died just two months previously. It had to have been a traumatic event for her and her two younger sisters, Allena and Susan. Fred returned to Camp Petawawa. Fred's older brother Jack was left to take care of his siblings when their Dad wasn't around, but often Jack had to work in the evenings, so Sis was in charge of her sisters.

I drove over to her house almost every evening. I wanted to be with her, but I also wanted to be out of the dull world of the Army barracks of Windsor Park. I thought it was unfair that married guys could live off the base in apartments and sleep next to a warm female body, but single guys like me were compelled to live in a cold, gray military building. I wanted to be like those married guys.

After Sis's sisters were in bed, we got cozy. I wasn't in love. I was in love with the idea of being in love or at least being married and playing house. It didn't take long before we acted like an old married couple. Sis and I began squabbling. I was jealous of any guy that she knew. I angrily accused her of screwing around with other guys while I worked nights. She told me to get lost. I blew up in a temper tantrum, which made matters worse. Sis packed up and moved to Toronto. When she came back a month later, not much had changed.

A week after she returned, I went over to her house on a Saturday afternoon to apologize. She hesitantly accepted my apology, and eventually, we resumed our lovemaking. She was clearly not enjoying it as much as I was. We broke up again and again, but I kept coming back. Then the bombshell dropped.

In early April, seven months after we had met, Sis gave me the news. "I haven't had a period in two months."

"Are you sure, Sis?" I hoped that there was a mistake.

I had known the risks. The pill had not hit the big time yet, and using condoms was a nuisance for impatient guys like me.

"Yes, I'm sure. I'll have to go to a doctor."

I tried to be positive. "Maybe you'll still get your period."

I knew that it was wishful thinking, and then I made the big announcement. "If you're really pregnant, we'll get married, okay?"

"I don't want to get married. I'm only 17, and besides, we fight too much."

"No, Sis, we'll be okay when we get our own place. I can move off the base if I'm married." Secretly, living off the army base was more important to me than a life of married bliss with Sis.

"If I'm pregnant, I'll have to tell my father. He'll kill me and probably you too."

"I'll talk to him, and I'll tell him that we're getting married. In fact, he doesn't even have to know that you're pregnant. I'll just say that I want you to marry me."

Sis and I were married on June 8, 1963, in a Catholic ceremony in Fairview, Nova Scotia. I was 22, she was 17. I had a vicious hangover and a severe case of diarrhea from a bachelor party thrown by Jack and his best friend, Smitty, the night previously. In the middle of the toasts at the reception, I abruptly darted from the head table and down the hall while whipping my tux pants down around my knees. Things were about to get shittier.

Sis and I found an upstairs flat, where we shared a bathroom with a cranky old lady downstairs. It wasn't penthouse living, but it was ours, and I wasn't living in military digs. The nosy lady downstairs didn't like us and gave me the evil eye when she heard me call my wife *Sis*.

Five months later, with mounting bills and a baby on the way, we were forced to move in with Sis's Aunt Sally, which made me wish that I was back on the Army base. My dream of marital ecstasy faded like smoke. We had little privacy, while Aunt Sally's hot-tempered husband made me feel unwelcome. To trigger a deeper depression, my prized Olds Starfire convertible was gone.

I had not learned my lesson. Against my best judgment, I had loaned my white Olds to my ex-Army friend, Gerrard Darlington. He needed to drive out into the country to meet his girlfriend. When he arrived at her home that night, he parked my car on the right-hand side of the narrow country road, facing the wrong way. He left the headlights on while he walked up to his girlfriend's front door. The driver of an oncoming truck was temporarily blinded by my car's headlights. The driver naturally assumed that the car he was seeing was on his left. However, he recognized too late that the car was parked on his side, facing him. Too late! He had transformed my sweet white Oldsmobile convertible into an accordion.

*   *   *

November 22, 1963. I was browsing in the TV department at Sears in the Halifax Shopping Center.

"Here is a bulletin from CBS News."

It was Walter Cronkite. Nothing was on the screen except the words, *CBS News Bulletin*. Sis was somewhere in the mall while I browsed the television department. Shoppers stopped and stared towards at the multiple screens.

"In Dallas Texas, three shots were fired at President Kennedy's motorcade in downtown Dallas. The first reports say that President Kennedy has been seriously wounded by the shooting..."

More people gathered around the TVs as Cronkite's face came on the screen. Shortly afterward, Cronkite removed his glasses, paused, replaced his glasses, and for a moment appeared as though he was about to weep, and announced, *"From Dallas, Texas, the flash, apparently official, President Kennedy died at 1:00 p.m., central standard time."*

Customers, sales people, and store managers, all stood in silence. Some wiped their eyes. I found Sis in a nearby store.

I held her hand. "We need to go home. President Kennedy was shot. He is dead."

The next day, Sis went into labor. Fathers were not permitted in the delivery room, and it seemed like it was going to be a long labor so I went back to Aunt Sally's, our temporary home. The next day we watched Jack Ruby shoot Lee Harvey Oswald live on TV. That night, we had a son. We named him John Roderick Kennedy Campbell.

Seven months after Roddie was born, I received orders to move to Camp Debert outside the farming town of Truro to work in a secret, high-tech underground military installation in an inconspicuous hayfield. Sis and I eventually bought a small house in Bible Hill outside of Truro. We paid less than ten thousand dollars.

We painted and made some home improvement and thanks to the new craze, CB radio, we developed a large circle of friends. My Aunt Ethel lived in Truro as well, so this provided us with a family connection. Sis and I grew up a bit and enjoyed a more harmonious life together.

On August 19, 1965, our son Mark was born. Sis made it through labor quickly after a tire-screeching ride to the hospital. As usual, I was not permitted in the delivery room, but I got closer. I waited in the lobby.

I was 24, and Sis was 19. We had two kids that we could barely afford to raise. I decided that it was time to quit the Army. Five years was enough, and I figured that I could do better with my electronics technician profession in the civilian world. I searched for work in Truro. We loved that little town with our circle of friends, and it was only a three-hour drive to Iona to see Mom and Pop.

My search for meaningful work hit a dead end in Truro. I even applied for an electronics technician position at a cement plant. In a search in the *Halifax-Chronicle* newspaper, I saw an ad where E.M.I.-Cossor Electronics Ltd. of Dartmouth, Nova Scotia, was hiring technicians. I drove to Dartmouth for the interview and was hired on the spot at significantly better pay than I earned in the Army. We sold the house for ten thousand, nine hundred, nine hundred more than we had paid for it a year earlier.

Sis and I rented an apartment in Dartmouth, across the harbor from Halifax. I was happy in my new job but became despondent at home. I drank more. The hangovers grew worse, and what should have terrified every airline pilot, and indeed every airline passenger, was the fact that I was an auto-pilot system technician. Mercifully, I didn't hear of any air crashes as a result of my hangover testing.

I did enjoy my work, but I enjoyed observing the department secretary, Linda Chambers, even more. She was stunning, sexy, and sociable. Her spectacular lusty appearance was not lost on the other male techs, either. She reminded me of a darker, doe-eyed young Brigitte Bardot. In a lunchtime conversation, I learned that she lived not far from us in the north end.

The buzzer rang to end the work day.

Linda whizzed past me breathless. "I have to run to catch my bus. If I miss this one, there won't be another one for half an hour."

I tried to develop enough courage to offer her a ride home, because she lived in my neighborhood, but I choked on the words. In spite of her friendly attitude, her beauty intimidated me.

At lunch the next day, I purposely sat next to her at the picnic table behind the plant.

"Linda, I understand that you live in the north end, right?"

"Yes, I live on Woodland"

"Oh, I live nearby on Victoria Road near Albion."

"Oh."

"I see you have to take the bus every day."

"Yes, I hate it. It's usually so packed that I can't get on, so I have to wait half an hour for the next one."

That's the opening I was waiting for.

"Linda, you are welcome to ride with me."

"Really Stan? That's so nice of you."

"Sure, no problem." I couldn't wait until the guys saw her getting into my green 1960 Chevy with the 10-foot CB whip antenna on the back.

The next afternoon, I held the door for her as she slid into the passenger seat. I looked around. No one was watching. Damn! That was disappointing. I wanted the guys to burn up with envy. For the first week, Linda and I shared small talk on the way home. We became closer. A *lot* closer. Somehow I forgot that I was married with two kids. The striking beauty seemed to like me a lot, and that made me feel good. I felt accepted again.

The timing was right...for trouble. Sis said that she wanted to go to Ontario to visit her uncle Tim. I agreed. We bought train tickets for her and the kids. I drove Sis, Roddie, and Mark to the train station in Halifax and kissed them good-bye.

On Monday, on the way home from work, Linda moved across the seat closer to me.

The wicked timing was right. "Linda, how would you like to come to my place on Friday evening? We can order Chinese and have more time to talk.

"Sure, I'd love to, Stan."

I was tempted to take her to my place that moment and tear her clothes off, but on the other hand, I thought that maybe she simply wanted us to be friends.

Friday afternoon at 5:05 I helped her into the car, and we drove toward my apartment. We didn't talk as much as we usually did. It was as if we knew that something was going to happen.

I hoped that my neighbors weren't too nosy. Once inside, I put an album on the record player. I chose something romantic. The Beatles, The Rolling Stones, and the Four Tops might have been big, but I figured that Pete Fountain would put her in the mood. I was already in the mood. To quicken the mood, I made a couple of potent daiquiris. We decided on pizza instead of Chinese.

While we listened to Pete and sipped our Daiquiris, I moved next to her on the couch. I slipped my arm around her. She kissed me. Her second kiss could only be described as an attack. My fantasies had been realized. I thought about the guys at work. If they only knew.

Linda spent that night and the next two nights with me. It was intense. The reality that I was married with two young children never came up. I wanted to feel guilty, but I didn't. I did worry about getting caught. I did.

Sis's Toronto vacation ended on Tuesday. So did my nightly delight. I picked Sis and the kids up at the train station. She seemed happy to see me. It was especially great to hug Roddie and Mark. I was resigned but not committed to being a married guy. I was depressed to be back to my mundane life. I couldn't see Linda anymore without the risk of being caught, and if I did, where would we go for a few hours of ecstasy, anyway? What really had me in a panic was the vision of her with another guy, sharing her animal-like sexuality.

Sis and I unloaded her luggage, as she talked about her relatives in Ontario. I didn't hear her. I could only think about Linda. I had to get over Linda. I couldn't get her out of my head. Besides, I had to face her at work every day.

"I missed you," Sis whispered in my ear as she pulled the covers over us in bed.

"I missed you too." I lied.

She ran her hands over my back. "Hey, what happened to you?"

She abruptly sat up in bed and rubbed her hands up and down my back.

"Nothing. What do you mean?" I had to think fast.

"Your back is bumpy." She snapped on the light. "Here, sit up and bend forward."

"No, it's nothing. Just a few scratches."

Her voice seemed to raise several octaves.

"No it's not. Your back is scratched from your shoulders to your butt. What the hell happened while I was gone?"

"Okay. Hold on. I'll tell you the truth." I was about to begin my string of lies.

"You were fucking some whore while I was gone, weren't you?"

"What? No! I'll explain." I was angry that she had called Linda a whore.

"Go ahead. I'm listening."

"Well, my buddy Jamie and I were out one night a week ago. We were both drunk out of our minds, and we were, uh, driving down a gravel road, and I was acting like a fool. Well, I jumped out of the car. I slid one hundred feet down the road on my back. So, that's how my back got scratched like that."

There was dead silence. She checked my back once more and exploded.

"You fucking son-of-a-bitch! Don't lie to me. Those are fingernail scratches. I'm not stupid. I can tell the difference. You were screwing some bitch."

The fight escalated until she got up and slept on the couch. I assume that she slept. I didn't sleep for fear of being castrated with a kitchen knife.

The next day, I assumed that it was the beginning of the end. However, we eventually resumed sleeping in the same bed, but we both knew that we weren't happy. We never really had been.

I left E.M.I.-Cossor and accepted a job in Sydney, Nova Scotia, with Pye Electronics as a service tech. While living in Cape Breton, I spent a lot of time with my old friends Howard and Sheldon. Also, I was only forty miles away from Mom and Pop in Jamesville West. Life at home was tolerable, but I still had Linda on my mind.

My manager at Pye Electronics regularly required me to go to the head office in Halifax for training and supplies. This gave me a chance to meet up with Linda again, but eventually my bouts of inebriation, coupled with my jealousy and hot temper, caused our lusty relationship to end with a lamp-throwing fight one night, and it was over.

* * *

"Hey, Stan, look at this," Sis said, from behind the pages of the *Cape Breton Post*. "ITT has a job posting for electronics technicians in the Arctic, and the pay is great. Here, check it out."

I read the ad. Interviews were to be scheduled in Halifax in two weeks. I read further. The pay was one thousand dollars a month, which was great in 1966, when the average annual salary was around seven thousand. The company took care of one's lodging and food, but employees could not take their families with them, plus, each tour of duty in the Arctic was from six to eight months before being eligible for a month of vacation. I thought it over.

Sis suggested that the high-paying job could be the answer to our financial mess, or maybe she had an ulterior motive. "Stan, we could pay off all our bills and even save some money."

I agreed. "Yeah, and probably in just the first year."

It was true. We were behind on our car payments. We had just bought a mobile home, and I owed a finance company a bundle.

"Okay, I'll call ITT tomorrow." I smiled at the thought of paying off all our bills and maybe being able to buy a new car for the first time.

On November 18, 1966, we drove to Halifax for my interview. I thought about Linda and who she was with. A pang of jealousy hit me in the gut.

I met an ITT representative in a meeting room at the Nova Scotian Hotel. He handed me an electronics test and a general questions test, along with some kind of psych evaluation. The test didn't seem too daunting. I completed it easily and handed it back to the ITT guy.

"Mr. Campbell, we'll give you a call in a few days and let you know if you've been accepted."

A week later, I received a letter and a contract. I was accepted and had to be in Streator, Illinois for training on December 6th. All travel, meals and hotel expenses would be paid by the company.

"Holy shit! I've been accepted," I yelled to Sis.

"Yaaaaay!"

I wasn't sure if she was happy about the money or about the fact that I was going away.

For me, the reality of leaving Sis, but especially Roddie and Mark, hit me. I had mixed feelings. I was sure that the job would eventually give us a better life. The memories and effects of my affair with Linda were fading, and I felt that Sis and I were growing closer again. We hauled our mobile home back to Dartmouth so that Sis could be closer to her family.

The first day that we arrived in Dartmouth, we met a neighbor. His name was Jerry. He seemed to be a nice guy and was quite helpful. Two weeks later, when the day arrived for me to leave for nine months, Jerry offered to drive me to the airport. I said a tearful good-bye to Sis and hugged and kissed Roddie and Mark. It pained me profoundly to say good-bye to my kids.

I loaded my suitcase into Jerry's car. At the end of the driveway, the highway to the airport was to the right. He turned left.

Jerry's left turn changed the course of my life.

Arctic Cat

This was the USA. I had been inside the United States of America only once on a weekend with a few Army friends from Camp Gagetown at an Air Force base in Maine. The one thing that I clearly remembered was the smell of American cigarettes. They had more of a cigar aroma compared to Canadian cigarettes.

From O'Hare Airport in Chicago, I took a train to Streator, Illinois. I met up with a few other guys on the train who were also on their way to that Midwestern town in the middle of nowhere for the same job. Maybe I wasn't so special after all.

We checked into the Plum Hotel in the heart of downtown Streator. The hotel décor was early black and white movie, run by a spooky husband and wife team. The rooms for the ITT trainees were modified to accommodate three or four people. It felt like the Army all over again without the Monday morning inspection.

On Monday morning a brown, unmarked school bus picked us up and took us out of town to the middle of a cornfield, where a radar dome dominated the dead corn stalks. We were ushered inside to a lecture by a guy who reminded me of Rod Serling from the *Twilight Zone*. He advised us that we were being processed for clearance to top secret. I thought that was pretty cool. I was going to be a super-sleuth, top-secret agent man, except for one problem. I had a big mouth.

We studied meteorology and air traffic control procedures. At night, we studied the strippers at Rokey's Bar across the street from the hotel. I had never seen a girl take her top off in public before. It was very exciting for a guy from Jamesville West.

Actually, she wasn't that impressive. Her name was Sam, and she could have been a guy. I had bigger breasts. I wasn't sure why, but for some reason, she liked me. I reasoned that maybe she could like me better at the Plum Hotel. I persuaded her to come back to my room...well *our* room. I was sharing. Jean-Paul and Samuel, my roommates from Québec, were not happy when they awoke and saw that I had female company in my bed. Once again, I had neglected to remember that I had a wife and kids at home. I forgot to remember this detail on a few occasions during my three-month course in Illinois.

*   *   *

"Mr. Campbell, come with me," the air traffic instructor whispered in my ear ten days after the course had begun.

"What's the problem?"

"We have a car waiting outside. You have to leave the class and return to the hotel."

"Why? It's only 1:30."

"Your security clearance has run into a snag."

"Why?"

"We don't know, but the Royal Canadian Mounted Police in Canada has come up with something of concern, and until it is straightened out, you cannot continue here."

I slept for most of the day and drank Schlitz Beer at Rokey's from 4:00 p.m. until closing. I was bored and speculated on what the hell the Mounties had found out about me that they considered a threat to national security. I was a womanizing drunk from Cape Breton. I couldn't damage national security if I was handed a nuke. Then I thought that maybe they had found out from someone in Jamesville West that I had a big mouth and couldn't keep a secret. Maybe the boob-challenged Sam was a Russian spy. I was worried. I began to drink alone at the hotel instead of watching Sam surprise the patrons.

Phone calls were expensive, but I gathered a pocketful of quarters to call Sis. She didn't sound happy. In fact, she sounded frosty and yet wouldn't tell me what was bothering her. I missed her, but especially Roddie and Mark. It crossed my mind that maybe she knew about my nighttime flings. Maybe the Mounties had told her. Something was not right at home.

Four days after I was sent home from school, I was permitted back in class. I asked my instructor if he knew what the problem was. He told me that the Mounties had apparently found nothing. At least, nothing that would have helped Leonid Brezhnev or Fidel Castro.

The course in Streator came to an end. I graduated as a *radician,* which is a combination communications and radar technician. My classmates and I were to be shipped off to the Arctic. The Arctic in mid-winter! I was told that I would be going to a DEW Line station called Cam-3, a place so isolated that geographically it didn't even have a name. We were all reminded that we would need to put in at least six months of service before we got a vacation. Oh, and we were also reminded that there were no women where we were going.

Maybe I should have spent a few more nights of sin with Flat Sam. Too late. We were leaving in the morning on a Northwest Airlines flight that would take us from Chicago to Minneapolis to Winnipeg and then on to Cambridge Bay, one hundred seventy-five miles north of the Arctic Circle. From this remote outpost, I would be sent to Cam-3, even more remote.

We flew from Chicago to Winnipeg, where we spent the night in a hotel. The next morning, a bus took us to the airport for our flight north by northwest thirteen hundred and forty miles to Cambridge Bay.

There was no heated ramp out to our Trans-Air plane, a World War II DC-4. The interior looked more like a WWI vintage flying machine. It smelled of fuel oil, grease, and stale tobacco smoke. Twenty seats were situated behind mounds of cargo, including a large diesel engine which was tied down securely for the flight.

We had been issued Arctic gear, consisting of parkas, thermal pants, and something I had only heard about in the movies, mukluks. They felt like slippers. I wondered how these oversized socks could keep us warm. We were also issued thermal underwear. My first thought was, always having women on my mind, that I didn't want be to seen in long underwear by a girl. Then I realized that I wasn't going to see a female for months.

First one engine fired up, sputtering and belching blue smoke, then a second, and a third, which took far too long to start, and finally the fourth engine on the old DC-4 roared to smoky life.

"Chris', I hope dis ting gets off d' ground," my new buddy, Paul Depuis, screamed into my ear over the din of the engines.

We taxied down the ramp, turned to line up on the runway. The engines roared for a few more minutes and rose and fell again. Then, all four engines increased to deafening vibrating levels. We bounced down the runway as the old clunker went faster. The plane bounced some more. I nervously watched the diesel engine up front and hoped that it wouldn't break loose. If it did, I knew enough about flying to know what would happen.

We went faster, and the bouncing and swaying decreased. Just when I thought we were running out of runway, we lifted off and gradually ascended up into the gray clouds. We were on our way, almost fourteen hundred miles straight north. As we climbed, I missed my boys Roddie and Mark more and more.

The flight felt like a lifetime. It grew dark, even though it was around 3:00 in the afternoon. Finally, we began our descent and broke through the clouds. As the old DC-4 touched down, Paul made the sign of the cross.

We stepped outside the plane into forbidding frigid air. My nose hairs felt like they were electric. My eyelashes became frosty within seconds.

"What's the temperature here?' I asked the Eskimo bus driver.

"Fifty-five below," he answered with a smirk.

He was amused by the new crew of spoiled, warm-blooded babies from the south.

We stopped in front of a long building raised high off the ground on posts. Snow drifted under the building. This was an overnight stop. The next day I was scheduled to get on another flying antique.

The next morning, we rode on a stubby blue school bus to the Quonset hut airport where a half a dozen Inuit men, women, and children waited for the next flight. Two other shivering radicians from the south looked apprehensive as they awaited their flight to Arctic isolation.

The aircraft on which we were scheduled to fly must have been built by the Wright Brothers. I found out that it was a C-46, which was similar to a DC-3. It looked like a flying killer whale. It was a tail-dragger, meaning that instead of a nose wheel it had a tail wheel, so when I climbed up the ladder and went inside, I had to walk uphill to my seat. I envisioned the old days when the traveling public flew on these planes. I imagined how many times grandma had fallen down the aisle or some drunk had ended up in the tail somewhere.

If the DC-4 was loud, the engines on the C-46 were deafening. Conversation was impossible without shouting directly into your seat-mate's ear. I noticed that the same diesel engine was on this plane that had been on the DC-4 from Winnipeg, obviously going to some DEW Line station across the Arctic.

We took off in what seemed like a bounding leap into the air. Wind and snow blew in through the cracks by the door. This aircraft was obviously not pressurized. I peered out the frosty window to the most amazing bleak white landscape peppered by rocky spots. I knew that if we had to make an emergency landing, it would be over, one way or the other. We would either be smashed to smithereens or become human popsicles within minutes. Better not to think about that.

The plane circled a few times in whiteness, as the pilots searched for Cam-1, our first stop along the way. Suddenly, the engines fired up, and we lifted into the air. I learned two new words that day. *Whiteout* and *abort*. We flew on to Cam-2 and landed without any problem, if you don't include bouncing down the runway like a kangaroo, with the diesel engine ripping at its tether chains.

We stayed on the ground for twenty minutes and took off for Cam-3, my stop. I was anxious to get off that flying whale. The C-46 looked as though it was never meant to be a flying machine.

We circled Cam-3. There was nothing but whiteness above and below. For a moment, I could see what I thought was the ground, and I hoped the pilot could too. Magically, we touched the runway and came to a stop in front of a hangar. I climbed down the stairs, along with an Eskimo man and his wife and child. This was going to be home. I was met by Ken Johnson, the DEW Line station manager, and a driver with a crew cab pickup truck.

We watched as the plane took off for the next DEW Line station with two pilots, a newbie radician, and an Inuit (Eskimo) family of four. It disappeared quickly into the low overcast sky. Ken and I loaded my stuff into the long, raised train-like building, which was to be home until August.

On either side of the building were two huge flat antennas that looked like double drive-in theatre screens. I remembered them from my course in Streator, Illinois. They were called Forward Scatter Tropospheric Antennas. They were part of our only means of communication with the outside world, including NORAD. Dominating the long white building was a radar dome, the external part of the twin radars we monitored twenty-four hours a day to be on the lookout for Soviet bombers in case they decided to come over the polar cap.

I was proud that I was a minute part of a team guarding North America against the Evil Empire. The Soviets did come to visit, and my job was to advise NORAD, which in turn sent jet fighters up to send them back home. Nikita Khrushchev was simply toying with us.

I settled in to my new digs with ten other guys in the lonely outpost for the next six months. It was true. There were no women, but the lonely outpost had a well-stocked bar and great food prepared by a superb chef.

"Hey, Campbell, welcome to Cam-3! Join us for a drink in the bar." It was Larry, one of the veteran radicians.

"Sure! I need a drink. It's been a long trip from Illinois."

Larry said, "I'm buying."

Before Larry could pour the drinks, Ken entered looking grim. "Guys, I have bad news."

We stopped. We knew that something serious had happened.

"What's up, boss?" Larry asked.

"The C-46 crashed at Dye Main."

"Oh, my God!" we all said together.

"There were no survivors. They were coming in low in the soup. The C-46's wheels hit a knoll half a mile from the runway. Apparently, they had a diesel engine on board. It broke loose and went through the cockpit. That was it."

I'm sure we all thought that it could have been us. For me, I felt sick to my stomach. I imagined that Inuit couple and the horror they must have felt in the last few seconds of their lives. I thought of the pilots as we had watched them navigate the aircraft through the open cockpit door. What if I had been sent to Dye Main instead of here to Cam-3?

I slept fitfully that night. I tried to get drunk but couldn't quite do it. I think we all did. The next day, I was on my first day shift. They were nine-hour shifts with three hours working as a technician, repairing and installing complex electronic equipment for which I was trained, and another six hours manning the twin radar screens, waiting for the Soviets and occasionally talking to captains on commercial flights flying overhead from U.S. and Canadian cities to Europe.

Once in a while, we got a chance to talk to a flight attendant who wanted to say hello to us lonely guys in the Arctic. That's as close as we got to women...thirty-five thousand feet away.

The rest of my six months was spent working, drinking, and sleeping. My excessive drinking almost got me sent home. My friend Paul Depuis, who got transferred to Cam-3, told me that he had heard the station manager, Ken refer to me as an orangutan and that if I didn't straighten out, I would have to go.

Summer arrived in the Arctic. It was delightful compared to the almost continuous darkness of winter. The evenings were warm and sunny, even at 11:00 at night. The snow disappeared, and flowers sprouted everywhere on the tundra. Most of all, the long sunsets were perfect for long walks on the tundra.

I sat on a rock one night and watched the sunset and wondered what my friends were doing at home in Halifax. I tried to imagine what Sis was doing and how the kids must be growing. I missed her and my kids more each day. Increasingly, I felt remorse for my unfaithful ways. I was anxious to get home to see her. I had a month to go.

We talked on the phone from time to time, but it was expensive. The really great part was that I was sending money home every two weeks and paying off all our bills. I hoped that when I got back from the next tour of duty, we could start saving for an actual house instead of a mobile home and maybe buy a new car. I would be home soon, for a whole month. I was about to discover that home is not necessarily where the heart is.

Payback Back Home

The businessman next to me on the Air Canada flight from Winnipeg was busy writing in his planner. It didn't matter. I had to tell someone.

"I can't wait to see her."

He didn't look up. He didn't care. I didn't care that he didn't care.

I kept babbling. "I haven't seen her in nine months."

"Uh, huh."

"I am so excited. She, my wife that is, is meeting me in Toronto."

"Hmm...great."

"She lives, I mean, *we* live in Halifax, but she made this trip to Toronto to meet me, and then we'll fly to Halifax tomorrow."

It was a delicious sunny evening on August 5, 1967. My trapped seat-mate jumped into the aisle to get away from me, but I followed closely behind, shivering with excitement to see Sis. She had left the kids back in Halifax with her aunt.

I shuffled down the aisle and then the long hallway and stepped onto the escalator down to the arrivals area. I scanned the waiting crowd as we descended, and then I spotted her. I waved madly. She smiled. I ran to her and threw my arms around her. I hugged her tightly. She patted my back. I moved to kiss her. She turned away. I remembered that she was shy about kissing in public. She always had been.

I asked about the kids as we waited for my bags. Finally, after some uncomfortable conversation, I picked up my luggage, and moved over to the car rental kiosk. I talked non-stop. She said nothing. After we picked up the car, I leaned over to kiss her in earnest. She pulled away again. I chalked it up to nerves on her part. After all, I was probably like a stranger to her. We drove down to the hotel strip near the airport. As I pulled into a hotel parking lot, Sis suddenly became alert.

"What are you doing?"

"We're checking into a hotel. I can't wait to be alone with you."

"No, we're staying at my Uncle Tim's. Remember, I told you that."

"What?" I asked a bit too dismissively. "I don't want to stay at anyone's house. I want us to be alone. We haven't seen each other in nine months!"

She stared straight ahead. "I don't want to stay here. Uncle Tim is expecting us."

"Sis, come on! We need to be alone. I do not want to stay at your uncle's. I'm sure that he would understand. All right? So that's it, we're staying here tonight, and besides, we can afford it now. If you feel more comfortable, we can go for a drink first, okay?"

She was silent for a few seconds and then relented. "Fine! But first, let's get a bottle of something and take it to our room."

"Sure! Let's go get a bottle of gin." I was relieved.

We returned to the Holiday Inn and checked into our room. Sis was still standoffish, but I continued to attribute her aloof manner to nerves. I poured a tall one for her. She drank it down quickly and went to the bathroom.

I downed half a water glass of gin and got undressed. I figured that after her drink and once she got into bed, she would loosen up.

I was snuggled under the bed covers when she came out of the bathroom. She sat on a chair.

"Come on, sweetie, get undressed. We have a lot of catching up to do."

"No, I'd rather not. Stan, I still want to go to Uncle Tim's."

"What? Why?"

"In fact, if you want, you can drop me off there, and you can come back here."

I sat up. It hit me like a bullet in my heart. I stared at her without saying a word for a moment, waiting to see if maybe she would smile or explain.

"Sis, tell me what's going on."

"Nothing is going on."

"Please tell me the truth."

I was suddenly terrified to hear the truth. I didn't want to accept what I had begun to believe.

"Do you not want to be with me? Is that it?" I asked so softly that my voice broke.

I waited.

"Sis?"

She paused. "No."

"No, you don't want to be with me anymore?"

"Yes."

"Oh, my God!"

The bullets stopped. It felt more like sledge hammer blows to my chest. We both sat in silence. Then the worst possible scenario exploded in my brain.

"I'm afraid to ask, Sis, but is there someone else?"

She didn't respond. The hush was nauseating.

"Please answer me. Have you been seeing someone?"

After a moment of silence she uttered, a barely audible, "Yes."

Her reply led me to the next question, however, I wasn't sure I wanted to hear the answer. "Have you slept with him?"

She looked straight at me for the first time and said, "Please take me to Uncle Tim's."

My massive chest pain and nausea turned to rage. "I won't take you to your fucking uncle's or anywhere else."

"Fine, I'll call a taxi"

"Not until you answer more questions. Who are you fucking? I want to know because I am going to kill the bastard."

"Go to hell. I'll never tell you," she yelled at me as she became more assertive.

"Sis, tell me who the son-of-a-bitch is!"

"Listen, you bastard, don't act like you have been a saint. You were fucking Linda in Halifax and God knows who else, and I'm sure that you dipped your dick in Streator, Illinois, too."

"The affair with Linda was over a long time ago."

"Bullshit! The day you left to go to Streator with Jerry, instead of going to the airport, you asked Jerry to turn left to go see your little bitch Linda to say good-bye instead of making a right turn to go to the airport."

"That's not true. Jerry had to get gas before we drove to the airport. We were not going to Linda's." It was the truth.

"Oh, bull-fucking-shit, Stan! Don't lie to me. Jerry told me that he took you to see Linda."

"What? That lying bastard! That is not true. Why would he tell you that?"

"Well, he did, and Jerry doesn't lie."

"Aha! That cocksucker! *He's* the one you're fucking!"

"No, he isn't."

"I never trusted that asshole. So he convinced you that I was still seeing Linda so that he could drive a wedge between us and then get into your pants while I was gone."

"No. Jerry is simply a good friend."

"Not to me."

The fight lasted for hours, as we finished the gin. I stayed undressed in bed, and she slept on top of the covers. Later, I got up and walked around the room naked just to irritate her.

We both flew to Halifax the next day without speaking to each other. The plane could have gone down like a flaming torpedo into the Bay of Fundy, and we wouldn't have said good-bye to each other.

I hugged the kids and finally had some peace and love in my life. Sis was aloof. At 6:30 p.m., on the first evening at home, Sis applied her make-up, did her hair, and then squeezed into white jeans that were so tight that one would think that she had painted them on.

I had to ask, "Where are you going?"

"I'm going out with some friends, if it's any of your business."

"Is *is* my business, so where are you going?"

"I'm going out with some friends," Sis said, as she added more hair spray.

"Who? What friends?"

"It's not important, and you don't need to know."

At that moment, a car horn blew, and she ran out the door and jumped into the front seat with a guy I didn't recognize, and off they sped.

I burned up with anger and jealousy, and I couldn't get rid of the images of the two of them screwing in the backseat of his car. I desperately wanted to kill him. At times, I wanted to kill her, and then I thought of my own sins. Then I wanted to kill myself. I reasoned that yes, I had screwed around, but I would never flaunt an affair to intentionally hurt her. At least that was my logic.

I wanted to get in my '67 Mustang rental and chase them, but Roddie and Mark were at home, and I was their absent Dad. Sis arrived home at 1:00 in the morning. I tried to initiate a calm discussion. She didn't want to talk, and in fact, she became more derisive. She even informed me that she was going again the next night.

My old friend Howard had dated a tall, attractive girl by the name of Marilyn. After he moved to Ontario, Marilyn relocated to Halifax, just a few blocks away from Sis and me. I called Marilyn and asked her if she would come and baby-sit the next night. I also called my friend, Dave Cunningham, to come with me to follow Sis and her boyfriend around town.

It took over an hour, but eventually we saw Sis and the guy driving down Halifax's main drag, Gottingen Street. I tailgated them. He drove faster. I stayed on his tail. He suddenly pulled over next to a police car, obviously had a short conversation with the cops, and drove on. Two cops stepped from their car and flagged me down.

"Are you harassing and following that gentleman and his girlfriend?"

I was enraged at the *girlfriend* description.

"That's my wife in that car!"

"Is she being kidnapped, or is she there of her own accord, sir?"

I lied. "She is being kidnapped."

"Sir, I spoke to her, and she told me that she is there of her own accord."

"But..."

"Sir, I'm warning you. If you attempt to follow them any farther, you will be arrested. Is that clear?"

"But that's my wife in that car!"

"Sir, go home and hire a lawyer if you need to, but stay away from that car."

I was irate, but I had no choice. Dave suggested that I go home and get a good night's sleep and make a decision the next day. I dropped Dave off and went home. I was also getting sexually frustrated. I had not been with a woman in over eight months while in the Arctic. I was resigned to the fact that sex with my wife was not going to happen.

I told my sad story to Marilyn, who seemed to feel my pain. We had a drink and then two. I felt better in the company of a woman who was not my enemy. In fact, we became friendlier. The kids were asleep. I handed her a second glass of wine, and as I did, my hand touched her arm. I kissed her. I took her hand and led her down the hall. The eight-month drought was over.

We never got together following that night, but neither one of us regretted our one-hour fling. I had hoped that Sis would come home and find us in bed together. Marilyn didn't share my vengeful vision and left before Sis got home at 2:15 a.m. I had a surprise package waiting at the door for her.

I was ready. A car pulled up out front and parked. I peeked through the kitchen window and watched as the two heads in the front seat became one. My anger and jealousy evolved to craving revenge. I didn't care anymore. At least not about her.

Finally, a car door slammed. I heard her try to turn the knob on the door. I had locked it simply to demonstrate to her that I was in control. I leisurely strolled to the door and on the way picked up a large suitcase and a garbage bag full of assorted clothing, opened the door, and threw both items past her onto the lawn, as she dug deep in her purse for her key.

"Hey, you'll need this wherever you crash tonight," I calmly said.

"What do you think you're doing?" she screamed at me as she evaded the flying garbage bag.

"I'm throwing you out of my house. This is your clothing and the rest of your useless junk. Take it, because you're not coming in here."

"Fuck you! I live here!" She attempted to squeeze her way past me.

"Not anymore, you don't. I make the payments on this place, and you have given up your right to live here. "

"Screw you, you son-of-a-bitch!"

"No you haven't even done *that*, Sis!"

"This is my home, and I'm fucking staying here." Sis tried to squeeze past me.

I stopped her on the threshold.

"Don't touch me you bastard!"

The *bastard* word hit a soft spot.

I grabbed her jacket and the back of her belt and tossed her out onto the lawn. By this time, there was no doubt that the neighborhood was awake.

"You fucking bastard. I am calling the police!" she screeched, as she ran in the back door and picked up the phone in our bedroom.

I quietly lifted the kitchen extension in time to hear a policeman on the line.

"My husband just threw me out of the house!" she cried.

"Are you hurt?" The cop inquired.

"No, but..."

"Why did your husband throw you out?'

"Because I came home late."

"With a boyfriend." I interrupted, deciding to add to the conversation.

"Sir, get off the line. And, madam, I suggest that you do not go back into the house. Go and stay with a friend or a relative, and then tomorrow, if you want to file charges, come by our office."

"But it's my house too." Sis argued with him.

"Well, for your own safety, I suggest that you stay out until you settle your differences or see a lawyer."

She hung up. I hung up. She left through the rear door and walked down the street at 2:30 in the morning, leaving her suitcase and Glad garbage bag luggage on the lawn. I felt sorry for her. I knew that Sis was out of my life permanently. I knew that ultimately I was responsible for our marriage mess.

The next day, I saw a lawyer and filed a separation agreement. Then, Sis sprang a second surprise. I had been sending money home faithfully every month to pay off all our loans and put money away to buy a house when I finally left the Arctic. Surprise! We owed more money than we had when I had left. We had no savings. The money that I had been sending home to her was gone.

She wouldn't tell me where it had gone, but after talking to my neighbors and friends, allegedly a lot of the money had been spent on parties and booze. One of her not-so-close friends claimed that Sis was hanging out with people who were drug users. It was all hearsay. I had no evidence, but the party stories were not surprising, given her new lifestyle and attitude.

I was angry and frustrated that my six months in isolation in the Arctic had been for nothing. Not only did I not have a wife but I was also broke. What payback for my philandering ways! Had I learned a lesson?

I planned to file for divorce when I returned from the north permanently. I had three weeks left in my vacation, and I wanted to enjoy the warmth of the summer before I returned to the north. I needed time to go home to Jamesville West to see Mom and Pop and spend time with my kids in peace, and I craved female companionship.

I spent a week at home with my parents and took Roddie and Mark with me. My kids loved their grandparents, so much so they were happy to stay with them. Sis and I agreed on one thing...that Roddie and Mark should stay with their grandparents until I finished my tour of duty in the Arctic.

Back in Halifax, I tried to find a date for dinner and drinks but had no luck until my ex-friend Jerry, who insisted that he had not bedded my wife, invited me to join him and his girlfriend on a double date. His girlfriend shared an apartment with a roommate who wasn't seeing anyone. She was an up-and-coming singer around Halifax and had even been on TV locally. Her name was Anne Murray. I was impressed. I had heard of Anne. To me, she was already a star because she sang onstage at a local club. I agreed to go, but at the last minute my nervousness and intimidation by a *star* gave me a grave case of cold feet. I opted instead to get slightly drunk with my friend Dave.

Dave's neighbor, Mary, worked at a supermarket in downtown Halifax. He thought that she wasn't seeing anyone, so maybe I should meet her. We drove by the store where he introduced us. She was good-looking and kind of shy, like me. Being a coward, Dave had to ask her if she wanted to go out with us for a drink and maybe a movie. She agreed.

We met at a bar in Fairview, after which I dropped Dave and his girlfriend off at his place, and Mary and I kept on to her house. She lived with her mom and dad, but fortuitously they were out of town. I liked Mary. For the remainder of my vacation we spent every moment we could together. I began to like Mary...a lot.

I kissed Mary good-bye at the Halifax Airport and told her that I loved her. Of course I loved her. I had known her for two full weeks! Mary responded with the same words...I think, or maybe I just imagined it. I really did care about her. She was 19, and I was 26, but she was more mature than her years.

I signed up for one more year in the Arctic in an attempt to get caught up financially. I was assigned to a different DEW Line station, but after six months, I was eligible for another four-week vacation. I spent my time with my kids, my mom and dad, and of course, Mary. I loved her. It was hard to say good-bye to her and my kids again, before I left for my final six months in the far north. However, I knew that I would come back this time with some money in the bank and get to be a dad full time. I planned to ask Mary to marry me.

The remaining six months in the Arctic were spent working, sleeping, eating, and drinking, but this time, I saved money. I paid off all my creditors and saved for a new car. I had it picked out before I flew home, a 1968 Ford Torino GT, my first new car.

I would never see the Arctic again. My first stop in Halifax was at Mary's house. My second stop was at a Ford dealership. I wanted the one on the showroom floor, the green Ford Torino GT with the gold accent stripe down the sides and the extra wide tires. The sales guys ignored me. When I suggested that I could go down the street to buy the Dodge Charger, they became helpful.

My third stop was at Pye Electronics, where the general manager agreed to re-hire me as the Cape Breton service rep. I was about to be home in beautiful Cape Breton Island in Nova Scotia, near my kids and among old friends, with a great job. I might be able to finally find the identity of my birth mother. Life would be good again.

I had only three more days in Halifax, so I spent as much time as I could with Mary. I didn't want to go to Cape Breton without her. I was in love, as I was with every woman who showed even the slightest interest in me. The next step was obvious, at least to me. I asked Mary to marry me. She didn't hesitate. She said no.

I was shocked that she would say no. I thought she loved me. She had told me so.

"I can't. I'm not ready to get married yet, and I may not be ready for a long time."

"But, you said you love me."

"Yes, I do care for you, but I think we both need to get our lives together. I'm only 20, you are almost 28, and you aren't officially divorced from Deanna. At least, let's give ourselves some time."

I was bewildered. I was sure that Mary would say yes without hesitation. It became even more obvious to me later that her level of maturity was no match for my irresponsibility.

"Don't get upset, Stan, but you have to get control of your drinking and especially your nasty temper when you're drunk."

I knew that she was right. I was aware of my ugly temper, especially when I drank hard liquor. Pop had warned me years before not to drink hard liquor because it often ignited a violent temper. I promised Mary that I would try. I meant it.

I left Halifax for Cape Breton promising to come back on weekends to see her. I kept the mobile home that Sis and I had shared and had it towed to a trailer park in Sydney. My two bosses from Pye showed up on Monday afternoon with my new fully-equipped mobile electronics van in which I would travel all over Cape Breton installing and repairing two-way radios and repeater stations on mountain tops. I loved my job.

I saw Roddie and Mark several times a week as I passed through Jamesville West going to and from jobs. I spent most weekends with them at Mom and Pop's or had them with me in Sydney, but I missed Mary. Once a month I drove to Halifax to spend time with her. I booked a room at the Bluenose Motel in Bedford, and we left only to eat. I continued to try to convince her to marry me. She was adamant. The trips to Halifax decreased. I had to have a permanent woman in my life. I was lonely. My friends all had regular girlfriends or were married.

In the late sixties, the phone company was local everywhere. If a person dialed zero or 411 for Information, a local telephone operator in his own town answered. I hatched a plan. Late at night, after I had crawled into bed, I picked up the bedside phone and dialed 411 and asked for the number of a nonexistent person. I had the act well rehearsed.

Most nights, I followed a script for the role of the confused caller. "Hello, do you have a number for Herman Gnudsun in Badger, Newfoundland?"

I was reasonably sure that there was no one with that name anywhere.

"Let me check, sir."

I waited.

"Are you sure of the spelling, sir?"

"Oh, yes. He is my real father, and I recently found out his identity. I was adopted. I have to meet him before he dies."

"Well, let me check some other listings."

"Oh, please, this means so much to me." I did my best to sound despondent.

I also turned on my softest resonant radio-style voice. Sometimes it didn't work, but other times I was able to draw the operator into a conversation. One operator talked to me through her entire shift while answering calls for real customers. Another operator, after a long, intimate conversation, engaged in phone sex with me. Obviously, she was working alone.

One night, as I picked up my bedside phone, I drew an especially sexy-sounding operator into a long conversation with my devious plan. After some prodding, she eventually told me that her name was Arlene. I talked her into meeting me for coffee when she got off work at 7:00 a.m.

I saw a somewhat attractive brunette sitting alone in the second booth in Java Joe's diner on Charlotte Street in Sydney. Our eyes met. We both smiled. I asked her if her name was Arlene. She nodded as I sat in the booth across from her.

I was amazed at my own clever strategy, but I was painfully shy. I could play the role of the smooth-talking radio guy on the phone, but face-to-face, I was a bumbling fool until I got to know someone...*much* better.

We managed to fumble our way through a primitive conversation, but she did agree to meet me for a drink the next night, on her day off. However, a thorny snag existed. Arlene cautioned me that we would have to have a platonic friendship. She could not get involved with anyone because she was engaged.

"Engaged? You're engaged...to be married?"

"Yes, we're getting married next summer when he gets back home."

"Is he in the military?"

"No, he's a Mountie."

"He's...a Mountie?" My mouth dried up.

"Yes, he is in Regina right now."

I thought that maybe she was right. We definitely should keep it platonic. I didn't want to mess with a Mountie. Mounties carried guns. I had heard that they always get their man, although I don't think that they had this scenario in mind.

By the time I had picked up Arlene at her house in North Sydney, I had already changed my plan. I hadn't been next to a girl in months. I prepared dinner back at my place. I invited her to share a cozy meal and a bottle of cheap bubbly wine. Arlene hesitantly agreed. We drove to my blue ten-wide mobile home on Prince Street. I whipped up spaghetti and meatballs, unscrewed the top of the wine bottle, and filled two water glasses. I had plans.

After dinner we watched TV and talked about her work at the phone company. I poured more wine, but she placed her hand over the glass and signaled for me to stop. I moved up closer to her. I slid my arm around her and attempted to pull her closer.

"It's getting late. I think I should go home," she announced, as she pulled away from me.

"What a shame. Are you sure?"

"Yes. I like you, but I have to remind you that I'm engaged. I have to behave myself."

I said, "Behaving yourself is no fun."

I assumed that intimacy with Arlene was a long shot, so we agreed to meet the next night for a movie. In fact, we dated for several more weeks, until one night when she concluded that good behavior is no fun. She stayed overnight with me often and I grew to like her (like almost all the other woman that I had ever met). I foolishly thought that maybe she would leave the Mountie guy and marry me instead.

Sunday, July 20, 1969, a bright, sunny day in Sydney, Nova Scotia, felt like a holiday. Arlene and I were riding in my Ford Torino GT, listening to The 5th Dimension on the radio, when the song was interrupted by an announcer from NASA informing us that the Eagle lunar module was about to land on the moon.

"Oh, wow! Let's go to my place. We have to see this!" I said.

She wasn't nearly as excited. "What? You're kidding!"

"This is a huge event. A man is about to land on the moon. It's one of the biggest events in history, and it's live on TV."

"Stan, it's a beautiful day, and you want to go home and sit inside and watch TV?"

"Are you serious? This isn't just another TV show. We can't miss this."

"Well, forget it. Take me home first."

"No! If I drive all the way to your place and back, I'll miss it."

"Well, I don't want to sit around all afternoon and watch people standing on the moon."

"What? I'm sorry, but we're going to my place, like it or not."

She uttered the wicked word that still sends me to the moon. "Fine!"

I knew then that Arlene wasn't going to be in my life indefinitely. She could go back to her Mountie. He didn't need to know what we had done in my mobile home bedroom.

Three days later, I called her house. Her Mom answered the phone. "She left for Regina on the train this morning."

"Regina? Why? Is she coming back?"

"I don't think so, Stan." Her Mom liked the Mountie, not me.

I was shocked. I was hurt. I felt lost. I couldn't understand why she would do that without at least talking to me. I missed her. I was surprised at my own level of distress, especially after I had wanted to end our racy relationship just days earlier. I broke every speed limit racing to the station in Sydney, hoping that the train hadn't left yet. I couldn't stand the image in my mind of her with him, in his arms, in his bed after she had been in mine. I had thought that the engagement was dead.

I wandered around in circles all day and drove up and down streets where we had been. I picked up a bottle of Pop's favorite rum, Seven Seas. I went home and filled a water glass and added a touch of Coke. Then one more without Coke. I chased it with a beer. My memory withered and died while harebrained ideas flashed through my head.

Here Comes Santa Claus

"**H**o! Ho! Ho!"
I awoke to the sound of belly laughing. It sounded like Santa Claus. It was! He sat across the aisle from me. The aisle? I was on an airplane, and it was night time. It was July 24, 1969, and yet, Santa Claus was seated just three feet away on an Air Canada flight. What the hell was I doing? Where was I going? *Am I dreaming? If this is real, how did I get on this airplane?*

I dug through my pockets and found a ticket. I peered through blurry eyes and saw Sydney to Regina, Saskatchewan. The plane was already descending in Toronto to change flights to continue on to Regina. Then it occurred to me why I was going to Regina, but I remembered nothing about buying a ticket or boarding a plane. I couldn't believe that the flight attendants had let me on the plane if I was that drunk.

I decided that since I had bought the ticket, even though I didn't know how, I would keep on my epic journey. I boarded my connecting flight to Regina in Toronto. I would find her, and maybe I would bring her back, but on second thought, I didn't know why I should. I didn't care as much as I had earlier.

After landing in Regina, I checked into a motel near the airport. I found the RCMP training camp and then called hotels and motels nearby. I asked each hotel receptionist for Arlene MacInnis. Bingo! On the second try, I found her, but she didn't answer the phone. I left a message. Probably out with Mr. Mountie on a *Musical Ride*. I prudently assumed that it would not be a good idea to get caught with a Mountie's fiancée. I imagined a platoon of Royal Canadian Mounted Police chasing me through Regina on horseback. I also imagined her Mountie being mounted at that moment. The image infuriated me. I tried to go to sleep, but I kept seeing images of a red-coated man on a horse with a naked woman. And it wasn't Lady Godiva.

Ring! The phone startled me straight up out of what must have been a five-minute nap.

"Hello..." I mumbled, trying to sound more asleep than I really was in an attempt to make her believe that I was sleeping like a baby with no thoughts of her.

"Stan, are you out of your mind? What are you doing here in Regina?"

"I'm joining the RCMP." I tried to be funny.

"Stop!"

"What do you think I'm doing here? I'm here to take you back to Nova Scotia!"

After an uncomfortable pause she spoke softly. "I really care for you, but I have made a promise to Kenny."

"You broke that promise a long time ago in my bed."

"Yes, and I feel so guilty about that. You were too persuasive."

"Arlene, can I see you one last time?" I said in my softest, sexiest radio voice.

"I don't think that's a good idea, Stan."

"Come on, Arlene. We never even got to say good-bye." I pleaded as I began to feel my love fading away and evolving into late night lust. "I rented a car. I'll come pick you up. Just for a few minutes?"

"Okay. But only for a few minutes. I don't want Kenny to call here and not find me in my room."

I dressed, splashed on some Old Spice, ran out the door, and sped away.

Arlene waited in the lobby. She backed away when I tried to kiss her. We searched for a place to have a drink or coffee, but everything had closed. It was 1:30 in the morning. There was only one option. I suggested that we go to my hotel room. We did, and we did. I was persuasive one last time. We said good-bye an hour later.

I arrived home in Sydney the next evening and rushed out to the airport parking lot. I had been drunk, so I had no idea where I had parked my car. I searched. It wasn't there. I closed my eyes and then opened them, hoping that maybe I just hadn't seen it the first time. My Ford Grand Torino GT was not in the lot.

I reasoned then that maybe Lloyd, my geeky teenage next door neighbor, might have taken me to the airport. I called Lloyd. His Mom, who assumed that I was a pervert, handed him the phone without speaking. After all, I had verified one afternoon that his girlfriend liked older men.

"Lloyd, did you drive me to the airport the day before yesterday?"

"Hey, man, what are you talking about?"

"I guess you didn't, right?"

"Are you drunk again, Stan?"

"Fuck off Lloyd! Hey, look out the window. Is my car in the driveway?"

After a minute he came back to the phone. "No, there's no car in the driveway, except your Pye Electronics van."

"Shit! Where the hell is my car?"

"Don't ask me, but I saw you drive out of here like a bat out of hell night before last."

I hung up and called a cab. When I arrived home, I found my place scattered with half-full glasses of rum and Coke and an empty Seven Seas rum bottle along with three beer bottles on the kitchen counter.

I searched for my Torino GT for three days. The police demonstrated little interest in investigating. Meanwhile, I used the Pye Electronic company van for transportation. I peeked over the ocean cliffs in Glace Bay, fearful of what I might see. Kids had been known to joyride with cars and then push them off the cliffs into the Atlantic Ocean.

On Wednesday morning the phone rang as I was about to leave to repair a repeater station on Cape Smokey. "Mr. Campbell?"

I suspected that it was a bill collector. I was behind on my electric bill, the telephone bill, and my car payment.

"Yes?" I hesitated.

"Mr. Campbell, this Sergeant MacLeod with the Sydney Police. You called us a few days ago about your missing Ford Torino?"

"Oh, yes! Have you found it?"

"Oh, we found it all right, Mr. Campbell."

I held my breath. I imagined that it had been totaled.

The cop had a chilly tone. "We found it at Sampson's Auto Pound. You car was repossessed."

"Oh, okay. I—"

"If you want it back, you will have to see your car finance company, plus it will cost you one hundred and fifty dollars to get it out of the pound."

"Oh. Okay, Sergeant."

"Make your payments on time, and if you don't, do not call us if your car is missing. Is that clear?"

"Yes, Sergeant."

My life was going downhill. I had lost my car and my girlfriend. I was drinking more, and by myself. DJ, Eric MacEwen, was on the radio in the background. I wanted to be like him...a star on the radio.

I refinanced the car at an astronomical interest rate and went back to flirting with telephone operators late at night. I made a date with an operator named Corrie, but she would only go out with me if two or three other girls from the telephone office came along. I figured that three girls were better than none, and besides, maybe I could then just choose one. It would be kind of like picking out the weak deer from the herd.

I liked to cook, even if it was only spaghetti and meatballs, so I invited them to my place to party. The downside was that I couldn't get cozy with any specific one, while all three were present. However, I made a play for Barbara, who seemed to be the most aggressive. I got a kick out of her. She was a bit of a cocky smart-ass. I liked that.

After a few beers, I found the nerve to ask her to go out. She agreed. I thought that she was cute and kind of sexy with her dark hair, full lips, and big eyes. She also was steeped in Celtic culture and even knew a bunch of phrases in Gaelic, mostly swear words. I thought that maybe a Cape Breton girl with a connection to the Scottish culture and music and love of the rural roots of the island was just what I needed in my life.

Barbara and I started dating. We drove up to Jamesville West almost every weekend. My father disliked her instantly, mostly because she was a devoted Liberal and he was a dyed-in-the-wool Conservative. She loved to harass him. My mother thought she was a smarty-pants. Her assertive, brash style even annoyed me at times, but I mostly considered it part of her impudent charm.

Barbara's father, Mick-Sandy, was an *Archie Bunker* character who poked fun at all races and anyone who wasn't a Roman Catholic. He cursed and used the *fuck* word, even when he talked to nuns.

I was legally separated from Sis. This bothered Mick-Sandy because I had not yet filed for a divorce from her. It was hard to tell, but I thought that I was getting closer to him, close enough to ask him to come with me in my Pye Electronics van on my road trip through the Cape Breton Highlands National Park.

I had an underlying reason. Barbara was pregnant, and we decided that we had better get married soon. We had already talked about getting married, but the missed-period surprise had caused the date to get moved up. I asked Mick-Sandy if he would come with me while I serviced the forest ranger radios in the National Park.

"Fuck, yes, bye!" he shouted. "You're all right Campbell, you little bastard."

"Great, I'll pick you up tomorrow morning at 7:00."

"Here, follow me out to the garage," he whispered. "We'll have a fuckin' hooter."

That was Cape Breton-speak for a drink of rum right out of the bottle.

Mick-Sandy reached inside an old tire and pulled out a flask of Governor General rum.

He handed it to me. "Jesus Christ, bye, take a good swig."

I swallowed.

"Fuck! What are you, a baby? Take a Goddamn good one."

I took a bigger drink. I handed it back to Mick-Sandy.

He drained it down to within an inch from the bottom and then handed it back to me with an order. "Finish 'er off, bye."

I emptied the bottle, and we went inside, as gave me a warning. "Now don't open your fucking mouth to Helen about the hooter in the garage, or I'll cut your nuts off."

Helen was Barbara's mother. She liked me and I liked her.

Thursday morning I picked up Mick-Sandy in the Pye Electronic Van. He carried a long case under his arm that looked suspiciously like a rifle.

"What's that?" I asked hesitantly.

"It's a fucking 308," he said as he winked. "You never know when you might see a deer or even a moose up there in the north."

"Mick, we're going through a national park, and you're not allowed to bring weapons into the park."

"Fuck 'em! What those fuckers don't know will never hurt them."

"But I work for the park rangers. They are one of my company's best customers. I could get fired."

"Jesus Christ, Campbell, don't be such a pussy!"

I could have argued with him, but I needed to stay on his good side because I had to pop the big question.

*   *   *

By late afternoon we were far inside the Cape Breton Highlands National Park, two miles from Park Warden McRae's house.

"Holy fuck! Look!" Mick-Sandy shouted as we cruised slowly through the breathtaking, peaceful scenery.

"Shit! What?"

"Jesus Christ! Look! There's a big buck over there in the field by the trees."

I glanced to the left, and there was indeed a deer grazing in the field.

"That's nice. What a beauty." I replied, hoping that he was only admiring the animal.

I had stopped the van. Meanwhile, he pulled out the 308 rifle.

"No! No, Mick we can't do that here. We'll end up in jail."

"Fuck them! They'll never know. Here, grab the rifle, and take your best shot. Hurry up!"

"What? Me? No. No way."

I hoped that the deer would run away, but the big buck seemed oblivious to our presence. Maybe he knew that no one would harm him in the National Park.

"Mick-Sandy, the warden's house is only a mile away. He will hear a rifle shot, and that 308 is loud. Please, no!"

"Jesus Christ, you're wasting time!" Mick yelled. Goddamn it! I'll do it myself."

He pulled back on the bolt and put a round in the chamber as he swung it across his knees preparing to exit the van.

BANG!

It was one of the loudest noises I had ever heard.

I stared at Mick-Sandy.

He turned in slow motion and looked at me.

I waited. I thought he might fall over.

He didn't.

He gawked at me.

"Are you okay?" I asked slowly, as though he might not understand.

I could hardly hear my own voice. It sounded like I had a pillow over my ears.

He continued to gaze at me, bewildered. I thought that he might be dead with his eyes still open.

Finally, with a stupefied gape, he spoke. "Fuck."

Mick-Sandy had accidentally squeezed the trigger in his excitement at the thought of shooting a big buck as visions of venison steaks danced in his head. He looked down. He had shot the side of the sole off of his steel-plant work boot on his right foot. I saw a glimmer of daylight through a hole in the floor of the van.

Suddenly, I feared that the Warden had heard the rifle shot, although in retrospect, the sound was likely contained mostly within the van, partially deafening us. I got out and walked around the passenger's side. A fluted gaping hole was apparent in the steel bumper. The bullet had penetrated the floor, both sides of the wheel-well, grazed the tire, and exited through the bumper and buried itself in the asphalt. It could have been so much worse. I got in and drove toward the warden's house to make a modification on his two-way radio.

I backed the van into the warden's station so that the bullet hole in the bumper would face the highway. He came out and greeted us cordially. I held my breath waiting for him to mention something about gunfire, but he said nothing. I opened his radio, replaced a part, replaced the antenna, and got the hell out of there.

On the way home, I took advantage of the fact that Mick-Sandy was feeling sheepish after his close call with a 308 rifle.

"Mick, you know that I'm divorced. Well, almost and I..."

"You want to marry Slanty, is that what it is?"

Slanty was his pet name for Barbara. I never quite understood why.

"Uh, yeah, but I didn't know if you were worried about my being divorced and the Catholic Church and..."

"Go ahead and marry her, bye, but let me tell you, you little Iona bastard, if you treat her bad, you'll wish you had that fuckin' 308 in your hands."

"Oh, you don't have to worry, Mick, I love her."

"Ah, Jesus Christ, I've heard that from a fella before, and then he beats the livin' shit out of her, and then the next day he claims that he didn't mean to do it 'cause he loves her'."

"Well, I don't do that kind of crap."

"Well, you got my blessing. You're all right, even if your father is a fuckin' Tory bastard!" He paused. "By the way, is she knocked up?"

"What?" I faked a few seconds to decide if I should tell the truth.

I waited. My face felt hot all of a sudden. He knew the truth, thanks to my hesitation.

"Ah, forget it. It's none of my business. It's between you two. Just take good care of her and...holy fuck. Stop!"

My heart stopped. For a moment, I guessed that it was another deer. This time, it was a rabbit sitting on the side of the road, frozen in the headlights. I stopped on the narrow dirt road. Mick-Sandy crept out of the van.

"Mick, what the hell are you doing?"

"Shut the fuck up!"

I watched as he snuck up on the rabbit, still frozen in the glare of my headlights. Mick-Sandy was careful not to block the headlights but came at the unsuspecting rabbit from the side. Mick-Sandy lunged. The rabbit jumped, but sadly for the bunny, not quite fast enough for old Mick-Sandy. He seized the rabbit by the neck and deftly twisted.

"We'll have rabbit stew tonight when we get home, Stanley bye. Let's go!"

You're Fired!

Barbara and I were married at the Sydney Court House. After a speedy budget honeymoon in Halifax, Barbara Ann and I settled into my ten-wide mobile home in Sydney. On our first weekend we brought Roddie and Mark to live with us. On Monday I went back to work at Pye Electronics while Barbara returned to her job with the phone company.

We settled into something that resembled domestic bliss. On most Saturdays, we drove with Roddie and Mark up Highway 23 to Jamesville West to see Mom and Pop.

One weekend, while we were visiting my parents, I was approached by a few high school students from my old alma mater, where I hadn't graduated, Rankin Memorial High School in Iona. They wanted to know, since I was an electronics technician with a Pye truck, if I could assemble some equipment and find some records to play music for a high school dance. The equipment wasn't a big problem, but finding the music wasn't as easy. I had a Neil Diamond LP and a scratched Pete Fountain album that I had played to seduce Linda in Halifax a few years earlier. Not exactly high school material in 1970.

I rented two speaker columns, an amp, a microphone, and two turntables from McKnight's Music Store on Charlotte Street. I wanted to buy 45 RPM singles, but that wasn't in the budget. Nothing was in the budget. The McKnight's man suggested that I talk to Eric MacEwen, who was the rock 'n' roll host at CJCB Radio in Sydney. Apparently he had *dupes,* radio-speak for duplicate records from the record companies. I called Eric. I welcomed any excuse to get inside a radio station. My dream of being in radio lived on, but so did my shyness.

Eric came out of the studio with a handful of records. I thumbed through them while he waited. This was great! There was *War* by Edwin Starr, *Get Ready* by Rare Earth, Eric Burdon's *Spill the Wine, Green Eyed Lady* by Sugarloaf, and dozen or so more.

The high school dance in the Iona parish was a hit. I even got a chance to pretend that I was a real radio DJ. The high school kids requested an encore for the next weekend. I agreed. I got more records from radio star Eric MacEwen and found some older 45s in the bargain bin at McKnight's Music. I added a few flashing lights and a black light, which made one of Angela Morrison's teeth glow when she smiled.

In the mid to late '40s, I had attended school at a one-room schoolhouse at McKinnons Harbour, a mile from home. There were eight grades in one room and no more than fifteen kids.

In early 1949, we kids were entertained daily by local workers constructing a new church and hall in the field next to our school. It was the church was where I had attended Mass with my parents, and where I had served as an altar boy.

However, over the next couple of decades, the hall was used less and less for bingo, card games, and dances. It had a superb hardwood floor, perfect for dances, but sadly, the hall had become an over-sized storage area for the church and anything else that local parishioners wanted to dump there.

My somewhat younger but good friend, Richard Jankowski, and I decided to snoop inside the church hall to check out the space as a possible venue for teen dances. What a mess! There was mold, spilled paint and rotting trash throughout, and tattered curtains on the windows.

"Why don't we clean it up?" Richard suggested, as he kicked an empty paint can across the floor.

"It will take us months to get this place into shape by ourselves" I said.

"Stan, maybe we can get some help. You know, maybe Carlie MacNeil and some of our friends can help."

"Not a bad idea. And maybe we can get some of the teens around here to help too."

"Okay, let's put the word out for a meeting here next Saturday."

I was thrilled at the thought of creating a place where the kids could go locally and enjoy themselves, provided that the parish priest agreed.

Father MacDonald was hesitant. He had visions of kids drinking and driving and God forbid, having sex, as if they needed a church hall for lovemaking. He eventually agreed, with a warning that if kids were caught drinking or a disturbance occurred, he would close it down. I wasn't sure if he would close us down if there was sex in the parking lot.

The next Saturday, the meeting was short but attended by local teens who wanted to get to work immediately. We cleaned, painted, and put up new curtains. On the third weekend, we formed a club. We called it the *Iona Sports Club*. I was elected president, Richard was chosen as secretary, and a young lady, Allison, was selected as treasurer. Our goal included buying uniforms and equipment for a softball team and maybe even building tennis and volleyball courts.

We hosted our first dance on a Friday night in July of 1970. The hall was half full. On the second Friday, the word was out, and we had a full house. I drove from Sydney with six teenagers in the Pye truck, with a load of soft drinks and snack food for the hall canteen. It was a party! The third Friday night was a problem. We turned people away at the door. We hired a bouncer to control any unruly teens. Sadly, he instigated more fights than he stopped. We brought in a hundred dollars or more each Friday.

The dances became more popular. After each dance we did a fast money count. By late September we had accrued approximately fifteen hundred dollars. Our treasurer, Allison, took the money home after each dance to deposit it at the credit union in Iona...or so I thought.

One Monday morning in September, I received a call from the Pye Electronics vice president, Knobby Sampson, in Halifax. Actually, I *thought* that he was at the head office in Halifax. He was actually down the street at a motel in Sydney.

"Stan, I want to come with you today to see the progress at the installation in Glace Bay at Nova Scotia Power."

I hesitated. "Uh, sure. But there hasn't been any progress there, because I have been so busy with maintenance for National Parks up north."

"Fine. Well, let's go out together to take a gander to see what needs to be done."

"Okay. I'll pick you up, Knobby."

I drove to Keddy's Motel on Kings Road in Sydney, where Knobby waited out front. He didn't seem happy. As he climbed in, I tried to make small talk about the weather and local news. He only wanted to grill me about what I was doing with my time. He asked me if I had sent in my expense report yet.

"No, I planned to send it tomorrow."

"Don't send it in, Stan. I want to review it first."

"Oh. Yeah, sure." I didn't like his tone.

We arrived at the Nova Scotia Power building in Glace Bay. The station manager met us in the front office. He appeared visibly annoyed and complained to Knobby that he had needed his communications system set up weeks ago.

"I'm terribly sorry, sir," Knobby said. "We will get on it next week, and that's a promise."

"Well, I damn well hope so, or we'll find another company to do it. There's always Motorola you know."

I knew that I was in trouble.

Knobby and I left power plant and got back in the Pye van...almost. When he opened the door, a beer bottle rolled out from under the seat and hit the pavement.

"So, is this what you do when you are on the road?" Knobby demanded to know.

"No, I don't know how that got in here." I realized that my response sounded like a childish lie.

"Stan, take us to the hotel so we can discuss what we do next."

We pulled into a parking space in front of Keddy's Motel. I shut off the motor and expected to get out and go to lunch with Knobby, as we usually did when he came to town.

"Stan, give me the keys please."

"Sure. Here you go." I assumed that he wanted to take the van himself and maybe see some of our other customers.

"Do you have anything at home that belongs to Pye Electronics?"

"No, I don't think I—"

"Stan, you're fired."

"What?"

I was shocked. I had never been fired before.

"If you have any personal stuff in the van, get it now. You can go inside and call your wife or have someone pick you up."

"But—"

"I don't wish to discuss this. You have obviously used this vehicle as a party van for months. You have charged us for the gas you burned while driving the van for personal use. On top of that, you did not even begin the job at Nova Scotia Power that you were supposed to have finished last month."

"Knobby, I uh—"

Your replacement is already here, so we no longer require your services, such as they are."

I envisioned my replacement smugly peeking out the motel window.

"Oh, by the way, I was going ask why there is a bullet hole in the bumper, but it might be best that I don't know."

Dismayed, I left the van and went inside and called Barbara to come to pick me up, without telling her what had happened. We had just sold our old mobile home and had taken out a large loan to buy a new twelve-wide mobile home, which had been delivered two days earlier.

I arrived home, where Mick-Sandy and Barbara's brother, Phippy, were busy blocking up our new mobile home for us. I stepped out of the car and blurted the news.

"I just got fired." I choked back tears of anger.

"Holy fuck!" Mick-Sandy yelled.

"What the hell am I going to do?"

"Fuck em!" Mick-Sandy shouted, in an effort to make me feel better. "You'll find something better."

"I'm not so sure. This is Cape Breton. There aren't a lot of jobs here in my field."

Mick-Sandy had a solution. "Phippy, run to the liquor store and get us a bottle of Captain Morgan rum. That'll make the little fucker feel better."

Phippy sped out of the driveway and was back in five minutes. I got drunk and considered my fate, until I didn't care anymore.

* * *

The next morning the phone rang early.

It was Mick-Sandy. "Campbell, go read the *Cape Breton Post*. A new electronics factory just opened on Prince Street, and they're hiring."

"Geez, Mick, I can't work in a factory"

"Jesus Christ, it's a fuckin' job, and unless you want to be eatin' your supper at the Salvation Army, you better get off your arse and go see about it."

"Okay, okay. I'll go check it out" I had no plans to work in a factory.

I searched the newspaper anyway and found the classified section. There was indeed a huge ad for General Instruments, Inc., with a job description, but this wasn't a factory assembly job. General Instruments was searching for a qualified electronics technician foreman.

I called the number in the paper. The lady on the phone sounded interested in my technical background. She invited me to come in to meet with the general manager, Mr. Petersen. I arrived five minutes early dressed in my only suit and a white shirt. Mr. Petersen peered over his large aircraft carrier-sized glass-topped desk. "Mr. Campbell, we assemble car radio tuners for various automobile radio manufacturers. You would be in charge of some seventy-two assemblers and testers here at our plant. You think you could handle that?"

"Oh, absolutely, no problem at all." I lied, not knowing what I might be responsible for.

We talked for fifteen minutes or so about technical issues, my experience, training, and the type of radio tuners the company made and the problems General Instruments needed to address.

"Mr. Campbell, if you are interested, the job is yours."

"Thank you very much, sir. I can begin tomorrow." I knew that I would have to bullshit my way through the first week.

"Excellent! Now, let me give you a tour of the plant."

We walked from Mr. Petersen's office into a room the size of a Walmart store. I saw rows of metal tables, otherwise known as test benches, from end to end of the big room. Something caught my eye as we strolled farther. I didn't see another male in the plant except Mr. Petersen and me! A few girls looked up from their work to check out the visitor. This would be interesting.

I drove home, ecstatic that I had a job. I told Barbara all about the job and the plant and not much about the fact that I would be the boss of seventy-two women.

* * *

Crowds of teens poured in from miles away to the Friday night dances at the McKinnons Harbour hall. I transported soft drinks and snacks from Sydney, but in my own car, the Ford Grand Torino GT, which broke down at the most inopportune times. It made me furious. It was still a relatively new car. There were days when I wanted to drive it into a concrete wall.

I began calling the Grand Torino *The Lemon*. The name stuck. My dance DJ work became more popular, so much so that I was in demand to play music for dances elsewhere in Cape Breton. I bought my own equipment and became so active that I had to hire help for the nights when I was too busy or when I had two dances on the same night. It was a growing business, which I decided to name after my breakdown Torino. I called my DJ business, *Lemon Limited*.

I was proud of my DJ work spinning records and tried hard to emulate the people I heard on the radio, especially late at night on faraway stations like WKBW in Buffalo and WABC in New York. I met a part-time DJ at CHER in Sydney, Ron Tynski, through Barbara's brother Mickey. On one Friday night, I invited Ron to host our dance at the church hall. Ron was happy to oblige, and I was thrilled to be able to invite a celebrity DJ from the rock 'n' roll station, *The Big 95-CHER.*

Ron introduced some records at the dance, and I did my best impersonation of a real radio guy.

After the dance Ron said, "Hey, you have a good voice. You should be in radio."

"Nah! Me? Really?" I faked humility, but this was as close to my dream as I had ever been.

I was still too shy to actually visit a station, given my embarrassing encounter after high school.

"Yes, you're as good as some of the part-time guys on the air."

"Really? I have always wanted to be on the radio, Ron."

"Hey, why don't you come to the station on Monday, and I'll introduce you to Weldon Boone, the news director?"

"Are you sure?"

"Sure, I'm sure."

On Monday, I arrived at the station at 10:00 a.m. sharp. Ron Tynski met me at the door and introduced me to the news director, Weldon Boone.

"Weldon, I think Stan has a great voice for radio, and I thought that you might get him to read something."

Weldon didn't appear pleased with the interruption, and having to deal with a greenhorn wannabe DJ, but he agreed to give me a shot. "Okay, Stan. I am going to give you a couple of news stories to read. You can record on this cassette recorder in the conference room."

He handed me a long sheet of teletype paper and a cassette recorder.

I carried the recorder and the teletype wire copy to the conference room. I read and recorded two short stories.

A few minute later Weldon came back in, punched play button and listened.

"Wow, that's not bad for guy who has never been in radio before." Weldon motioned to the music director, Dave Hay, to come in.

Dave didn't appear to want to be a part of the amateur audition, either, but in he came. After listening to thirty seconds of my recording, Dave stopped the tape. He left and returned with four 45 RPM records.

"Here, take these into the production studio and pretend you're doing a radio show, okay?" Dave handed the records to me and escorted me into the studio, where he showed me how to turn the microphone on and off, record on the big Ampex reel-to-reel recorder, and start and stop the turntables.

A half hour later, I had recorded a 10-minute radio show. Dave, Weldon, and Ron entered the studio to listen.

"You've never worked in radio before?" Dave asked, after hearing my audition.

"No." I was ecstatic that he had asked such a question.

"Stan, I'm going to pass this tape on to our program director, Dean Hagopian."

I didn't know for sure if they were just being polite or if the program director would really get to hear my audition.

Meanwhile, supervising seventy-two girls was tough on my self-discipline. I was responsible for assisting any girl who had trouble aligning a tuner on her oscilloscope. For a few girls, trouble seemed to crop up frequently.

Coincidentally, those same girls seemed to be perpetually horny. While I worked at their work stations, they stood behind me and attempted to repay me with back rubs or other teasing tickles. Several girls attempted to rub more than my back. One girl asked me to stand behind her and look over her shoulder to check her work. As I did, she reached around behind her to rub my pants in an effort to see if she could create a response. I was 29, so the reaction was rapid, but I wisely moved on, but only after I was able to walk straight for fear of being caught by the assistant foreman, Fran, a woman who hated me and wanted my job.

In Iona, I arranged a formal meeting with the Sports Club. I was becoming too busy with Lemon Limited and my job at General Instruments. I decided that it was time to resign as president of the Sports Club. Also, my friend Richard had finished college and decided to move to Toronto. He was the secretary. We both felt that it was time for the kids to assume responsibility for their own club.

We met on a Sunday afternoon in October in the renovated church hall, of which we had become so proud. Richard read the minutes of the last meeting. I requested the treasurer's report. Treasurer Allison hesitated. She appeared confused.

"Allison, can you give us the treasurer's report, please?" I repeated.

I was excited to learn how much money we had collected over the summer.

She appeared as though she might cry.

"Allison, are you okay?"

"Yes."

"Can you tell us how much money we have in our credit union account?"

"No."

"No? You don't know or no you can't tell us?" All eyes were on Allison.

"We don't have any money," she suddenly exclaimed through tears.

"What? What do you mean, we don't have any money?"

"We don't have any money." Allison repeated as the tears flowed.

"How could that be?" I asked. "A few weeks ago we had almost fifteen hundred dollars!"

"I don't know"

"You are the treasurer, Allison. You and you alone handle the money. How can you not know?"

"I don't know." She kept reiterating the same phrase, offering no other explanation.

For almost an hour we tried to get her to explain where the money had gone but got nowhere.

She answered every question the same way. "I don't know."

I was sure that she hadn't spent it. I trusted her but couldn't understand what had happened.

The next morning I drove to the Iona Credit Union and caught the manager, Arthur Campbell, (not my uncle or a relative) and asked him if he could tell me what might have happened to the money in the Sports Club account.

"What account?" He replied in an annoyed tone. "You have no account here at the Credit Union."

"Yes, we do. It's the Iona Sports Club account."

"There is no such account here. Never was."

For the second time in two days, I was speechless. This was bizarre. The harder we tried to find out what had happened to the money, the more we were stonewalled. We began to suspect Allison, but she was such a sweet, almost naïve, young lady that we figured that there was no way that she could have spent or stolen the money.

Richard left the following week for Toronto, and I was left to try to get to the bottom of the missing Sports Club money.

* * *

Two weeks later, I was blindsided again. This time by my father.

"Did you take that money from the Sports Club?" Pop demanded to know, point blank.

"What?" I couldn't believe what I heard from my own father.

"People are saying that you and Richard stole money from the Iona Sports Club."

I exploded. I rarely, if ever, swore around, and especially at, my father. But I was incensed.

"Jesus Christ! How do you fucking dare ask me such a question? You, my own father, are accusing me of stealing from the very club that I created and worked so hard for?"

"Well, that's what people are saying."

"What fucking people? Give me their Goddamn names."

"Well, Father MacDonald as much as accused you last Sunday at mass."

"Fuck Father MacDonald and his self-righteous sermon. That son-of-a-bitch needs to come and say that to my face!"

Now my father fumed. He was outraged that I would swear at him and against a priest and the church. I didn't give a damn. I wanted him to feel my rage.

"Stop it Stanley!" It was Mom, who had heard the commotion from the kitchen. "You should be ashamed of saying things like that, God forgive you."

I calmed down at the sound of Mom's voice.

"Well, if you didn't take it, then who did?" My father interjected.

"You still suggest that I might be responsible. You don't even trust your own son," I yelled, as I took hold of Barbara's hand and stormed out the door with Roddie and Mark.

I fumed all the way back to Sydney. I was convinced that I would never set foot inside a Catholic Church again. I didn't want to see my father for a very long time, if ever. I was angry and I was hurt that I would be accused of stealing from the organization that I helped build. I was also upset that Richard was also one of the suspects, and he couldn't even defend himself, because he had moved to Toronto.

On Monday, before I put on my lab coat, I was summoned to Mr. Petersen's office. He asked me to close the door behind me. That was never a good sign. Then chubby, squat, bitchy Fran, my assistant foreman, came in to join our meeting.

"Mr. Campbell, I need you to gather your personal effects together and leave the plant. You're fired."

"Excuse me?"

"Yes, you have been observed flirting with the ladies on the line and making sexual advances towards them."

"Wait a minute! *They* came on to *me*!" I protested.

"Well, our assistant foreman Fran here has a different story."

"Yes, I'll bet she does," I said as I glared at her with her condescending gotcha smirk. "Fran is lying. I did not make advances towards any of the ladies."

Okay, so I didn't always reject their advances.

"Just pack up any personal effects and leave now. This conversation is over."

"You can stick this job up your fucking arse!" I slammed his door on the way out.

"Well, I'm doing great!" I sarcastically told Barbara as I came home early. "I've been fired twice in two months, and I was accused of stealing money from the Iona Sports Club."

"To hell with all of them. Here, have a hooter of rum."

A hooter of rum seemed to be the solution to most crises in the family, and I was a willing participant in the trauma program. We talked about what was next. We had a big fat loan on our new mobile home, and she was pregnant and due in days.

I was pleasantly plastered when the phone rang.

"Stan Campbell, this is Dean Hagopian, program director CHER. What are you doing now?

"Just got home early from work." I lied.

"Well get off your arse, bye, and come see me." He tried to talk like a Cape Bretoner even though he was originally from Malta.

"Sure, I'll come right over," I replied, trying to impress him with the most resonant radio voice that I could muster.

"Holy shit! That was the program director at CHER Radio! He wants to see me." I reached for another hooter, this time to celebrate and calm my nerves.

Downing a straight shot of dark rum was the medication for depression, over-excitement, or celebration. It was the answer to whatever was going on, good or bad.

I brushed my teeth and swished a mouthful of mouthwash. I couldn't let the program director smell booze on my breath. I drove to downtown Sydney and pulled up in front of Kentucky Fried Chicken on Prince Street. The station was on the second floor. I was going to smell fried chicken for nine months.

I'm Stan Campbell!

Dean didn't waste time with small talk."Can you start on Monday night?"

"What? Sure. Yes!" I felt dizzy.

"Okay, get together with Dave Hay. He'll go over all the stuff you'll need to know. You'll be doing midnight to 6:00 a.m. You have to keep this confidential, though. We're firing Mike McAskill. He's not cutting it, but we haven't told him yet."

"Sure, Mr. Hagopian."

Keep this confidential? I'm bursting. How could I keep my mouth shut? I had never been good at keeping secrets, even when I was given a top secret clearance working for NORAD, but this one was a bombshell.

"I'm Dean. This is radio. There are no formalities here or anywhere in radio."

"Okay, Dean, no problem. The secret is good with me."

I knew that it wasn't. I wanted to scream it to the world. *I am going to be on the radio!*

I flew down the station stairs, three steps at a time. I peeled the last of the rubber on my Torino tires on the way out of the parking lot. I laughed and screamed to myself over and over all the way home. I had dreamed of this moment since I was old enough to reach the radio on the table. I was going to be on the radio, on CHER, which was the hip rock station in Sydney in 1970. My parents would hear me, my friends would hear me, my old high school buddies would hear me, my former boss who had fired me would hear me. Screw him! The girls at General Instruments would hear me. I was going to be on the radio!

I raced in the door and hugged Barbara and the kids. "I'm going to be on the radio! I have been hired to be on the air every night. I'm going to be on the air...on the radio!"

"That's great," Barbara said with far less enthusiasm. "I'm having labor pains."

My thrill-priorities were suddenly readjusted. "Oh shit! Do you think we should go to the hospital?"

"No, I'll know when my water breaks."

On Friday, Saturday, and Sunday I called all my friends and even people I barely knew to tell them that I was going to be on the radio. I warned all of them to tell not a soul. None of them were as excited as I was. I was torn between the excitement of being a radio DJ and being a new Dad. Barbara wasn't nearly as elated as I was, but Roddie and Mark thought it was cool that their Dad was going to be on the radio. They were leery about having a new brother or sister though.

I paced the floor, announcing invented weather reports and introducing the Doors, Santana, George Harrison, and some new guy with a first name last, Elton John.

On Monday, I drove to the station and went through fundamental training with Dave Hay. It was enough to terrify me. He told me that when the news ended at midnight, I was to punch on the mic and say *I'm Stan Campbell, and this is the Big 95, C-H-E-R* and then roll the record, which I was supposed to *cue up* on the turntable, ready to go. In fact, I had to cue up two records. I learned the new words *cue* and *segue* and *sweep* on the first day. I was thrilled and terrified.

As I poured over the music format sheet, the gorgeous secretary from the front desk came in and told me to pick up line three.

It was Barbara. "Stan, come home right away. My water just broke!"

"Okay, I'll be right there!"

"Hurry! The pains are ten minutes apart."

As I ran past the front desk I shouted, "I have to go. My wife is having a baby."

"Go man!" Dave yelled after me.

I broke all the speed limits driving home to pick up Barbara and rush her to the hospital. My mind raced faster than the Torino. What the hell was I going to do? I was supposed to be making my debut appearance on the radio at midnight. It was the biggest event of my life, but I was going to be a Dad again, probably tonight.

Could I tell the program director that I couldn't show up on my first night on the air? I didn't want to be a no-show and possibly lose the chance to be on the radio. It was my lifelong dream. What if another radio opportunity never came along? I concocted my own line of reasoning.

If I spent the evening in the hospital waiting for Barbara to have the baby, as soon as she started into serious labor, they wouldn't let me in, anyway. This was 1970. Fathers weren't permitted in the delivery room in most hospitals. My rationale made sense, at least to me.

I helped Barbara into the car, hoping that she wouldn't deliver right there. I didn't have a clue what to do. We arrived in record time at St. Rita Hospital after dropping Roddie and Mark off at her mom's. We checked in and got Barbara settled. A bossy nurse ushered me out of the room while Barbara was being examined. That pissed me off. Did she think that I was going to see something that I had never seen before?

I was finally permitted to go back into the room. Barbara's labor pains were far enough apart that it could be hours before she delivered.

"Stan, go ahead and get ready for your big night on the radio. I'll be all right." Barbara seemed to be a bit sleepy.

"Are you sure?"

I was going to be on the radio, even if she was having quintuplets.

"There's nothing you can do here."

"Okay!" I kissed her and rushed out the door and down the stairs.

It was early evening. I had to get a nap before I went on the air. I raced back home and tried to find something trendy to wear, even though this was radio. I needed to look like a hip, happenin' *Boss Jock*. I had nothing. That had to change.

I reclined for two or three minutes on the couch but flew back up on my feet again.

"Am I nuts?" I asked myself out loud. "I can't sleep now."

"*The Big 95 CHER with George Harrison and My Sweet Lord,*" I announced in my best affected radio voice with my left hand over my ear.

I liked the sound of my own voice, even though I faked a lower range with more resonance than usual. I paced the floor and thought about throwing back a hooter of rum for courage but feared that the gang at the station would smell it and I would be fired before I started.

I called the hospital to see if I was a new dad yet. The nurse advised me that Mrs. Campbell was not close to delivering for several hours, maybe not even until tomorrow. I was relieved and hoped that the baby could wait until my show was over at 6:00 in the morning.

I showered, shaved, and splashed on some Old Spice and drove to the station. I continued to do a pretend radio show in the car. The car acoustics were great.

I actually had a key to a radio station! I climbed up the stairs above KFC. The Colonel's secret spices filled the air. I realized that I had not eaten since noon. I didn't care. If I ate then, I would likely throw up. The smell of KFC blended with the aroma of radio. Radio stations have a distinct smell. It comes mostly from acetate reel to reel tapes.

I peeked through the newsroom window into the on-air studio. Andy Kay was on the air. I was just a bit jealous of Andy. He was only 17 and already a radio star. I was 30 and just beginning. He sounded to me like one of those New York DJs I used to listen to late at night. In less than ninety minutes, it would be my turn to sit in the big chair and flip on the microphone, and all of Cape Breton would hear me. I didn't know whether to throw up or dance.

A peculiar thought crossed my mind. I wondered if my birth mother was out there somewhere and might hear me. Would she recognize her own son? The thought made me angry. Not because she had put me up for adoption but because she had never made herself known. She simply abandoned me and disappeared forever.

I called the hospital again to see if there was any change. There wasn't. Andy Kay stepped out of the studio to run down the hall to the bathroom.

"Hey, man, you must be the new guy starting at midnight, right?"

"Yeah, I guess I am."

"Hi, I'm Andy Kay. Welcome to CHER, man."

"Thanks, man, I am really excited to be here, man." I resonated back, calling him *man*, since that seemed to the cool thing to do among us cool radio guys.

Andy ran back to the studio, as his record ended.

I observed closely as he donned his headphones, known to us radio guys as cans, and flipped on the microphone. "*The Big 95 CHER, coming up after the midnight news, get ready for the newest addition to the CHER Good Guys, Stan Campbell! Now, here's Rare Earth.*"

Oh, my God! Andy mentioned my name on the air! I imagined that my entire family and all of my friends were listening. In reality, likely none of them had the radio on at 11:45 at night. It was my turn to go to the bathroom. I stepped inside and stared at myself in the mirror. I did not portray the star radio DJ image. After all, it was peak of the hippie era. I would have to do something about that.

I cupped my hand over my ear. I had seen Gary Owens do that on *Laugh-In* on TV, and he was definitely a radio guy. If only I had known that night that I would work with Gary Owens one day. I had to pee again, and as I did, I rehearsed.

"This is the Big 95 CHER, and I'm Stan Campbell with racks and stacks of hit—"

The door to the bathroom opened. It was Weldon Boone, the news guy. I felt like an idiot.

He closed the stall door behind him without saying a word. I slithered out the door and into the production studio, where I called the hospital one more time. No baby. It crossed my mind that Barbara's parents, Helen and Mick-Sandy, likely figured that I was the most uncaring father in Cape Breton history. But, what the hell would I do at the hospital, anyway, when the nurses wouldn't even let me in to see her? Besides, this was my lifelong, childhood dream.

"Okay, man, you're on!" Andy yelled as he popped open the studio door. "If you need any help, I'll stick around for few minutes."

"No, that's okay. Uh, well, yeah, maybe for a few minutes until I get started," I said with a voice that trembled with cold stone fear.

The timbre that I had earlier was gone. My voice had risen in pitch to a whispery squeak. I entered the on-air studio, sat in the big swivel chair, and did a practice run, sliding back to the turntables and up to the console, as I had seen Andy do.

I took my first record on the printed list, a new album by George Harrison called *All Things Must Pass,* and attempted to cue it up to *My Sweet Lord.* I tried dropping the needle on the groove at the beginning of the second cut but scratched the needle across the album with my trembling hand. I tried again by bracing my elbow on the counter. I managed to set the needle down this time without causing more damage.

Andy watched me through the window from the production studio. I ran the LP back and forth to find the beginning of the cut, so when I pushed the turntable play switch, the music would be right there within half a second.

"Stop!" Andy yelled, running into the studio. "You're cuing on air."

He reached over me and turned down the *pot,* which is radio-speak for the volume control.

"What?" I gasped, fearful that I had done something terrible.

I had. I had run the record back and forth on the air instead of on cue, which is the in-studio system and speaker that is used to cue up the record to within a second of the beginning of the song. I had made a huge backward and forward *rrrruup* sound on the air over Weldon Boone's news. I glanced over at Weldon in the booth. He looked peeved. No wonder.

Andy helped me cue my album cut. When cued up, he turned the pot up. All systems were go. Except for me. I was instructed to come on immediately after Weldon's news and say, *Its 12:05 and I'm Stan Campbell,* and then hit the first button on the cart machine that played a CHER jingle, and then hit the play button for the turntable to play *My Sweet Lord.* My Sweet Jesus! I was petrified and ecstatic at the same time.

While George sang *I really want to see you Lord,* I cued up my next record on the second turntable, a 45 RPM single, Edison Lighthouse's *Love Grows Where my Rosemary Goes.* I was careful to not cue it up on air this time.

After six songs, I finally got up the guts to turn on the mic to read the weather forecast in my best radio DJ voice. Even though it was almost 2:00 in the morning, I imagined all my friends and Mom and Pop still awake and listening to me, and just maybe, my real Mom out there somewhere, hearing my voice for the first time. In reality, I might have had a cop, taxi drivers, and a few nurses listening.

When I became more comfortable, I called the hospital again. Barbara was still in labor but no arrival yet. I thought that maybe she was waiting until I got there. I also got up enough courage to leave the studio and go down the hall to pee again and race back, zipping up my pants before the record ended. I wasn't sure how I would handle more serious bathroom visits. Dave Hay never explained that.

I screwed up a number of times through the night, including cueing up on the air again and one radio nightmare that haunts me to this day, forgetting to cue up the next record, leaving me attempting to do it while simultaneously talking on air and reaching off to the side to put a record on at the same time. My shift ended at 6:00 a.m. Dean Hagopian, who doubled as the program director and morning guy, took over. I was relieved...and worried about what he thought.

"Hey, man, you did a good job, especially for a guy who has never been on the air before."

I was about to leave when Weldon Boone stuck his head in the control room door. "Stan, you have a call on line two."

"This is Nurse Sampson in the maternity ward at St Rita's. You have a healthy baby boy!"

"Oh, my God!" I shouted, capturing the attention of everyone in the station. "That's wonderful! Thank You!"

I raced out the door and to the hospital. What a night! I had inherited a new career and a new son in one night. As for radio, I hoped that it would be a new career, if the station bosses liked me. Dean did. The general manager had a different opinion.

*   *   *

Is there a parent gene? I envy doting dads in those moving scenes of fathers who stand tearfully in awe of the birth of their son or daughter. I did adore my newborn son, but my growing self-centered focus on myself and my career took center-stage in my life. Through radio, I received the attention that I desperately craved.

Barbara and I named our son Michael Alexander, as in Mick-Sandy, the father that Barbara venerated. Alexander was my first name, and I figured that at least one of my kids would bear one of my names. For sure, no kid was going to be named Stanislaus, my legal middle name. However, it was apparent inside Barbara's family that our son had been named Alexander to honor Michael Alexander MacLennan, Barbara's Dad, not me. Years later, I discovered that Barbara had the hospital records list him as Michael Alexander MacLennan. The MacLennan name was sacred.

In our new twelve-wide home in Howie Centre, we settled into our version of marital harmony with Roddie and Mark and our new son, Michael. I drank at night, and Barbara and I often consumed a few hooters of rum on weekends. When I wasn't drinking, I was flirting with my first love, radio, even when I wasn't needed at the station.

I admired the hip people there. My mentors were pros brought in from Montréal to manage the station while it was in receivership. The bank picked some of the best in the business. I began to believe that I was pretty cool too. I did receive compliments for my on-air work but none at home. I was becoming a radio celebrity. Not everyone thought so.

* * *

Getting drunk didn't happen every day but rather when it was convenient. It was convenient often. I never refused a drink or a second or a fifth. Somewhere between the first drink and passing out, I fell into the nasty custom of making a fool of myself and an enemy of others by insulting and irritating people around me, people that I cared about. That included my new radio colleagues.

An example of my out-of-control drinking came on a Saturday in mid-summer of 1971. I was assigned to broadcast live twice an hour from a used car lot on the Glace Bay Highway. Usually, the sales people who sell the on-location promotions show up and act as a liaison between the client and the host...in this case, me.

For that remote, the CHER sales guy didn't show up, so there were no goodies to give away, such as free records, balloons, and other promotional items. I was angry that our sales rep wasn't there, and therefore, I had no prizes to give to potential customers.

However, the car lot sales manager was happy to have a *celebrity* at his location, so he invited me into his back office for a shot of rum. I broadcast my first two on-the-air reports and talked about the car deals. Then we had another shot of rum and another on-air report followed by another swig of rum, straight from the bottle.

By the second hour of the three-hour remote, I was on my way to being stupidly drunk to the point where I forgot where I was. I told the listeners that I was in Sydney River, ten miles away. Then, I forgot the name of the dealership in my third hour. None of my reports were particularly good for business.

In my final report, I made a garbled, drunken announcement, while fumbling the microphone. "It has been a distinct pleasure working for Johnson Motors (wrong name) today. I wish I could say the same about this radio station. Good-bye."

Then, I drove home...drunk.

It was a fabulous summer weekend for a drive. Bob Ancell, the CHER Radio general manager, had been traveling with his wife on the magnificent Cabot Trail approximately seventy miles away. He could hear the station loud and clear from atop Smoky Mountain. I was told that he almost drove over the cliff into the Atlantic Ocean when he heard my drunken reports, especially the final one. He was not a fan of mine, and suddenly he knew why.

Barbara hadn't heard about the on-air disaster until my father-in-law Mick-Sandy called her. In his unique style he declared that I was a fucking arsehole for screwing up my first radio job. After a few hours, I sobered up enough to realize that he was correct. I had likely trashed the one career that I had dreamed about all my life.

Bob Ancell raced back to town. Presumably, the long drive calmed him down...a lot. For some reason that I will never comprehend, he didn't fire me. My mentor Dean Hagopian saved me. Instead, inexplicably, Ancell sent Barbara and me on a short evening dinner cruise around the Bras d'Or Lakes, where I got drunk again and threw up over the side of the ship, near the open portholes of the dining room, thereby prematurely ending most patrons' lovely dining experience. I remembered nothing of the cruise, which I understand was delightful.

I began to dress differently from my usual conservative fashion. I let my hair grow longer. I bought paisley pants and beads and checked myself more often in the mirror. It was the early seventies, and the hippie era had not yet passed. I was morphing from Pat Boone to Jerry Garcia. My head also got substantially bigger, but it wasn't until an evening in February that my head changed inside.

My new radio friend, Mike Cohen, called. "Stan, what are you doing this evening?"

I liked Mike. He had a brilliant sense of dry humor. He had a hippie appearance, wore a beard, and was tall. Most people were taller than me.

"I'm not doing anything important, Mike. Why do you ask?"

"Want to come to a movie with me and Ron MacKinnon?"

"Sure. Which movie?"

"*Easy Rider* is back at the Vogue Theatre, and we want to see it again."

"Yeah, sure. I've never seen it."

Mike and Ron picked me up in Mike's rusty Ford Falcon. The theatre lights dimmed, and the movie started at the same time that I noticed Ron lighting up a cigarette. Smoking wasn't banned anywhere in 1971. It didn't smell like a normal cigarette, though. In fact, it smelled like the grass that we burned back in Iona in the early spring. Ron took a long drag and held it in. Then he handed it to Mike. He sucked in hard and held it for a long time, then blew out the smoke and passed it to me.

"What?" I said, looking at Mike for an explanation.

I suspected what it was, but I wasn't entirely sure.

"Here, take it before someone sees us."

"Okay, okay." I sucked in a lungful of the smoke and coughed out most of it. I had only smoked in high school but always hated it. It was the only vice that I *didn't* have.

Mike whispered, "You didn't get any. Do it again."

This time I sucked in and held it until I ran out of air. I handed it back, and we repeated the process. Eventually Ron killed what I later learned was the roach with his bare fingers.

The movie got much better. *The Weight* by The Band really impressed me. The music jumped out at me. In those one hundred and five minutes, I experienced a metamorphosis. Between the movie and the marijuana, my view of society, the law, and bigotry changed. Overnight I evolved from a straight, conservative guy to an anti-establishment socialist. The scene in *Easy Rider* where one of my heroes was blown off his bike in a blast of gunfire infuriated me.

Barbara, my father-in-law, and my friends, noticed my new unfolding personality and my growing ego. Several months went by. I was promoted from the midnight shift on air to the afternoon drive and then to mornings. The morning show was the top shift on radio.

I became so over-confident in my ever-expanding opinion of myself that I applied for a morning show job at CKWS in Kingston, Ontario, a much larger market. I sent the program director an aircheck (a five to ten minute edited tape of my morning show). Within a week, I was hired. Even with my inflated ego and increasing self-indulgence, I was shocked. I had only been in radio for nine months.

We rented out our mobile home to three radio DJs. Barbara and I and the kids loaded up a U-Haul and moved to Ontario. The first week at work, I was trained by a young assistant program director. He could only be described as a brown-nosing suck-up who answered to the older, ultra-conservative program director, Ian Chesterfield, whom I instantly despised. These people were not cool like my old gang at CHER in Sydney.

The music format was more Doris Day than the Doors. To a guy who had just begun to enjoy a joint now and then, the music was deadly boring. The general manager was even more of an ass than the program director. I discovered in the first week that I was in over my head. I screwed up badly during the first few weeks on air. I was nervous and intimidated by the cold conservative atmosphere. I made technical errors and constantly caught shit from the pompous, toady, assistant program director. I also got grief from the listeners. Kingston was a center of higher learning, home to Queen's University and a herd of pointy-head professors, who called me to complain each time I made a grammatical error on the air.

My overblown ego had the air sucked out of it. I realized that I wasn't as good as I thought I was. I was not happy. Barbara wasn't happy with her job working at a tanning factory. She came home smelling like a dead cow. On top of that, Roddie and Mark hated school.

The day that put me over the edge was in the same week that I was rescued.

Sophie's Bad Choice

There will be a meeting this evening at 7:00 p.m. sharp in the general manager's office for all staff. Be on time. Wear proper attire. It was memo from the kiss-ass assistant program director sent to all station personnel.

The tone of the memo and the scheduled time infuriated me. I had to get up at 4:00 a.m., and now I was being summoned to a meeting at 7:00 p.m. in the oak-lined cavernous office of general manager, Cyrus Vanarsdale. He was a big shot in town and brimming with pomposity. He had once warned the on-air staff that he would fire anyone who dared play Anne Murray on the air. In his snooty mind, she was low class because she was born in Nova Scotia. He called her *Maritime Mafia*.

I arrived with the rest of the crew of twenty-five other radio and TV people and crowded into Mr. Vanarsdale's starchy office wondering why he couldn't host the meeting in the conference room. Most of us had to stand, except the suck-up assistant program director, and His Grace, Ian, the program director. Even though there were a few chairs, we peons were not permitted to sit. It took twenty seconds for me to be singled out.

"You there!" Mr. Vanarsdale pointed his boney finger straight at me. "What is your name?"

"Stan Campbell, Sir."

"Mr. Campbell. Where is your tie?"

"Excuse me?" Had I really heard the word, *tie.*

"Why aren't you wearing a tie, like the rest of the staff here?"

I scanned around the room. Sure enough, everyone wore a white shirt and a tie.

"Campbell, were you not informed of the dress code here at CKWS?" He scowled.

"Well, yes, but I assumed that after hours it would—"

"Never assume, Mr. Campbell. You are in the office of the general manger of this radio and television station. Therefore, you do not enter this office unless you are dressed appropriately. Do you understand me?"

"Yes, sir," I mumbled obediently but wished that a bolt of lightning would zap through the ceiling and fry his arrogant ass to his vinyl chair.

"Go home and get a tie right now. The rest of the staff will unfortunately have to wait here until you return. And let this be a warning to the rest of you."

Great! Now the whole staff will be pissed off at me.

I burned several blocks of rubber leaving the station to go home to get a tie. Not that I was in a hurry. I was seething. I downed half a water glass of rum at home and then burned more rubber on the way back, cursing him while fantasizing about being heavily armed with sharp objects and alone with him in a tiny concrete room.

I arrived back at his office and was welcomed with icy stares from my fellow workers and a smarmy smile from Mr. Vanarsdale. I knew that my days were numbered there, even if I had to find a job announcing arrivals at a Greyhound bus station. I don't remember what the meeting was about.

* * *

I was scheduled to work six days a week, something I rarely had to do back in Sydney at CHER. God, how I missed that place! Saturday morning at 9:45 the request line rang. I figured that it was one more pinhead professor from Queen's telling me that I had pronounced *schedule* incorrectly.

"Hello. Is this Stan?" a friendly gentleman inquired.

I hesitated. "Yes. Can I help you?"

This caller didn't sound like an elitist Queen's professor. I assumed that it was a man. A few days earlier, I had embarrassed myself with a female caller with a rather masculine voice. I called her, sir. I wasn't about to repeat that awkward moment.

"Maybe you remember me. My name is Dave LaFave. I'm married to one of your high school friends, Myrna MacLean, from Grand Narrows, across from Iona."

"Yes!" I answered excitedly. "I know who you are."

"Would you like to join me for breakfast when you get off the air?"

"Yes! I'm off the air in a few minutes."

At 10:01, I flew out the door, glad to be out of the building that I had learned to hate.

Dave sat in a booth not far from the door. He had thick red hair and wore a big toothy grin. He offered a firm handshake and invited me to sit down.

After some small talk, he said, "I listened to you on the air this morning. You sound great."

"Thanks." I stammered, no longer accustomed to getting compliments since I had left CHER.

He got to the point. "How would you like to be my production director and do a short on-air shift at CJSS in Cornwall?"

I was amazed. He asked how much money I was making at CKWS.

"I can match it, and we'll pay for your move. You'll love it there. I have great staff, Cornwall is a great city, and it's only an hour from Montréal."

"Well, Dave, it sounds good. I think that I might accept your offer."

"Well, talk it over with your wife on the weekend, and give me a call on Monday."

We finished breakfast while we talked about his wife Myrna and Cape Breton. He told me a dirty joke and laughed at his own stories. I didn't want to seem too anxious, but I knew that this offer was the answer to my prayers, even though the money wasn't much better. I couldn't wait to tell the wimpy, fawning assistant program director and the self-important Mr. Vanarsdale to shove it all up their royal rectums.

I raced home and told Barbara. We began packing immediately. Roddie and Mark would be happier too. They hated school in Kingston. Michael was too young to care.

I called Dave on Monday and set a start date. Then I sauntered into Ian Chesterfield's office and gave him the news. He called in the general sales manager and the suddenly-agreeable assistant program director. They all tried to convince me that it was bad career move.

A week later, Barbara and I loaded up another U-Haul and moved to Cornwall and CJSS Radio. The station was welcoming, and Dave turned out to be more than my boss. He became a friend. Our house was party central for entertainers who came to town, including one of the hot groups of the day, The Bells.

Not long after we arrived, Barbara announced that she was pregnant again. I wanted a girl. On December 5th, 1972, I got my wish. We named her Helen Christena, after Barbara's mom and my mom. I preferred to call her Chrissy because I thought it sounded cute and feminine. Barbara reluctantly agreed, even though she wanted to call her Helen.

For a while, life at home was peaceful, although my drinking and pot-smoking continued off and on. The job was a delight compared to Kingston. We had fun on and off the air. A year and half went by before Dave was offered a job in Halifax and moved on. I took over from him as operations manager.

The station was owned by a pleasant gentleman who also owned the Cornwall Royals hockey team. It seemed that he was obsessed with the winning hockey team and seemed to invest little or no money into the radio station.

One day, while running to the control room, my leg went through the rotting floor. For a moment, I thought I had broken my leg. On the floor in pain, I came to the realization that we had better move on...again.

I found an opening for an on-air job at CJON in St. John's, Newfoundland. I had never been to Newfoundland, and it sounded like a great adventure. After all, *Newfies* had a reputation as party people. I sent off an aircheck tape and a resume. Two weeks later, I was hired.

Barbara was eager to get back east, so after packing up, she took the kids to stay at her mom and dad's in Sydney while I finalized business in Cornwall. She took our baby-sitter, Sophie, with her for a few weeks. Sophie was French and 16 but looked like she was 26. She was very pretty.

A month earlier, I had been lured by her sweet, sexy look one evening at home. While Barbara was at bingo with a friend, Sophie was baby-sitting. I arrived home after enjoying a local band downtown. As I went down the stairs to our rec room, Sophie got up off the couch, and without saying a word, opened her bathrobe to reveal her stunning, young, naked body. I gasped. I gazed, completely speechless. Somehow, I controlled my dizzying desire to fall to the floor with her. Instead, in a rare moment of restraint, I walked to her and closed her robe.

"I love you," she murmured in my ear.

She smelled delicious.

"No you don't," I whispered back, although I felt something for her more than raw desire.

We were both probably saved by the fact that it was one rare evening that I had consumed only two beers.

When Barbara decided to take Sophie with her to Nova Scotia, I feared that it might be a dangerous move. I also wondered whose idea it was.

* * *

The last night in Cornwall was a night of celebration. I went out to a club to see a favorite band and have a beer with some friends, including a few girls that I knew. I had too many beers and had a hit from a joint. Inhibitions faded as I became more than friendly with a tall acquaintance named Brandi. We spent the night together at her place, even though I had to get up at 4:30 a.m. to do my last morning show in Cornwall. I wasn't proud of another infidelity, but as with every woman who had ever taken her clothes off for me, I thought I was in love, again. That feeling lasted for two weeks.

* * *

I arrived in Cape Breton to spend a few days there before moving to Newfoundland. Barbara enjoyed time at her parents' summer vacation home in Big Beach along with the kids and Sophie. I studied Barbara's mood to see if she could read the guilt on my face for my latest transgression.

The day before we left for Newfoundland, I needed to pick up a few supplies in Sydney. Barbara's cousin Jack joined me for the half-hour drive to Sydney. We bought packing tape and boxes and odds and ends for the last part of our move to Newfoundland. As we pulled up in front of the cottage back in Big Beach, Barbara practically flew out the door toward us in a fury.

"Oh, fuck, I'm in shit, Jack."

"What did you do?"

"Nothing." I couldn't tell Jack or anyone about my Cornwall fling, but I was convinced that somehow, someway, Barbara had found out.

"That little bitch!" Barbara screamed at me.

I thought that was refreshing. *She's mad at her and not me.* Great! I wasn't sure how to respond, so I kept my mouth shut.

"I want to kill her! And to think that I trusted her."

I was confused. Did she know Brandi? Had Brandi called her and confessed? I had to say something.

"Who are you talking about?"

"Who?" she screamed even louder. "Who the hell do you think?"

I wondered if this was an entrapment ruse. I was not going to be stupid enough to volunteer any names in case she was talking about her sister Leona, with whom she had recently had a spat.

"She told me that she is in love with you!"

Now I was really confused. I couldn't take it anymore, even if it meant an on-location castration.

"Who the hell are you talking about?"

"That little whore, Sophie, that's who!"

"What? Pardon me?" All of a sudden I feared that Sophie had confessed the open bathrobe incident to her.

At least I was off the hook for my transgression with Brandi.

"Sophie confessed to me this morning after you left that she is in love with you."

"Really?" I choked. "Ah! That's cute."

Oops! Bad choice of words.

"Cute? You think that's *cute*? Do you feel the same about her?"

"No. No! She's just a kid. It's only a teenage crush, you know, infatuation."

"You're approving that comment to me, your wife?'

"No! Uh, by the way, where is she now?"

"On the train to Cornwall, Ontario."

"What? You're kidding? How? When did you—?"

"As soon as the little bitch told me that, I packed up her shit in a bag and drove her to the train station in Sydney and put her on the Goddamn train to Cornwall."

I was angry, but I couldn't admit it. I thought that Barbara had over-reacted to a teen infatuation. I felt sorry for Sophie. Then I imagined what would have happened if I had actually had sex with Sophie, including a possible extended stay in a federal penitentiary. She might have told Barbara. I had dodged another bullet. St. John's, Newfoundland was waiting, and I was about to become a local TV star and get caught without my shoes.

No News At 5:00

At my new job at CJON Radio & TV in St John's, I was assigned swing shifts on radio and part-time news on CJON-TV. I had never been on TV before. After several weeks, I became the 11:00 p.m. news anchor on NBC. No, not the big New York-based NBC network...the Newfoundland Broadcasting Company. I was also scheduled to anchor the 5:00 p.m. newscast on Saturdays.

One sunny Saturday, two hours before my scheduled newscast, I flirted with and innocently teased the attractive receptionist, Marlene.

Marlene challenged me. "Stan, you'll get yours!"

Normally, that's an innocent taunt, but the teasing escalated.

"Oh yeah, you'll get *yours*," I retorted with an evil smiling threat.

"Really? When?"

"How about right now?

Another reckless choice was made on the spot. I chose sex over sanity. I asked Ken Doyle to fill in for me on the 5:00 p.m. news while I succumbed again to feminine temptation. Lust dulled my logic. I didn't stop to consider that Barbara might watch me on the 5:00 news. She saw a new face anchoring the news, yet, I wasn't home. She called the station. A helpful individual told her that I had left with Marlene. The obliging character, obviously not a friend of mine, offered Marlene's address.

As Marlene and I were busy upstairs in her bedroom studying the latest ratings report, Barbara showed up at Marlene's door. Against my most fervent advice, Marlene foolishly answered the door and the screaming began immediately. She lied to Barbara, telling her that we had, in fact, left the station at the same time but not together.

Barbara might have bought the story except for the fact that I had left my shoes at the front door, which she identified as irrefutable evidence. I wisely did not come to the door. After a lengthy screaming session and questionable entertainment for Marlene's neighbors, Barbara left.

I knew that the shit was going to hit the fan when I got home. It did. The yelling was eventually replaced with a few weeks of cold silence. Barbara and I began a downhill slide.

After seven months in St. John's, the company transferred me to Grand Falls, Newfoundland, as general manager of the radio and TV stations there. For temporary accommodations, until I found a permanent home for the family, the company rented a boarding house for me.

My pathetic self-control failed again with the boarding house lady. She was a sea captain's wife. He was off sailing on the bounding main for several months at a time. She was lonely. I was accommodating. For a few weeks, I had visions of castration by Captain Hook.

After a month with the bawdy boarding house lady, Barbara and I rented a house in Windsor between the Salvation Army on one side and a Pentecostal Church on the other. Our weekends were spent drunk and/or stoned in the backyard with our crazy army friends, Bill Patterson and Rod Murphy, while next door they sang *What a Friend We Have in Jesus*. We assumed that on one side they prayed for us and on the other they condemned us to hell. There was no doubt that I needed spiritual guidance and a moral compass.

I enjoyed managing the radio and TV stations with a great but sometimes odd staff. On Sunday mornings, a long-haired, Harley ridin', mad DJ guy, Larry Donnelly, was scheduled to be on the air at 6:00 a.m. He drank and smoked weed more than I did.

One special morning Larry arrived at the station at 5:55 a.m., partially drunk and hung-over after only an hour's sleep. He kicked off the show, as usual, by playing a few gospel songs after which he was scheduled to read the long, drawn-out marine weather forecast. Larry was quite ill, so he placed a metal trash can by his chair, in case he had to vomit. He began reading the endless marine weather forecast but placed and cued up a record on the turntable, just in case he had to stop to puke. He read the forecast for a full minute before he felt it coming. He knew that he was going to barf. He rolled the music under his voice as he hurriedly tried to finish the marine weather. Too late! He shut off the mic. Or so he thought. He proceeded to vomit violently.

Retch. *Fuck!* He punctuated his retching sounds with more swear words.

"Jesus Christ! Ruuuup!"

He threw up last night's pizza, Black Label beer, and pickled eggs, while making a distinctive schlep-splat into the metal pail. He articulated a few more creative swear words and finally wiped his chin. That's when he noticed it. His music had stopped, but the microphone was still on. Instead of shutting off the mic, he had stopped the record that he had just started earlier. Technically speaking, there was no music or recorded sound to cover his retching, metal pail splats, and colorful profanities. He was live on the air to hundreds of nice folks on their way to church, tuning in to hear a few moving spiritual numbers.

I had fun in Newfoundland, but I felt trapped on the big island, known to some as *the rock*. We at least needed a break. Barbara and I left for a week-long vacation in Toronto.

I had earlier met up with a lady named Julie, who had visited Newfoundland as the lead singer with a band. For the record, I did not sleep with her. She told me that she was a member of a spiritualist church in Toronto. I had always been interested in the paranormal, so she invited us to be a guest at her church while we were in Toronto.

After some prayers and a reading from the bible, we all sat around in a circle in the church hall. An elderly lady, who we were told was a medium, approached a few people and allegedly delivered messages from departed loved ones. I wasn't completely buying the performance until she came to me.

"You work in front of knobs and dials, do you not?" she asked.

"Uh...yes. I guess." I didn't to share too much information.

"I see you turning in your swivel chair and walking away from it."

"Really?"

Then she said something truly ridiculous. "Do you plan to work at General Motors?"

I laughed. "No!"

"I see you going to work for G.M." She moved on to the next person, leaving me, if not confused, amused.

Barbara and I reluctantly returned to Grand Falls, Newfoundland. I wanted to be back on the mainland. Like most other radio people, I dreamed of being on the air in Toronto. To be in the radio biz in Toronto was the pinnacle of broadcast success in Canada.

Two weeks after we returned from Toronto, I received a surprise phone call from an old radio acquaintance. "Hi Stan, this is Bill Anderson, how are you doing?"

Bill was the program director at the biggest country music station in Canada.

"Hey, Bill, it's great to hear from you. What's going on?" I tried to guess why he was calling me.

"Stan, are you interested in working in Toronto?"

"Of course, Bill, I'd love to be in Toronto."

"Well, I have a job for you here doing swing shift, if you are interested."

"Yes! Absolutely!"

"We would need you here within three weeks. Can you do it? We'll cover the cost of your move."

"Consider it done," I said, as evenly as I could manage.

I hung up and screamed my brains out.

"Toronto! We're moving to Toronto!

Then it dawned on me. The old medium had been right.

* * *

It was Canada's biggest country station, CFGM, but known to everyone in the radio business as simply GM. I was thrilled. I had loved country music since I was a kid listening to CJCB in Sydney. This was big. I was going to be on the air on the huge Toronto station with a signal that covered most of southern Ontario and the northern U.S. And we would live in the big, trendy Toronto. Success in the radio business had finally arrived, even if I had been assigned a swing shift. I was not ready for the cost of living in Toronto.

Barbara and I rented a townhouse in suburban Downsview. She found a job across the street at a carpet and tile store. Roddie and Mark were enrolled in school, and Michael had just begun in kindergarten. Chrissy wasn't nearly old enough for school. I became a daytime dad.

Six months into my job, the program director assigned me to a Monday through Friday permanent evening shift from 6:00 p.m. to 10:00 p.m. I had to be in the station at 4:00 p.m. to voice commercials and prepare for my show. I was thrilled that I had my own regular show, but there was a downside. I didn't have time with Roddie and Mark. As they arrived home from school, I had to leave for work. When I arrived home at 11:00 or later, they were in bed.

However, I did get to spend my days with Chrissy. We watched *Sesame Street* together, took midday drives in the country, and ate mushrooms for lunch. The missing parent gene from four years earlier finally showed up. I cherished my time with Chrissy.

The first two years in Toronto were uneventful, but I became increasingly frustrated with working nights and not being able to see my kids. I couldn't help Roddie, Mark, or Michael with their homework or see them play little league softball or hockey in the evenings. Barbara and I were at each other's throats more often, and on the weekends, I drank more. The bickering escalated at times into pushing and shoving. I drank more, which added more fuel to the tension. The only peace I felt was when I spent my days with Chrissy.

Barbara and I befriended a couple, Don and Debbie, who liked to drink as much as we did. Barbara became closer to them while, over time, I drifted away from all of them. Often, when I arrived home from work at 11:00 p.m., I found them sitting around the kitchen table, inebriated. Barbara and her new-found drinking partners often had most of a 40-ounce bottle of rum finished off. There are few situations as irritating as walking into a room full of drunks when you are sober.

"Come on, sit down and have drink with us." Debbie made this demand as she pounded the table with her hand.

"No, that's okay." It was late, and I wanted to go to bed and dream about being somewhere else with that same elusive idyllic girl in my head.

Occasionally, I did join them in an effort to get equally plastered and forget where I was.

It crossed my mind, as I lay in bed at night, that maybe I deserved this harassment in return for my screwing around on Barbara.

I realized that I didn't love her anymore. In fact, I began to dislike her more with each passing day. I didn't want to come home at night. Some nights, I didn't. Occasionally, I accepted enticing invitations from sexy-sounding female callers on the request line, for an hour of mutual ecstasy at their apartments, a motel room, or my car. I didn't feel guilt anymore. I didn't care.

On weekends, I drank with my new friend, Ken. I did whatever I could to avoid being home with Barbara. To add to the angst, Roddie was becoming a problem as he grew older. He was living in a troubled environment at home, and he rarely heard from his mother, Sis.

In an effort to find something to do away from home, I teamed up with a co-worker, Joe Lefresne, to create a live radio show in a theatre setting. We both loved country music. We agreed that Canadian country artists and bands had few alternatives but to play in smoky bars and depressing dives. Many of them deserved better. We reckoned that maybe we could create a venue like the Grand Ole Opry in Nashville, Tennessee, where country artists performed in a concert setting in front of a live audience...an audience that came *only* for the show, not to drink, smoke, date, or mate.

After months of campaigning, it happened. The first of many live concerts was held at Seneca College's 1,100-seat Minkler Auditorium. The show was called *Opry North.* A remarkable success, it was broadcast coast to coast in Canada and on a few stations in the U.S. However, my attitude on the air and in the hallway at work grew decidedly sour. I was miserable at home *and* at work.

Breaking Up Is Hard To Do, Again

"Hey, man. Did ya hear the news?" It was CFGM madman Mike Manson, our afternoon guy.

He wore a zanier than usual expression as he pulled on one side of his large moustache and glanced sideways to check to see who might be listening. "Alan Slaight's son is the new program director, starting next week."

Alan Slaight was the owner of CFGM Radio. He had two sons, Greg and Gary. Greg, the youngest, was about to be the new guy in charge.

"No shit, Mike!" I said. "He started here in sales only a few months ago. He has no experience in radio, does he? Fuck! I can't believe it. The owner's son is going to be our boss?"

Greg moved into his office on Monday morning. He seemed like an okay guy. The changes didn't take long.

Things were screwed up at home too. I began going home later in the hope that Barbara would be asleep and not drinking with her friends. Sometimes, after work, I engaged in a quick and easy racy rendezvous with a persuasive female fan. There were plenty to choose from, including one lady who became a scary *Fatal Attraction* nutcase.

I was fed up with working nights, which I had done for five years which meant that I only got to see my kids on weekends. I implored station management to give me a day shift. I searched for radio jobs elsewhere in Toronto, but I had no offers.

The fights grew more intense at home. Almost everything about Barbara irritated me. Sundays were spent at the Minkler Auditorium as a producer of the live syndicated *Opry North* show. At least I was out of the house and not drunk.

I felt an ever-increasing longing to find out who the hell I was. I wanted to know who my birth mother was. My adoptive mom, Tena, refused to discuss the topic whenever I brought it up. Gradually, I began to suspect that she knew my birth mother and that maybe my mystery birth mother was a prostitute or a homeless drunk. Increasingly, I felt sorry for myself, the orphan, the helpless drunk and philanderer. I didn't like who I was, and yet I needed to cover my shyness with booze and demonstrate my sexual prowess with women to reaffirm my sagging self-worth.

Barbara decided to take Chrissy and Michael back to her mom and dad's in Cape Breton for a couple of weeks. I was happy to get her out of my hair and enjoy some peace. Besides, I had to work all weekend on Toronto Island at a CFGM-sponsored festival. It was a perfect, sunny, Sunday afternoon with thousands of people and fans.

One woman in particular caught my attention as she tapped my shoulder from behind. I spun around. She was an attractive lady in her mid to late thirties with big eyes. She looked vaguely familiar. I had her figured for a regular CFGM fan whom I had met previously.

She wore a teasing smile with her head cocked sideways. "You don't remember me, do you?"

"Hmm, I feel like I know you from somewhere."

"Really?"

"Help me out, where have we met before?"

"Well, we might not have actually spoken before, but think back to Newfoundland."

I guessed. "You are Bill Murray's wife?"

"Yes, I'm Debbie, and I *was* Bill's wife. We divorced a couple of years ago.

"Oh, I'm sorry, Debbie.

"Stan, I'll bet you didn't know that I had a crush on you. I used to follow you around town.

I laughed out loud. "Nah, you're kidding!"

"No, it's true. I thought you were cute."

"Am I *still cute?*" I asked, striking a mock pose.

"Even more."

We both chuckled.

We sat on the grass for an hour and talked about radio, Newfoundland, her ex-husband, and eventually the conversation became more personal. I confessed that I was also in an unhappy marriage and frankly wanted out. The sun was setting as we rode the ferry to downtown Toronto.

"Stan, would you like to come up to my place for a drink?" We have a lot of radio gossip to catch up on."

"Sure, I don't have much to do. Roddie and Mark are up north visiting their mom for a few days."

Sis was remarried and living northwest of Toronto. She had returned to her given name, Deanna.

I sat on Debbie's couch while she relaxed in a wingback chair opposite me. We went on talking about radio, people we mutually knew, and then about our lives. We each enjoyed a rum and Coke. I caught a glance of upper thigh as she attempted to get more comfortable in her chair. The conversation became more intimate. Debbie moved next to me on the couch. Another affair had begun, and this one was going to be marriage-ender. I knew it that night.

On a hot Sunday afternoon in August of 1977, I took the coward's way out. I left a card in my briefcase with an intimate note from Debbie expressing her love. Barbara liked to sneak a peek in my case. I knew she would. She did. That's when it all blew up.

Taking the biased advice from our friendly neighbors, John and Emily, Barbara and I agreed to a trial separation. She packed her bags and took the train to Nova Scotia with Chrissy and Michael. I knew that it was no trial. The only trial would be in court. Roddie and Mark remained with me.

With baby-sitters and Debbie's help, Roddie and Mark felt freed from the constant yelling, yet I was still stuck on evening shifts. Roddie was almost 14, and like many young teens, he was developing an attitude. Mark was 12 and played in the evenings on a kid's hockey team. It was tough not being able to see him play. Most of all, I missed Michael and Chrissy. I especially missed Chrissy because we had spent every day together. One day when I heard the *Sesame Street* theme, I broke down and wept. I was a mess. I knew that I had helped create the hell that I was in.

A few weeks before Christmas in 1977, I spent a paycheck on toys and clothes for Michael and Chrissy and packed them into a large box that measured three feet by two feet and sent it off to Nova Scotia. Roddie, Mark, and I spent Christmas at home with Debbie and my friend, Ken Legge.

In mid-January, the mailman knocked on my door. He wrestled with a giant crumpled box that looked vaguely familiar. I dragged it into the house. That's when I realized that it was the box of toys and clothing that I had sent to Michael and Chrissy. My first thought was that it had been returned for insufficient postage, or the mailman couldn't find Barbara's place. I opened the box and found that the toys and dolls had been broken and the clothes torn and dirty. The box contained a handwritten note:

The kids don't want your shitty toys and clothes. They wanted to throw them away, but instead we're sending them back. They don't want anything from you, you bastard.

I was heartbroken but only briefly until my sadness turned to intense fury. Michael was barely six, and Chrissy was five. A five- or six-year-old would not say no to toys, if they had come from Count Dracula. Barbara's vengeance was at work. I picked up the phone. What followed was a screaming match peppered with threats. If she had annoyed me before, I despised her then. She had tried to use our kids as a weapon to exact revenge. I declared war.

I wanted to get out of the house that Barbara and I had shared. I found a townhouse in Richmond Hill, less than a mile from the station and away from the bad memories. Roddie and Mark especially liked the new peaceful neighborhood and a more rural environment.

We settled in as the war of words with Barbara grew more intense. She refused to allow me to talk to Michael and Chrissy. She made excuses that they were at their Grandma's, or when she was really pissed off at me, that Michael and Chrissy simply didn't want to talk to me. In fact, I never again got to talk to my little girl that I had known as Chrissy. Barbara began calling her Helen, which was another way of removing any connection to me or my family, in this case, my mother.

I knew that it was a bad idea, but I chose to fight back by refusing to send support payments. This intensified the level of threats and counter-threats.

A consequence of my actions occurred on a Saturday afternoon, when I was pulled over by the Ontario Provincial Police for speeding. I expected to receive an expensive ticket. I did, but the police were in possession of something more serious...a bench warrant for my arrest. I spent a weekend in jail for failure to pay child support. On Monday, in court, the judge ordered me to pay up.

More trouble brewed on the home front. A chill grew between Debbie and me. She left for a long weekend with a male friend on his boat off Cape Cod. She tried to convince me that he was an old friend of the family and that their relationship was strictly platonic. I had been warned about rebound relationships, and my relationship with Debbie seemed to be suffering the fate that my friends had predicted.

On Sundays I was back at the Minkler Auditorium for the weekly live *Opry North* shows. We had no shortage of volunteers. After all, they got to hang out with stars backstage. One volunteer caught my eye. She was beautiful and wore a wide smile and had a loud infectious laugh. She had long dark hair and darker eyes. I asked her name.

"Hi, Stan, my name is Veronica."

"Hello, Veronica, thank you for helping out," I said, while still holding her hand.

"Sure, Stan, I love doing it. By the way, I listen to you on the air all the time. I love your voice."

I blushed. "Oh, thank you."

Now I *really* liked this striking lady.

After the show, along with my assistant producer, Sheila, and our volunteers, we spent half an hour cleaning up the dressing room, and then we all left through the backstage entrance. Veronica walked beside me as we talked about radio and her family. She told me that her family was from Eastern Europe.

"How do you feel about joining me for coffee or a drink," I asked, while fearful that she would say no.

"Sure, I don't have any kids or pets at home, so I have lots of time."

She followed me in her Triumph TR7. We drank coffee and talked for over an hour. I asked her if she wanted to have dinner with me the next night. She agreed. I really liked this girl with a laugh that got everyone's attention.

For two weeks we saw each other almost every day. In the meantime, Debbie had returned from her weekend sailing with Captain Bligh around Cape Cod. She called a few times and left messages with the baby-sitter, but I didn't call her back.

On a Saturday night I was at Veronica's apartment for dinner when her phone rang.

"Stan, it's for you. It's a woman. She sounds upset."

I knew that this could not be good. I guessed that it was Barbara harassing me. But how had she found me here?

"I need you to come here right now!" the hysterical lady screamed on the other end of the line.

"What? Who is this?"

She shrieked so loud that I couldn't tell who it was.

Too Many MacNeils

Ronnie Kartman was a singer-songwriter with a few mid-chart hits. He was originally from Manhattan but was living in Toronto in the late '70s. We had become friends and had shared a few beers and Christmas dinner once. We also had shared stories and a few secrets. One secret he didn't keep was my new-found love, Veronica.

When my out-going girlfriend Debbie couldn't find me and tried to understand why I wasn't returning her calls, she turned to my friend Ronnie for answers. He helpfully gave her Veronica's home phone number.

"I will kill myself if you don't leave there and come over here right now!"

"Stop!" I pleaded with her. "Please stop."

"No, I am going right now to the balcony, and I'm going to jump if you don't leave there this minute!"

I felt sorry for her pain, but I was not about to leave Veronica and go to Debbie's to resuscitate a dying relationship. I had heard that if someone tells you that they are going to jump to their death, they won't. I took a chance.

"Go ahead and jump because I am not coming over there." God, how I hoped that the myth about suicide threats was true.

"I will! I will do it," she shouted with a tad less enthusiasm.

I used the logic that it might be better if she was really pissed off rather than depressed. So I went on the attack.

"Listen, you cheating bitch! We are done! You were fucking your so-called platonic friend Herman-the-German on the high seas off Cape Clitoris while I was back here jerking off waiting for you!"

"I was not! Herman is just a friend!"

"Bullfuckingshit! I could tell by your face that you had been screwing him all weekend."

"Fuck you, Stan Campbell!"

Mission accomplished.

Veronica was not amused. Damn, maybe I had lost them both, but no matter. I had started down this road, and I was not turning back.

"You screwed around on your husband, so I know that you can't be trusted."

Something briefly crossed my mind about the pot calling the kettle black, but this was a strategy, and it seemed to be working. Hey, if I saved her life, it was worth it.

Debbie's attitude changed. "Go to hell, you son-of-a-bitch."

Click!

I paused and exhaled. It was over. I didn't feel good, although I felt more confident that the Toronto police would not be scraping a flattened body off the sidewalk.

Veronica and I saw each other almost daily. I stayed overnight at her place in Mississauga with Roddie and Mark, and she sometimes stayed with me at my place closer to the station in Richmond Hill. Meanwhile, Barbara was on the warpath. She had heard about my new love.

Because of my evening shifts, I was dependent on baby-sitters most evenings for Roddie and Mark. Roddie was 15 and was not dealing well with revolving mothers. Baby-sitters had no control over him. Veronica was not comfortable with my kids, even though she did keep them company occasionally.

* * *

In late '78 I had to travel to Nashville as a bus-tour host for country fans. Before Veronica and I departed for Music City, she left her Triumph TR7 with my mechanic friend, Ken. He was to replace the brake pads, so we left the keys hanging on a hook in my kitchen. Ken also acted as part-time baby-sitter when he wasn't at work.

We came back from Nashville a few days later and were met at my door by Ken. He appeared grim.

"Hey, guys, I have some bad news for you," he said, as he avoided our eyes.

"Oh, shit!" I was afraid.

He turned to Veronica. "Veronica, your car is smashed."

"Smashed? How could it be smashed? I left it with you to work on it." Veronica's voice trembled.

"Well, unfortunately, you left the keys here in the kitchen, but it was taken for a joy ride and got banged up pretty bad," Ken replied, while studying the floor, apparently not wanting to tell us the rest of the story.

"Who took it? Was it stolen?" I asked.

Ken hesitated. "Your son."

"What? No! Roddie? Not Roddie!"

"I'm afraid so."

"Is he all right?" I asked Ken, suddenly realizing that a smashed car might be less important.

"Yeah, he's fine."

"What about my car? How bad is it?" Veronica demanded to know.

"Bad." Ken went on to describe the damage. "The front tires are flat, the rims are flattened, the grill and fenders are smashed, and what's worse, the frame might be bent."

Roddie was grounded for months. I felt helpless. I was stuck on a night shift, and my anger at Greg Slaight and CFGM Radio grew. I desperately needed a day shift, but none was available. On the other hand, I feared that any day I might be fired for my bad attitude. At least I would be home, even if we did starve.

Some sense of normalcy came into my life when Roddie, Mark, and I drove to Nova Scotia for a two-week vacation. It was wonderful being able to spend two whole weeks with Roddie and Mark and for them to see their grandparents again.

After some persuading, I brought Mom and Pop back to Richmond Hill, Ontario. It was September 1979. It was a warm place for them to spend the winter, and most of all it was a warm feeling to have my parents living with me.

Some more help came my way. My first ex, Deanna, now lived north of Toronto with her new husband, Ed. Roddie moved in with her. She had her life straightened out, which made it a good environment for Roddie. Ed seemed to be the no-nonsense, strict father-figure that Roddie needed.

* * *

As the unpaid producer of the *Opry North* show, I received calls almost daily from new and unknown artists appealing for a spot on the show. A few were parents who twisted my arm to get little Jimmy or Jenny on the show. I hated saying no, but to maintain the integrity of the show, I had to draw the line somewhere.

An assertive mother called me in the autumn of 1979. "Hello, is this Stan Campbell?"

"Yes."

"Are you the *Opry North* producer?"

"Yes, but..."

"Well, my daughter is an excellent singer and songwriter, and I think that she would be great for your show."

I knew the pitch well. "Well, we are completely booked for the next few months and..."

"I think you will be surprised. She is quite talented."

"I'm sure she is, but I..."

"You have to see her. We drove all the way down from Timmins for her vocal lesson. So while we're here, I want to try to get her on the show. I hear that you have a studio. What if I bring her to wherever you are, and she can audition for you?" She was unrelenting.

I tried to think quick but not quickly enough.

"What do you think, Stan? It will only take a few minutes of your time."

I weakened. "Well, all right. When can you come over?"

"Right now! Give me your address."

"Okay, but I didn't catch your name."

"I'm sorry. My name is Sharon Twain. My daughter's name is Eilleen. She is 14 years old."

Minutes later, Mrs. Twain and her daughter were at the door. Sharon Twain was tall, slender, and imposing. She was a no-nonsense woman. Eilleen was cute with frizzy hair and a noticeable gap in her front teeth. She carried her guitar, which appeared bigger than she was.

Eilleen, even at 14, was entirely serious as she opened her guitar case, pulled herself up on the stool in front of the mic, and sang. I was impressed. I thought she sounded a lot like Tanya Tucker, which was a coincidence since Tanya also sported a gap in her front teeth. I offered Eilleen a chance to sing two songs on the *Opry North* show.

Throughout the winter, often when Eilleen and her Mom and Dad made the four hundred mile drive down from Timmins, Eilleen came by to spend a few hours in my studio recording songs that she had written. She was confident and usually sang through each song in one take. The more I got to know her, the more I believed that this 14-year-old really had something. She was focused and driven.

* * *

After Mom and Pop returned to Cape Breton in the spring, I resumed my angry, bitter mood at the station. Greg Slaight grew impatient with my obstinate, confrontational attitude. I suspected that the axe would drop any day. I frequently fought on the phone with Barbara. I received negative reports about Roddie's behavior at his mom's.

Deanna and I believed that Roddie might behave better if Mark and he were together. She and I agreed that Mark should move in with her and Ed in a more stable family environment. They wouldn't be that far away, less than an hour, so I could see them often. Mark seemed to be happy with the move. I had mixed feelings.

After Mark went to stay with Deanna, Veronica and I agreed that it made no sense to maintain two homes. She owned a condo in Mississauga, while I rented a townhouse in Richmond Hill. I moved in with Veronica, and we shared the household expenses. I was still unhappy and frustrated at the radio station, and to make matters worse, I was thirty miles from work rather than within walking distance and even farther from Roddie and Mark. The war of words and threats grew more intense from Barbara. As a result of the war, I rarely got to talk to Michael and Helen. One ray of sunshine occurred as I edged ever closer to employment termination. At a gala affair in Toronto at the Big Country Awards Show, I was bestowed with the honor of being named Canada's Top Country DJ. The award saved me. I heard a rumor that a pink slip had been waiting for me at the station. How could CFGM fire the Top Country DJ? They wisely didn't. However, I knew that I had not been named Top Country DJ for my on-air performance but rather as a *thank you* from the Canadian Country Music Industry for my efforts in promoting Canadian artists through the *Opry North* show.

Three months later, in January of 1980, I resigned from CFGM Radio before CFGM got to me. I felt financially comfortable, since I was voicing freelance radio spots and appearing occasionally in TV commercials. I was the TV spokesman for a TV retail store of questionable integrity.

I did bit parts in made-for-TV movies, including a tiny part in a movie with Suzanne Somers and Donald Sutherland entitled *Nothing Personal*. The movie was so bad that I fell asleep watching it. I was chosen for a Canadian Tire national TV commercial, and I scored big when I was hired as the on-camera announcer on the longest running network variety show, CBC TV's, *Tommy Hunter Show*. I also had a walk-on each week to talk to Tommy, the star of the show.

Mom and Dad were bursting with pride. They had watched the *Tommy Hunter Show* together for decades. Their son was on it! I wondered if Michael and Helen (formerly Chrissy) ever saw me on it.

I was doing better out of radio than on the air, but my success led to a series of stupid and enormously expensive decisions, which stained my reputation as an advocate of Canadian country music.

At home, Veronica and I engaged in a few verbal spats, mostly about money, my choice of friends, and my kids. After Roddie had smashed her car, she grew cold to both Roddie and Mark. I understood her resentment, but I dreamed that she would put it behind her and embrace my kids.

On a positive note, Veronica became interested in finding out my birth mother's identity. Together we began a letter-writing campaign to orphanages, hospitals, and parent-finders in Nova Scotia. All we knew was that I had been born in New Waterford, Cape Breton, Nova Scotia, on September 9th, or 13th, 1940, to Cecelia MacNeil. However, MacNeil was the most popular surname in Cape Breton. We found a dozen Cecelia MacNeils. Each time that I thought I was close and had possibly found her, the search went cold. The more we searched, the more I became haunted by my mystery mother.

Spinning Out Of Control At 45rpm

Veronica loved the music business and enjoyed being around the stars. She wanted to get closer. Thanks to my quasi-celebrity status, I had backstage access at most events, including the taping of the syndicated *Ronnie Prophet* CTV Network show. On a winter night in 1980 when we visited, a superb country music vocal group from Belleville, Ontario, called Cedar Creek appeared on the show. The quartet sounded a lot like the popular Oak Ridge Boys.

Following the show, Veronica and I, along with the Cedar Creek guys and the TV show band members, all went out for drinks at a hotel near the CTV studios. During a conversation about the TV show and the music business, someone mentioned that the guys needed a manager. Steve Smith from the TV show band suggested that I would be a good manager. I had managed a few Toronto artists, including Nancy Ryan and an awesome Eagles-like group called Foxglove.

I wasn't biting. I had learned early on that managing bands was like baby-sitting drinking-age adults. Besides, I was still the *Opry North* show producer, plus I was already working with two female artists, Eilleen Twain and a sexy blonde beauty with an edgy voice, Lindsay Taylor. My self-control with Lindsay was tested and passed...but just barely.

Veronica was motivated. "Stan, those guys are so talented. I think that you and I should do it."

"No, I have had my fill of baby-sitting bands. Besides, it will consume your life and our money."

"But those guys are as a good as the Oak Ridge Boys."

I wasn't biting."That's true Veronica but there's already one Oak Ridge Boys group. We don't need another."

"Stan, I am willing to invest some money into them, and you're making good money right now with the TV store commercials and the Tommy Hunter Show. We could handle it."

I didn't mention it, but I wasn't sure what Veronica could contribute to artist management.

I really didn't want to do it, but I had to agree that these guys, Dave, Ken, Ron, and Don, were damn good. They had begun their collective careers, as the Oak Ridge Boys had, as gospel singers around the U.S. and Canada.

The next day, after more urging from Veronica, I agreed to offer my services to the Cedar Creek guys as their manager. They happily agreed. I was going to have my hands full. The next phone call was not from the band.

Deanna was on the line. "Roddie got arrested last night."

"Oh, shit! What did he do?"

"He got caught drinking and driving, and the police suspect that he stole some stuff."

"Okay, I'll come up to see him."

Deanna then dropped a bomb. "Stan, we can't handle him anymore. Ed wants him out of the house. He thinks that we should take him to a family not far from here. Roddie has friends there. It's a foster care home.

"A foster home? You can't be serious. This is our son!"

"Well, they, the Coopers, have had a great reputation taking care of problem teens."

"But, a foster home, for my son?"

"Well, you can't handle him, either."

"I don't know. I would rather they both come back and live with me, *us*, that is, in Mississauga."

"Yeah, well, let me know how that goes." I caught the sarcasm in Deanna's voice.

I hung up and told Veronica the story and suggested to her that I would like to have my kids here with us. She flatly rejected the idea. She was still angry with Roddie for stealing and smashing her car, and her antagonism spilled over to Mark. I tried to understand her on-going resentment toward my kids, but I also couldn't see my own son go into a foster home, no matter how highly it was recommended.

I loved Veronica, but I also loved my kids. I thought it was strange that Veronica could say that she loved me but could not embrace my children. I was frustrated, and I was torn.

Between Deanna and Veronica, they persuaded me to let Roddie go the Cooper family, where he would be supervised twenty-four hours a day. Roddie swayed my decision too. He disliked Veronica and would not live with us...or at least with me with her.

I made the most disgraceful decision of my life. Deanna and I share the shame.

I weighed the options. If I left Veronica to bring Roddie and Mark back to live with me, I didn't know how I could handle parenting alone. Most of my work was still at night and on weekends. I knew no one responsible enough to supervise them while I was at work. I couldn't reverse careers and return to electronics. I would have to go back to school. At the time, it seemed like the Cooper family was the only option.

I visited Mr. and Mrs. Cooper. They convinced me that they had years of experience working with troubled teens. Yet, the decision was the most painful of my life.

I began working closely with Cedar Creek, planning their eventual rise to fame and, I hoped, fortune. I called Andy DiMartino, the New York producer for whom I had worked months before promoting an Iris Larratt record. I told him about the amazing Cedar Creek and asked him if he would be interested in being their record producer. He had worked with the Cascades, who had a huge hit in the 60s with their *Rhythm of the Rain* song, and he had produced rocker Captain Beefheart and Australian singer, Glen Yarborough. He boasted that he had a load of connections in New York and Los Angeles, including the legendary record producer Clive Davis.

"This is gonna cost money, you know," Andy said.

He thought he sounded like Joe Pesci.

"I didn't expect that you would do it for nothing, Andy."

"Well, we gotta see these guys first. Set up a showcase for me and Pete Bennett, and we'll fly up there to see them."

"Pete Bennett? Who is Pete Bennett?"

"What? You don't who Pete Bennett is? Pete is the guy who brought the Beatles to North America."

"He did? I though Ed Sullivan brought them," I said, having seen the Fab Four for the first time on that legendary Sunday night TV show.

"Fuck Ed Sullivan! Pete set that up."

"Okay Andy. Give me a few weeks, and let me try to set up a showcase for the Cedar Creek guys here in Toronto."

"Fine, but you gotta take care of our airfare and hotel and expenses. Pete is accustomed to first class treatment."

Veronica and I set up an evening showcase at a show lounge in the Roehampton Hotel in Toronto. We invited Toronto record executives, booking agents, and the media plus a few potential investors, including a rich lady with terminal halitosis. We paid for the food and drinks and special seating for our New York guests Andy DiMartino and, of course, Pete Bennett, who had the distinction of being the only promotions manager to work simultaneously with the Beatles, The Rolling Stones, Elvis, Bob Dylan, Frank Sinatra, Tony Bennett, Princess Grace, and Sophia Loren. He was undoubtedly well connected and billed as The World's #1 Promotion Man.

I learned later that Pete had changed his name from Pietro Benedetto to Pete Bennett. I wasn't surprised. I assumed that he made the name change to appear less Mafioso. It didn't help my first impression of him. Pete was big with jet black hair and spoke with a voice that sounded like he gargled with battery acid. He wore a pin-striped, double-breasted suit. Pete was straight out of central casting for a mob movie. On the other hand, Andy was short and talked rapidly while waving his arms wildly and punctuating every other comment with *fuck*.

Andy grew impatient within five seconds of taking his seat. "Let's get the fucking show started."

"Okay, Andy, take it easy," I said. "Give us ten minutes, and have a drink in the meantime."

"Is this all the fucking food you have? Me and Pete are hungry, and all you got here is these baby fucking shrimps and crackers and shit."

"Sorry, Andy, this is it."

While Andy demonstrated his Brooklyn tough guy attitude, Pete was laid back. He didn't say much. He didn't have to. His presence intimidated the shit out of everyone, especially polite Canadians.

The backup band kicked it off, and then, Cedar Creek appeared. For forty-five minutes, the guys knocked the crowd out of their seats! Their harmonies were flawless, and their presentation was first class. The assembled crowd gave them a standing ovation. I was elated. Andy and Pete assumed a more reserved attitude. After the show, we sat down with Andy and Pete.

Andy passed judgment. "They're good. I think I can work with them. Let me search for some song material, and we'll set up a recording date. The minimum it's gonna cost is fifty grand."

I tried not to appear shocked, but I was.

"Andy, I think we have to try to find an investor."

I didn't think that we could come up with fifty thousand dollars on our own.

Gravel-voiced Pete spoke up. "Lemme ask around. I know some people."

I figured that he knew people all right. People like Marco the Assassin or Mad Frankie. I envisioned Vito the Enforcer showing up at our house in a long black Cadillac with a bag of money with a gruff warning that we had better not fuck up.

Andy and Pete flew back to New York. Veronica and I pooled our resources and canvassed relatives to invest in this awesome group that was sure to be a smash hit. I was excited and fearful. What if the group was a flop? Some of these people could not afford to lose thousands of dollars. Neither could we.

Veronica knew nothing about the music business. Through radio, I had some knowledge of the inner workings of the record industry, and I had been an artist manager previously. However, the Cedar Creek management project was far bigger than any music endeavor I had ever encountered.

The fifty thousand dollar investment was earmarked for Andy DiMartino's professional fee, the New York recording studio at one hundred and twenty-five dollars per hour for several days, and eight studio musicians and a musical arranger. In addition, we had to pay the group's airfare from Toronto to New York and hotel expenses for Andy and the Cedar Creek guys while in New York.

Veronica and I visited the bank, which was a waste of time. We did meet a potential angel investor lady who loved the group but didn't look like she had a dime. She was interested until she got turned off by Andy's aggressive attitude.

Two weeks later, Andy called. "Okay, I hope you got the money together because we have a recording date set up at Media Sound in New York."

"Andy, we don't have all of it right now, but we hope to have enough to cover the studio and the musicians."

"Hey, *I* need to get fucking paid too, y'know."

"I know. I know, Andy. You'll get paid."

In early March, Veronica and I and the four Cedar Creek guys flew to New York. We checked into the Holiday Inn in Midtown Manhattan. The recording session was at Media Sound on West 57th Street. The studio was famous. Frank Sinatra, Neil Diamond, Barry Manilow, Barbara Streisand, Stevie Wonder, Aretha Franklin, Dionne Warwick, Diana Ross, and Duke Ellington had all recorded there. How could we lose? We were in good company. There was dark history down the street, though. John Lennon had been assassinated not far from there several months before. I figured that if I didn't pay Andy, I might be wiped out on the same block.

The session was a learning experience for me. Andy had hired the famous Billy Strange as arranger. Billy had worked with Elvis, Nancy Sinatra, Dean Martin, and the Beach Boys. I felt my wallet getting thinner. Andy the producer was pure entertainment, though. He yelled, jumped up and down, waved his arms, swore, and drove the studio musicians and the recording engineer nuts. I didn't know if Andy's act was producing or showmanship. He did seem to know what he wanted, even if the Cedar Creek guys and I didn't agree. I thought the songs were a bit too New York for a country group, but Andy was the pro, and disagreeing with him was not wise.

Back home in Canada, after three Cedar Creek songs had been recorded, Veronica and I mulled over our next move. We were deep in the artist management business. We decided that we needed a record label, so we pressed on to the next dumb decision. We created a record company named Acclaim Records. We established two publishing companies. We were getting in deeper and couldn't stop.

We decided, with Cedar Creek's encouragement and Andy's hesitation, to finish the album in Nashville instead of expensive New York. Andy had never produced in Nashville. In fact, he had never been in Nashville. This was going to be a learning encounter for Andy and an annoying experience for Nashville's studio musicians. I had been in love with Nashville since Barbara and I had traveled there on vacation in the mid-seventies.

After the Cedar Creek album was finished, the first single from the album was *Looks Like a Set-Up,* written by my Nashville songwriter friend, Alan Rhody. It was released to a lukewarm reception in Canada and a similar fate in the USA. It debuted at the bottom of the Billboard charts and stayed there for two weeks, then dropped off. Our relationship with the Cedar Creek guys was cooling fast, as they began to view us as, in their words, farmers. Their egos grew as our bank account shrank. We needed a life preserver, fast.

Twain Wreck

Back home in Toronto, Roddie got into more trouble. I felt helpless to do anything. After all, he was 18 now and wasn't about to listen to me or anyone else. Why should he? In a sense, I had abandoned him. Mark was 16 and doing okay, so far. I visited them as often as I could and felt like hell because I couldn't have them come and visit me. Veronica refused to embrace them. She made it clear to me that they were not welcome in our home, which was fuel for fiery arguments.

My relationship with Michael and Helen was worse. Make that non-existent. Barbara would not let me talk to them, and when I suggested that I wanted to travel to Cape Breton to visit them, she told me that she knew some cops in town. The inference was clear. I made one more irresponsible decision. I was furious at Barbara, so I chose again to stop sending support payments in retaliation for being prevented from communicating with my two youngest children.

Undoubtedly Michael and Helen suffered as a result of our war. I had heard a rumor from Cape Breton that Barbara was drinking heavily. I couldn't prove it, but the report further underscored my ill-advised decision to cease support payments. The war escalated.

* * *

While I was in Nashville, I had struck up a conversation with Charlie McCoy, who had been the Cedar Creek studio session leader, about living and working in Nashville. In spite of Andy being a pain in the ass in the studio, I learned a lot from observing him produce. I got a kick out of his Brooklyn style. Some of it rubbed off on me. I also saw that Charlie McCoy and engineer, Joe Mills, were doing most of the technical stuff. I was a former tech guy, so I figured that I could do the technical stuff too. Besides, I had creative musical arrangement ideas in my head. I wanted to produce a record or an album.

"Come on down," Charlie said. "I'll help you."

"Do you think I could do it?" It was though I was asking my daddy if I could drive the car.

"Sure you can, Stan. In fact, why don't you move down here to Nashville? It's a great place to live and work. Besides, y'all have a bunch of friends here already."

This became a serious idea. My chance to produce an album came along sooner than I had anticipated when I was approached by one of Canada's most respected, legendary country singers, Orval Prophet. He asked me if I thought I could produce an album for him. He was 60 years old and had been a country music star in the late forties and fifties under the names Orval Prophet and Johnny Six. Above all, he was a sweet, gentle man.

In 1982 I produced my first album with Orval in Nashville. He deeply appreciated the attention from the studio musicians and the joy of being in Nashville again after all those years. Personally, I loved the chance to be creative in the studio, even though my musical experience was limited to rudimentary guitar and a piano playing.

But I knew in my head, exactly what I wanted and what would make Orval stand out. Above all, I was aware from my radio years what radio would play and would not play. However, Orval, because of his advanced age, would be a tough sell on radio. The country music radio and record business is not kind to people over 40.

I didn't cut any corners but used the best musicians and background singers that I could find. Orval's album *True Blue* was released several months later on our Acclaim Records label. It was a creative success with amazing reviews. Larry Delaney wrote in the Canadian Country Music News magazine, *Stan Campbell should be canonized for his production on Orval Prophet's new album True Blue.*

I might have been canonized, but instead I became cannon fodder for a handful of Canadian music industry people who attacked me from the shadows for allegedly ripping off Orval by over-charging him for production. I was also assailed by other Canadian record producers because my background was in radio, not the music business, and therefore I had no business producing records, even though the results proved otherwise.

The album was a critical sensation but a financial disaster. Other than a few brave radio stations, most would not play Orval Prophet. In many minds, he was old and dated. Quality didn't matter.

Although Orval paid for the production on the album, we lost even more money on album and singles manufacturing and album cover artwork. Meanwhile, the Cedar Creek relationship worsened. Money drained away, and not just our money but investments and loans from friends and family. In spite of the financial hole we were digging, we still believed that Cedar Creek would hit it big and we would finally pay off investments and loans with dividends.

It got worse. Andy and I fought more each day. The Cedar Creek guys no longer wanted us to represent them as managers. After all, we had no more money to invest in them, and we weren't cool in their eyes.

I had been living with Veronica for a year and a half when I agreed to an additional dumb decision. We exchanged vows on May 27, 1983, at Old City Hall in Toronto. Video cameras were new and expensive, but I rented one for the occasion and asked a friend, Dave Hall, to shoot video of the ceremony. I don't know how he did it, but the entire wedding was shot upside down. It was an omen.

I was still earning income as a TV and radio pitchman for Big Daddy TV and as the Tommy Hunter Show announcer, but in spite of good money coming in, bad money was going out faster.

Veronica earned some income as a typesetter for specialized math books. It wasn't enough. Family and friends invested or loaned us money.

We still believed in our fledgling record label. We signed on new artists and even created a new service label, *16th Avenue Records*, whereby performers could buy a package deal for pressing records, distribution, and promotion. We signed a few good artists but we lost more money. We received moderate airplay but virtually no sales and no money from our publishing companies.

I had been away from radio for almost two years, but I was back on good terms with my former boss, Greg Slaight. My attitude had changed. I wasn't drinking as much except for the occasional night out, when I got plastered. One drink was never enough.

Veronica did keep me on a short leash and also influenced me to eat healthier. I lost twenty pounds and ditched the Pablo Escobar look with the afro frizzy hair and Fu Manchu moustache. My new image was slimmer and somewhat more conservative. I credit Veronica with cleaning up my act. I considered going back to radio, at least part-time.

In spite of the fact that a few industry insiders groused about a radio guy daring to produce records, a number of Canadian artists approached me to produce them. For recording sessions, I always chose leading Nashville studios along with the best studio musicians and background singers. Beginning with a simple demo from a songwriter, recorded on a cassette in his or her basement, and building it into a dynamic recording was pure joy.

Just as a painter aspires to create a masterpiece, the process provided me an opportunity to be creative with arrangements and direction. I would have done it for nothing if Veronica would have agreed. She didn't. She was an extra frugal manager. She was so frugal that we began cost-cutting on groceries and rarely dined out. Drinking was out of the question, unless someone else was buying.

I had not heard from Eilleen Twain for over two years. She had recorded demos in my studio in Richmond Hill when she was 14 and 15. I had helped her set up radio interviews and the occasional performance date, but then she stopped coming to Toronto. Instead, she had joined a rock band in her hometown of Timmins, Ontario. We reconnected in September 1984 when she called me one day to update me about what she was doing. She had moved to Scarborough in Toronto's east end.

Because I had been an enthusiastic supporter when she was in her early teens, she asked me if I would produce a few sides (songs) with her. She felt that it was time to think about a recording career. I never doubted her immense talent and drive, so I was quick to agree. Besides, I liked her. Not in a romantic way. I simply liked her, even though at times she was frustratingly assertive. Veronica instantly disliked her aggressive manner.

At Eilleen's apartment we spent an afternoon discussing style, music genres, and song material. Because we had discussed recording in Nashville, I assumed that she wanted to record country music material. I was wrong. She was a fan of artists such as Bonnie Tyler, Laura Branigan, Madonna, and Pat Benatar. She was adamant. Eilleen wanted to do pop/rock material. I was disappointed. I felt that she belonged in country music, but she and her parents were paying me.

Together we settled on three songs that I had found at Nashville publishing companies, *Kiss & Run*, *Ease Up*, and *It Only Hurts When I Love*. Eilleen and I agreed on a recording date in late November at the Music Mill Studios in Nashville. The Music Mill was owned by Harold Shedd, who was Alabama's producer. When I first met Harold in 1980, he was a struggling studio owner with the then unknown group, Alabama, from Fort Payne, Alabama. Now with Alabama's success, Harold was doing well, with a striking log cabin-style twin studio complex on Roy Acuff Place in Nashville.

Around the same time, I was approached by singer Tim Denis from St. Catharines, Ontario. He also hired me to produce an album for him and his CTL record label. CTL was financing the cost of production. I decided to also record Tim's session at the Music Mill Studio. I booked both Eilleen's and Tim's session dates and musicians back to back, in an effort to save money.

Veronica, Eilleen, and I drove to Nashville, Tennessee, in our tiny 1983 Pontiac Acadian. It was Eilleen's first time in Music City, USA. It was November 1984. I booked Eilleen into a motel on West End Avenue while Veronica and I stayed with our friends in suburban Green Hills. Veronica made it clear that she did not like Eilleen's attitude, so she avoided the studio. Eilleen was smart, headstrong, and knew what she wanted.

The recording session on the first day went smoothly, as it always does with Nashville studio musicians. On the second morning of the recording sessions, I stopped by the motel to pick up Eilleen, but she was not quite ready. She invited me in.

"Sit down, Stan. I'll be out in a minute," she said, as she disappeared into the bathroom with a hair dryer in her hand.

I sat on the edge of the bed and chatted about the plan for the day. I had to shout when she turned on the hair dryer.

"When do I get to do my vocals?" Eilleen yelled back.

"We'll probably do them tomorrow night, if the overdub studio is free and the engineer, Paul Goldberg, is available."

She unplugged the hair dryer and came into the room, stopped, and stared at me. Had I said something wrong?

"Oh, my God, Stan, you need to do something with your hair!"

"My hair? What's wrong with my hair?"

"Look at it. It's flipping up in the back. It's like wings. You need to fix it."

I chuckled. "Well, I can't see behind my head."

"Have you ever heard of a mirror?"

"You're funny, Eilleen."

She went back to the bathroom and returned with the hair dryer, plugged it in by the bedside table, and crawled onto the bed behind me. There was nothing sensuous or titillating about it. It was funny.

"Sit still Stan and let me fix your hair."

With the dryer and a brush, she straightened my hair. It was classic Eilleen. Just do it!

"There! That's better," she proclaimed. "You need to do that every day, okay?"

"Yes, Mom!" I answered, teasing her.

It was my most memorable Eilleen Twain moment.

Two days later, Tim Denis arrived. We had finished Eilleen's recording session and were both happy with the three songs. They were unusually pop/rock for Nashville and sounded current for the era, with Eilleen reaching some astonishing notes to do octave doubling.

I hired the background singers for Tim Denis's album and as a last minute idea asked Eilleen if she would like to sing with them. She did. Late the next night, over too many Long Island iced teas, someone had an idea to have Eilleen sing a duet with Tim on one of his song choices entitled, *Heavy on the Sunshine.*

The next night Tim and Eilleen sang together. I had never heard her sing so beautifully. Eilleen literally caressed the lyrics. I felt like both recording sessions went well, even if Eilleen, in my opinion, wasn't in the right music genre. Tim Denis' *Heavy on the Sunshine* album cut became Eilleen's Twain's first official commercial recording exposure in Canada.

We finished Tim and Eilleen's projects, and it was time to depart to Toronto. Veronica came to the sessions a few times but easily became irritated by Eilleen. I knew that it wasn't going to be a fun drive back to Toronto in the tiny Acadian. It was a typical gray December day when we left Nashville for the seven hundred and sixty mile drive. It started out quietly. Eilleen spoke to me and I spoke to her. Veronica talked to me and I responded, but Veronica and Eilleen did not speak to each other, except once when Veronica opened her passenger window.

Eilleen said, "Veronica, would you close your window, please. I'm freezing back here."

"We need some fresh air in the car," Veronica answered.

"Yes, but its freezing, and its blowing right on me here in the back."

"Fine!" Veronica cranked her window up in one quick twist.

I said nothing, not wishing to run through that minefield.

Later, Eileen asked, "Stan, could you turn up the heat a bit, it's really cold back here."

"Sure."

"No, it's already too hot in the car." Veronica glared at me.

"Never mind." Eilleen gave up.

It grew quiet until we reached Elizabethtown, Kentucky, when I spoke for the first time in a hundred and fifty miles. "Hey, I'm hungry. I could use a coffee and a snack."

No one spoke. I decided. I drove into a McDonald's parking lot and got out. The two warring ladies got out. They walked on either side of me. There was a chill in the mid-December air but not nearly as frigid as the icy atmosphere between Veronica and Eilleen.

I stepped aside to let them both go ahead. Eilleen walked through the door and Veronica attempted to follow but Eilleen let the door go. Smack! Veronica walked into it. I admit that I was shocked but not as stunned as Veronica. She mouthed words that I had never heard from her before, a few of them in her native Czechoslovakian.

Before attempting to enter again, she turned to me. "That's it! I do not want that girl associated with us in any way. Do you understand me?"

"Hey, you both need to take it easy and stop this war between you two."

We went inside and ate in an unnerving silence.

The car was too small and overloaded with two, but it was hell with three people when two of them hated each other and used me as an intermediary. After thirteen miserable, tense, infuriating, and tiresome hours, we arrived at Eilleen's apartment in Scarborough. Veronica opened her door on the two-door Acadian and practically launched Eilleen out of the car onto the parking lot pavement. I had to say *something* to Eilleen.

"Bye, Eilleen! I'll call you tomorrow."

I felt sorry for Eilleen. I wanted to hug her to reassure her that I was still her friend and supporter.

"Good-bye, Stan. Talk to you tomorrow."

Veronica added no good-bye or other pleasantries. None were expected.

"Stan, I don't want to do any more business with Miss Twain."

"That's crazy, Veronica."

"I will not deal with her cocky attitude."

"You don't have to deal with it. That's my job."

"Did you forget that I am half of this company?"

"I know that, but your role in the company is to handle the accounting and the other business stuff, and I deal with the creative side and work with the artists."

"Fine! Then you deal with her attitude."

"I don't have any problem with her attitude. Eilleen is strong-willed and driven. She knows what she wants. I don't have a problem with that. Besides, she is a remarkable talent and will be successful some day. I'm sure of it, and besides, her parents are counting on me."

"Well, I don't want her on our Acclaim Records label."

It was my turn to say it. "Fine! She will have a better shot at success on a major label, anyway. I will shop her around to Capitol, CBS, MCA, and RCA."

I knew that Eilleen could be a huge success, and especially in light of the fact that Cedar Creek was self-destructing, along with our huge financial investment in the group. Eilleen was our last hope.

After resting for a day following the long journey through hell, I got on the phone to major record companies in an attempt to set up meetings to play Eilleen's material for them. I felt energized. I figured that any record company would be interested in her. She had the talent, the determination, and she was attractive.

My first meeting was with Attic Records in Toronto. It was not a major record label, but the company had some impressive acts. I played the three songs we had recorded for the owner, Al Mair.

He was not impressed. Undeterred, I planned to take it a step higher and meet with some of the major labels. I drove home prepared to go after the really big fish the next day. Instead, I strolled into a buzz saw!

"Stan, I don't want to be associated in any way with Eilleen Twain."

"I'm sorry but I have an obligation to the Twains. They paid for not only the production costs, which they could ill-afford, but most of all, they expect me to do my best to try to acquire a recording contract for Eilleen."

Veronica was steadfast. "They can do that themselves or hire someone else. I want you to give them the master tapes."

The fierce argument grew louder.

"Veronica, I'm not going to let her go on her own. It's not fair. She doesn't deserve this!"

Then, the ultimatum came.

"Stan. Either she goes, or I go!"

I was astounded. Did I really hear her say that? I stood with my mouth agape.

"You heard me, Stan."

"You can't be serious. You would leave me over this?"

The argument escalated until I stormed out the door and returned to a favorite diversion. I bought a pint of vodka and sat in the car behind the Dominion Store on Glen Erin Drive and drank it down in two gulps. When I finished that, I stopped at a tavern and washed it all down with a beer. I foolishly drove home drunk. The argument erupted again with more alcohol-fueled fury until I lost my infamous temper and flipped my desk over. I slept on the couch.

I felt like crap the next morning, in several ways, including physically and mentally. What could I do? I thought about leaving Veronica. After all, she had also rejected my kids. Why shouldn't I move on?

The familiar basic-fear instinct gripped me. If I left Veronica, I would be alone, without a woman in my life. I couldn't. Maybe, for the first time, I realized that I had always been petrified at the thought of being alone. I had no choice. I had to deliver the bad news to Eilleen and her mom. This was going to be unpleasant.

Y'all Come

I broke the news to Eilleen and then to Sharon Twain, Eilleen's mother. They were justifiably angry. I had reneged. Secondly, I was certain that Eilleen would be successful someday, and I wanted to be a part of that triumph. More importantly to me, I liked Eilleen personally. She was a friend. I felt sad and guilty for walking away from her. I was a coward. I had acquiesced to Veronica's unrealistic intolerance. My fear of abandonment overcame what I knew was the honorable thing to do. It was done.

Several weeks later, we were served with a breach of contract lawsuit by lawyers for Eilleen's family. After some phone calls and letters, the matter was settled, and the master tapes were handed over to Eilleen and her new manager, Mary Bailey. We were now bleeding money, but most of all, I regretted how I had treated, not the rising star, but my friend Eilleen. Would she and I ever speak again?

* * *

A definite chill filled the air at home following the conclusion of our partnership with Eilleen. I felt angry and depressed. It was over. For our record company, we had Iris Larratt, who had good airplay but weak sales, which was a paltry source of revenue for us. We flew to Calgary to host a press reception for Iris. As with the Orval Prophet album, the reviews were excellent, but the revenues were insignificant.

We fought with Andy DiMartino and the Cedar Creek guys almost daily. There were now eight guys in the group instead of the original four. One was Chris Golden, the son of Oaks Ridge Boys singer William Lee Golden. The other was corpulent Garland Craft, the former flamboyant keyboard player from the Oak Ridge Boys band. Cedar Creek was composed of four Canadians and four Americans, so no matter which country they played in, the immigration paperwork was an issue.

With the new guys in the band, the egos became a larger problem. Garland Craft added to the multitude of opinions about how the group should be managed. Also, adding a semi-celebrity such as Garland gave the guys an inflated opinion of their worth. With a tour bus and an attitude that they were already stars in their collective minds, they were paying more out in fees than they could afford.

We had had enough. The feelings were mutual. They wanted us gone, and we wanted to say good-bye to them but also had to say farewell to any hope of recouping any kind of return on our huge investment, not to mention the loans and investments from friends and relatives. To the Cedar Creek members, our enormous financial investment in their careers was seemingly inconsequential. To be fair, one member of the group, Ken awarded us understanding and respect.

Andy suggested that we sign the group over to him and his Moonshine Records label in a licensing deal. No money exchanged hands, but Andy assured us that we would see royalty money when the guys finally hit it big. We were glad to be free of all of them so that we could concentrate on the artists that we cared about and who were willing to work with us.

* * *

I traveled to Nashville regularly to produce records and meet with industry associates. I felt comfortable doing business there. By contrast, I loathed the business climate in Canada. Whether it was a bank or a supplier, the answer was always no. Minor businesses like ours weren't welcome.

For example, when we requested five hundred 45-RPM record envelopes from a Toronto supplier, we were told that they would sell us a minimum of ten thousand, no less. The suppliers weren't interested in small-time operations like ours. The record pressing plants in Canada couldn't be bothered servicing a Mom and Pop enterprise.

Meanwhile, in Nashville, the answer was almost always yes. If we wanted only ten envelopes, a supplier would sell them to us. I was fed up with Canada's elitist business attitude and government bureaucracy.

One more bad financial decision in a long line of regretful decisions was made. Veronica and I decided to sell the house that we had bought less than a year before and move to Nashville, where we would be welcomed with open arms and a three-chord *Kumbaya*! Through a lawyer friend of Andy's in New York, we applied for and were approved for L-1 visas. (The L-1 visa is created for business people to live temporarily in the USA to operate their own business.)

*   *   *

In April of 1985, I said good-bye to Roddie and Mark, who were now both in their twenties and thankfully doing better. I traveled to Nova Scotia to visit Mom and Pop. They were visibly upset that we were leaving Canada to go live and work in the big bad United States. Veronica and I loaded up a truck and moved to Music City to seek our fortune. We sure as hell had lost it in Canada. Surprise! The Nashville welcome mat must have been at the dry cleaners.

Veronica and I rented a small but attractive apartment in Nashville's south end. We expected to buy a nice place in posh Brentwood when the record business turned around. Well, *one* of us would end up in Brentwood.

I loved living in Nashville. I loved living in Tennessee and in the USA. Everything seemed easier, whether it was picking up a can of Coors at the 7-Eleven or arranging a line of credit at the bank. Folks were friendly and accommodating.

But wait. Let me back up. Everyone *seemed* friendly.

When Charlie McCoy had said, *Come on down, you have lots of friends here, and you'll make new friends,* he apparently wasn't using the word *friend* literally. He really meant polite acquaintances...most of them business acquaintances. People in the south are exceptionally polite. The friendly part is only skin deep. Never confuse *polite* with friendly.

I had imagined us arriving in town, and all of the nice folks that we knew would show up at our door with a load of fried chicken and biscuits. I expected our new phone to ring off the hook with invitations.

"Hey, Stan and Veronica, why don't y'all come on over to our place for dinner tomorrow night?"

"After our recording session is done, let's go on down to my mansion in Brentwood for a few Jack and Cokes around the pool?"

None of those invitations materialized. Our neighbors in the apartment complex scurried in and out, and no one spoke to us and didn't respond when we said hello. The neighbors upstairs were certainly friendly enough...with each other. They had riotous, wall-banging, thumping, ear-piercing sex, usually at 2:00 in the morning. My imagination went off the charts, especially when I saw them. He was taller than Kobe Bryant, and she was around four-foot-six. No wonder she yelled!

For a while we felt good about business in Nashville, but our debts were catching up with us. We managed to get a line of credit from the Third National Bank, something the banks in Canada would not even discuss. However, money got tighter. We were becoming desperate.

I had to find work of some kind. I took a chance and drove to radio station WSIX with my aircheck audition tape from CFGM. I met with the program director, Wayne Campbell. I was unsure of myself and figured that he would think I sounded Canadian, even though in Toronto I had worked on not saying *oot* and *aboot*, as Americans hear it. After all, this was Nashville.

"Hey, you sound great," Wayne said, to my surprise. "You really sound like a pro."

"Wow! Thanks!"

"We don't have anything right now for full-time work here, but I think I could use you on weekends, if you are interested."

"Yes! Sure!"

"How about we start you on the air next Saturday?"

"Yeah, that would be great."

"Okay. We pay six-eighty for part-timers."

My eyes darted around the room as I attempted to understand him. *Six-eighty? Six-eighty what? Six hundred and eighty dollars a month? Six-eighty? Surely he doesn't mean six dollars and eighty cents an hour*!

I hesitated and said slowly, "Six...eighty?"

"Yes, it's not a lot, but that's the part-time pay scale here. Six dollars and eighty cents an hour."

"Oh. Six-eighty..."

I had been earning around fifty thousand a year in Toronto, more than three times what he was offering.

Wayne became serious. "You want it or not?"

"Of course! I need to break into the radio business here in the USA. Yes!" Most of all, I desperately needed money.

I debuted on US radio at WSIX on the following Saturday. It felt good to be in radio again. The attitude of the WSIX staff blew my mind. Staff members called to say that I sounded great on the air. This had never happened in Canada. In no time I felt like I belonged at WSIX. I also found listeners more friendly and interactive.

A few were *very* friendly! I received invitations from female listeners to come by for a visit or to meet and have a drink. Some got straight to the point, suggesting what they would do to make me smile. And I thought that they were all good church-goin' Christian folk in Tennessee, the buckle of the bible belt. Y'all fooled me!

At home, Veronica and I squabbled more and more about money. Most people in the Nashville music business awarded us moral support. It didn't help. We were literally pinching pennies. Veronica held the purse strings so tight that I was provided an allowance of twenty-five cents a day to take to work to buy a cup of coffee from the coffee-machine. It really ruined my day when the machine ate my quarter and gave me no coffee.

I sure cut back on my drinking. I was allowed to buy a quart of beer on payday. We lived almost exclusively on a diet of packaged soups. The chill at home had turned to a deep freeze. I knew that we were in deep financial trouble, but I refused to starve to death because of it. There had to be a limit.

Roddie and Mark called me once a month or so.

When Veronica answered the phone, the response to my sons was curt. "Hello. What do you want?"

Judging by her tone, I assumed that maybe it was a bill collector. After all, we were getting more of those kinds of calls more often.

"It's your son." She practically threw the phone to me.

Once, Roddie called to say hello and to tell me that he had bought a motorcycle. He was thinking of riding down to Nashville with his girlfriend. Inside, I was thrilled at the idea, but I knew that this would be a huge problem for Veronica. I talked him out of it. We chatted for a while, and after I hung up, I stormed into the bedroom and slammed the door. I was furious that I couldn't even invite my own son to the place that I loved, Nashville. I knew that Roddie would love it too.

Veronica invaded my retreat. "What did *he* want?"

"What the fuck do you think he wanted? He wanted to talk to his father! And I wanted to talk to him."

"Does he have to call *here*? Couldn't he call you at work?"

My patience with and love for my wife had run dry. I missed my kids. They obviously missed me, even though I had been a lousy father. I was depressed and felt sorry for myself.

At times like that, I saw myself as the orphan with no clue as to my origin. As I frequently did when I was down, I thought about my birth mom. Why did she abandon me without a clue? Who was she? Who was my father? Was I like him? Did he have an alcohol problem? Did he have marriage problems? If it took the rest of my life, I would find out where I had come from.

I wrote more letters to several individuals and organizations in Nova Scotia, who claimed to be experts in finding adoptee's birth parents, but either they led me down a dead end or I received no response. I felt disconnected and lonely. Even in my happiest moments with Deanna, Barbara, and Veronica, I had always felt like someone was missing from my life. I never stopped fantasizing about that perfect girl. Was the idea just an immature whimsy?

Third Rate Romance, Low Rent Rendezvous

Even though the pay was only slightly above minimum wage, I felt valued at WSIX Radio. My old self-confidence on the air was re-energized, without the overblown ego. To my friends and former radio colleagues back in Canada, it didn't hurt my image to be on the air in Music City, USA, where many of our listeners were country music stars like Johnny Cash, the Gatlin Brothers, Randy Travis, Reba McEntire, and Tanya Tucker.

I loved living in Nashville, even though getting beyond the polite *y'all have a nice day* was difficult. I did become close to my co-workers at WSIX, especially Devon O'Day, who became my confidante. Even though Devon was a tall, shapely blonde, former New York model, I was not romantically or overtly sexually attracted to her. Instead, I grew to revere her as a cherished friend over time. As I became more despondent at home and in business, I needed an occasional shoulder to lean on. Devon was always there for me. In fact, we supported each other.

Veronica and I were in serious financial trouble. We owed everyone. Our creditors grew aggressive and threatening. Our friends and relatives demanded to know when they were going to see a return on their investments. Friends of friends got in on the act. Someone left an unsigned hostile note at the front desk at WSIX. *We have called U.S. Immigration to tell them that you are working illegally in the USA. They will send you back to Canada where you will have to face the people you screwed out of thousands of dollars.*

The cowardly threat scared me, but it angered me more because I had never set out to defraud anyone. In fact, in my most idealistic dreams, I thought that we would make them all wealthy. I felt ashamed. I had gained a good reputation in Canada, not necessarily for my on-air performance but for my work in supporting Canadian country artists. Now, it seemed, I had fallen from grace.

Life at home was unpleasantly cold. I didn't want to be there, but I couldn't afford to be elsewhere on six dollars and eighty cents an hour, part-time. Besides, if I left, I would be alone. That fear loomed over me again, as it had for most of my life. I began to wonder if I would ever be able to be happy in my own skin without feeling that I had to be attached to a woman. I imagined what that would be like. I couldn't. I would fall apart.

Our new WSIX receptionist had one of those unique names and an inimitable personality to match. Dixie Lee Carrington. Dixie was an attractive brunette, of medium height, and sexy eyes. I guessed that she was in her mid to late thirties. She also worked on-air on the weekends on WSIX-AM, across the hall. She was a platonic friend, until the day that the relationship dramatically elevated to broil level.

I was working on-air on a Saturday afternoon when Dixie and a girlfriend stopped by the station. I exited the studio into the office area to say hello. Dixie didn't say hello but strolled straight toward me with a sly smirk, gripped me by the shoulders, and planted a hard, lingering kiss on my lips.

"Gawd, I think y'all are hot!" She gushed in her husky southern twang after she released me.

"Whoa!" I had nothing else to say.

I felt lightheaded. I did not recall any woman ever saying that I was hot. I've had cute (which I hated) and nice, but never hot, although at that moment I was hot, but not in the way that she meant. I didn't quite know how to handle this sudden burst of lust, at least not at that moment.

I said, "You're crazy, Dixie!"

"About you."

"Shit! I gotta go. My record is fading."

"Bye, Stan!"

Honor Bound by Earl Thomas Conley was ending, and I had to run to the studio. Dixie and her friend left. Her perfume had not.

Fate interceded the next weekend. Dixie was scheduled to be on-air at the same time as I was. She was AM and I was FM. She was female and I was male. I was unhappy at home, again, and wanted out but was too much of a coward to live with myself if I made the decision to leave.

Dixie and I got to know each other better. Much better. During newscasts and long records, we attacked each other in the hallway. Because it was a weekend, no one else was in the station. It was purely a ferocious physical attraction, but we were at work, so we could not take it to the limit.

It didn't take long for the rumors to fly through the station. *Dixie and Stan are hot for each other.* I became somewhat less popular and for good reason. My radio co-workers knew that I was married. At home, the weather got colder. I desperately wanted to leave what felt like a prison, but I had nowhere to go and wasn't making enough money to go it alone.

It was a Saturday afternoon, and Dixie and I were on the air again finishing our shifts at 6:00 p.m., AM and FM. Charlene Cannon had just arrived for her shift on AM. She stopped us in the hallway.

"Here you go. It's a little gift for you two. Go have fun!" Charlene wore an evil smile as she handed me a brown envelope.

It had a rattling lump inside.

"Pardon me?"

"Just open it, Stan."

Dixie watched as I tore the end off of the envelope.

"What the hell...?"

Charlene pointed to the door. "Go! Get out of here you two. Get it over with."

"You have got to be kidding, Charlene!" I felt my face burn.

I held a hotel key that had the words *Red Roof Inn* emblazoned on the plastic.

"It's paid for. That's my gift to you both."

Dixie laughed."Charlene, you're crazy."

"Hey, what are you waiting for? Go!"

I put the key in the door to open another chapter of my life. The song by the Amazing Rhythm Aces *Third Rate Romance* crossed my mind as we fell in the doorway of our low rent rendezvous.

Our lusty relationship was finally consummated. At that point, it was mostly a physical attraction. Dixie felt that it was more. Whatever it was, I couldn't live a double life, and I had to be straight with Veronica. I no longer loved her and hadn't for a long time. It was unfair to drag her along in a lie.

On the way home, I tried to conduct a self-analysis. I had done it again. Could I ever be faithful? Could I find someone to love forever and remain true? I still dreamed of that mysterious perfect girl. If I met her, would I know her? Maybe she only existed in my mind. Okay, perhaps she wasn't real, but my birth mother was. I needed to find her, dead or alive.

A few weeks later I summoned the courage to tell Veronica that it was over. I was terrified. I had always hated confrontation. I didn't love Veronica. I grew increasingly angry at her for barring the door on my kids, but this time, I knew that it was my fault for not demanding acceptance of my children as a prerequisite before we were married.

I invited Veronica to meet me at a Hardee's restaurant, not far from our house. I needed a drink before I could do this. I stopped at the Kwik-Sak and gulped a tall Coors on the way.

Veronica waited for me in a booth. I sat across from her and commenced with banal weather and traffic talk. Finally, I had to do it. I can't remember what I said or what she said. It did go smoother than I expected. There were a few tears from both of us. I told her that I would move out that weekend.

Moving out was far more painful, and there were far more tears this time. No, make that out-and-out sobbing. Walking up the stairs from the apartment that we had shared together with so much hope and so many dreams was one of the most heartrending moments of my life. I looked back down at her sitting on the floor crying, and it killed me. I wanted to run to her and hold her, but I had to have my life and my kids back, as much as I could after all that time.

Imagine that you can't swim but that you have to cross a lake on stepping stones, except that the stones are slippery on top. You have to jump from the top of one to the other. If you miss one or slip, you drown because you haven't learned to swim. I never learned to swim, figuratively or literally.

Dixie was another stepping stone because I didn't want to risk swimming. I knew that this was the wrong way to get there. Another slippery stone was waiting for my next jump. There were sharks in that lake.

Living In The Diplomat

"Hey, Stan, y'all can crash at our place." Dixie suggested after I told her that I had moved out.

"Are you sure that your roommate will be okay with me crashing on her couch?"

"Sure, no problem."

"Can you give me a ride as well?" I asked.

I had left the Pontiac Acadian with Veronica.

"Sure, I'll drive you anywhere, and if I can't, you can use my car."

Dixie had a '78 Dodge Diplomat.

I arrived at Dixie's place with my green Glad garbage bag luggage. Dixie's roommate, Sharon, was not happy to see me. We ordered pizza and watched TV, after which I slept on the couch until midnight. After Sharon and her 7-year old daughter were asleep, I crept upstairs to Dixie's bed

The next morning Sharon made it clear that she was not happy about Dixie and me sharing a bed in her apartment. The next night I didn't sleep quite as well, aware that I wasn't welcome.

* * *

A few days later, Dixie took me aside in a hallway after I got off the air. "I'm really pissed off at Sharon. I'm sorry, but you can't stay at our place anymore."

"Shit! I knew that this was going to happen, but where the hell am I going to crash?"

"I'll ask some friends to see if y'all can put your head down at their place for a short while."

"Yeah, I'll check with some friends too." It was becoming clear to me that I was truly homeless.

"Stan, let's look around for a place to rent together."

"Dixie, I can't afford a place right now, plus I owe money to the whole world."

"With my full-time salary and the weekend money you make here, we can do it."

"Okay, I have no options, so let's give it a shot."

We drove to Dixie's place, not knowing where I was going to spend the night. Sharon wasn't home yet, so Dixie invited me in for a beer. After my first sip, Sharon arrived. Her eyes shot daggers through me. Dixie handed me the car keys so that I could at least sit in the car and we could figure something out. We didn't.

I spent the night in her '78 Diplomat. For the next week, her car became my home. One night, I tried to get comfortable in the backseat covered with a smelly blanket retrieved from the trunk. I stared at the stained ceiling and had a conversation with myself.

How did you get here to this place? Look how far you have fallen. You were going to be the head of a stellar record company, attending all the awards shows, standing in the spotlight with your star artists accepting awards, and paying back all the loans and investments with dividends. You were living in a three-bedroom house in a nice neighborhood in Mississauga, Ontario. Now you are sleeping in a car in Tennessee with no home and no car of your own. How are you going to get out of this? Stan Campbell, you are homeless, living in a car. Maybe you'll end up on Lower Broadway with the rest of the homeless men begging for quarters and drinking cheap wine from a brown paper bag.

"Stop!" I yelled at myself in the darkness. "I have got to get out of this downward spiral. I caused it. I can get out of it."

I fell asleep with visions of my kids in my head, trying to imagine what they were doing and why I couldn't have a normal humdrum life in the suburbs, in love permanently with an adorable wife, and going to softball practice or school recitals with my kids.

*　*　*

After a week in Dixie's car, she told me on the way to the station that she had an oddball songwriter friend, Sammy Goldman, who was willing to let me crash at his place, but I would have to sleep on the floor. The floor probably wouldn't be as comfortable as the backseat of Dixie's car, but it was in a building that had an address. I accepted the offer.

We went over to Sammy's tiny house that evening. It was dilapidated, and that was just the outside. The inside looked like there had been an explosion and the Hazmat crew hadn't shown up yet. Sammy was a geeky songwriter guy. He wasn't home very much. No wonder. If I had owned the place, I'd never go home!

The first night was hell. The floor was hardwood and not soft, even with a mat under me. I woke up often and scratched a lot. I figured that it was the mat or the itchy woolen Army blanket. Sometime in the middle of the night, I had to get up to pee. As soon as I flicked on the light next to me, I saw movement in my peripheral vision. I looked down. A battalion of cockroaches scurried out from around where I had been sleeping and dashed into hiding. There were big ones and babies.

Apparently Sammy was out somewhere, presumably buying a few dozen Roach Motels. I was *living* at the Roach Motel!

I put up with the roaches and the hard floor for two more weeks and even got to drive Sammy's very old Mercedes car around town. I come across as an eccentric homeless guy with a Benz.

In the meantime, Dixie, who had a home that had a telephone, found us a potential apartment in of all places, Brentwood! Brentwood is to Nashville what Brentwood is to Los Angeles, without O.J. Simpson. It's where the most of the big-name country stars and high-paid record executives lived. We inspected the condo, owned by a cranky couple who seemed to like us, especially Dixie, who could have taught P.T. Barnum how to string a line of bullshit.

We moved in with our table and Dixie's 10-year-old daughter, Raylene who had just returned from a month-long vacation with her uncle in the Virgin Islands. We found two chairs at a garage sale. She owned her own bed, and since we hadn't had much alone time, that's all I cared about. Life was good. I was living large with an address in Brentwood! *Fucking Brentwood!* Within two weeks I had come up in the world, from sleeping in a car to living in Brentwood, Tennessee. We had no money for food, gas, or furniture, but we were living in Brentwood. We were the Brentwood Hillbillies!

We were in love for a while, or was it lust? I think that up to at least that point in my life, I couldn't tell the difference.

At work, at WSIX, there was rumor that I might get hired full time. As it was, I was getting all the part-time work that came up. I was also doing voice-overs for a Brentwood ad agency.

When Dixie and I moved in together, our living room had no furniture in it. We bought a second-hand couch and a tiny TV, the last of the old black and whites. With the help of the nice manager at the Third National Bank, who still believed in me, I managed somehow to get a loan for a car. We got a phone.

"Hello, Dad?"

"Roddie!" I was thrilled to hear his voice.

"Dad, how do you feel now about me coming to Nashville to visit with my girlfriend?"

"Yes! Yes! Y'all come on down!" Damn! I was picking up the southern twang.

"Dad, you're not back with Veronica are you?"

I had called him to let him know that we had split.

"No, the coast is clear." We both laughed.

"I will be so happy to see you, son." I choked back tears.

Two weeks later Roddie and his girlfriend came to visit us. I had saved every penny I could to entertain them. I felt proud of him and was so happy to have him with me again, and I wished that he could stay, but I knew that he could not remain in the U.S. legally. Even my L-1 visa status in the USA was in question, now that Acclaim Records was almost gone. The other label, 16th Avenue Records, was on life support.

Personally, I was done with the record business, except for maybe producing an artist now and then. I produced another album with Tim Denis and one of Canada's greatest country traditional country singers, Johnny Burke. I still loved the studio and the creativity. Fall approached, and the chill was inside our apartment. The fire had gone out. Dixie came home later and later and was often drunk. I guess it was her turn.

By late fall, Dixie had left WSIX and was working as a secretary at an oil company. She worked long hours. At least I assumed that she was working. On Thanksgiving weekend she announced that she needed to go to a company convention in Atlanta. A convention, on the second biggest holiday of the year? She swore that it was true. I was suspicious. She left on Thursday, and when I had not heard from her by Saturday afternoon, I called Dixie's office and actually found someone doing weekend work there. I asked the gentleman about the Atlanta convention.

"What convention?"

"The company convention in Atlanta."

"Sir, are you aware that it's Thanksgiving weekend? There is definitely no company convention in Atlanta, or anywhere else."

"Thank you." I felt stupid for even asking.

I visualized Dixie in a hotel room somewhere doing what we had done at the Red Roof Inn. I became insane with anger and jealousy. I wanted to kill her and the son-of-a-bitch who was with her. It crossed my mind that I probably deserved this fate. I was the victim this time.

Dixie arrived home on Sunday night at 9:00 p.m. After telling her what I knew about the non-existent convention, she admitted that she had spent the weekend with the company vice president. He was younger, better looking, and taller. Of course he was taller! Everybody was taller than me! I was about to get stuck with an apartment that I couldn't afford and...I would be alone. I had to live with me.

Some breakups are sad. Some breakups are hostile. Dixie and I broke up with a car chase through Brentwood. Our car, an '85 Pontiac Grand Am, was registered in my name and financed through a loan solely in my name at Third National Bank. Dixie viewed the ownership differently. While I was at work, she drove the car away from the station parking lot. Upon discovering that the car was gone, I borrowed a car from one of the girls in the office, in an effort to find Dixie, and my car.

I found Dixie at the apartment taking the last of the garage sale junk. When she spotted me, she jumped into the Grand Am and drove off. I followed. She drove faster. I tailgated her through the fashionable streets of Brentwood, faster and faster, ignoring stop signs and red lights, and at one point we drove over a sidewalk, arriving in a cloud of smoke, burning rubber and dust in front of the police station. She ran into the cop shop.

Twenty seconds later, two cops came out the door with Dixie. She was screaming that I was trying to steal her car. The police ordered me out of the car and commanded me to put my hands behind my head. For a few minutes, everyone was yelling, to the delight of a highly entertained crowd that rapidly materialized.

"Everyone shut up!" one cop shouted.

I thought that he was about pull out his gun. We shut up.

"Sir, show me your driver's license, car title, and proof of insurance," he shouted at me.

I obeyed and handed him all the paperwork. He took a few minutes to look it over and then declared the verdict.

"First of all, I should charge both of you with reckless driving. However, I won't if you both leave here, peacefully, in opposite directions. And you, Miss Carrington, must hand Mr. Campbell the keys to what is legally his car."

"But this is—"

"Miss Carrington! If you want to dispute ownership of this automobile, hire an attorney, but I don't want to hear from either of you again. Is that understood?"

"Yes, sir." We both chimed in.

I left the borrowed car across the street to retrieve later. I drove away with the Grand Am. Dixie called a cab. I had not learned anything. My dangerous liaisons with women were about to get deadly.

We Won The Lottery

I gave the Brentwood condo landlady notice that I was moving out. Normally that would have been a problem, but luckily she wanted the property for her son. In the meantime, Veronica and I still had unfinished business with the record company. We spoke more often and became friends.

Not long after I had moved to Nashville, I met up with a singer/songwriter friend I had known when I worked at CFGM in Toronto. His name was Bob Van Dyke. Bob was a big guy, rotund, with dark afro-style hair, and a darker sense of humor. I told Bob about my homeless situation. After all, I continued earning lousy money as a part-time DJ at WSIX, so I could not afford an apartment by myself. Bob suggested a roommate service. It worked almost like a dating service. I paid a fee, and the service matched me up with a couple of potential people.

One of the matches was a lady named, Kay Birdsong. The Birdsong name had me envisioning a little old lady with doilies, teddy bears and a pussy-cat. I figured that a home-spun, old-timey environment would be just what I needed. The roommate service people contacted Miss Birdsong and then called me to say that she could be interested.

I suggested a meeting during happy hour at the lounge at The Holiday Inn on West End Avenue. Frugal Bob Van Dyke tipped me off to this great place. With a dollar twenty-five cent draft beer, one had access to the free all-you-can-eat tacos on Thursdays. That was something else I needed. Cheap food!

The roommate people finally gave me Kay's phone number. I called her to confirm our appointment. She said that she would be wearing a red dress and carrying a white purse and that she had long, dark brown hair. Dark hair? Maybe she didn't crochet doilies, but she sure sounded older with a southern accent. I described myself and where I would be sitting.

I sat at the rear near the window as I spotted a red dress pass through the Thursday crowd. I stood to get a better gander at the stunningly gorgeous lady, maybe 30 years old, scanning the room for someone. *This cannot be her.* She looked my way. She gave me a smile and nodded as if to say, *is that you?* I hurriedly glanced around to see if there was a little old lady in the room wearing a red dress and carrying a white purse. There was not. I smiled and nodded too.

She moved slowly to my table and said softly, "You must be Stan."

"You must be Kay." I still thought that maybe she was the wrong Kay there to meet with another Stan.

"Yes, nice to meet you, Stan. How are you?" She spoke with a charming southern accent.

I couldn't believe that this could happen to me. I could be *her* roommate? My male friends were going to be so damn envious, but how was I going to survive living in the same apartment with this striking woman? She was sweet and soft-spoken. We engaged in casual conversation and then discussed her apartment which was out by Percy Priest Lake on the south-east side of Nashville. Then, the dream of living with Kay evaporated.

"Stan, because I don't know you, I will need references, and I would like to maybe meet a couple of your friends."

"Sure, I think I can do that. By the way, isn't it odd that you are accepting a male roommate?"

"No. I had a female roommate before, but she always wanted to borrow my clothes."

"I'll try not to do that." The ice was broken.

We set a date three days later for her to meet my friends, Devon O'Day, Bob Van Dyke, Charlene, and Chapel. She liked all of them. Our meeting turned into another happy hour party. I was approved to move in. My elation turned into another downer when Kay told us that she had a boyfriend. Damn! Kay had me follow her to check out the apartment, at night, in the most circuitous route imaginable. I guess she still wasn't completely comfortable with me.

I looked over the apartment that had been designed especially for roommates. It had a bathroom and bedroom on each end, with a living room and a kitchen in the middle. It was perfect, and the rent was right. I really liked Kay. But how could I control myself living with such an adorable, beautiful lady?

Over the next few months, my lust for lovely Kay evolved into a more sisterly fancy. We became best platonic friends. Occasionally we shared a bottle of wine in front of the fireplace, told stories to each other for hours, and then said good-night and went to our separate rooms. Our bond became one of the most endearing relationships in my life.

* * *

Two days before Christmas in 1986, Veronica called me to tell me that she was going home to Ontario to see her family for Christmas and New Year's. Several days into January, she called me from Toronto to tell me that she had applied for a U.S. Immigration Department lottery. I chuckled and suggested that she was wasting her time because millions apply for the lottery. I wished her good luck.

My legal status in the U.S. was becoming an issue as my L-1 visa was due to expire in September. I had already renewed it twice, and no further renewals were permitted. I needed to apply for a Green Card. If the INS denied my application, I would have to return to Canada. In spite of my down period, I had grown to love the USA and especially, Nashville. I was confident that I could eventually be far more successful south of the border. In my radio career, I enjoyed positive reinforcement in the USA that I had never received in Canada.

In May, Veronica called. "Guess what I got in the mail today?"

"I don't know. Probably a summons, right?"

"No! An official offer from US Immigration to apply for a Green Card!"

"No shit!"

"Yes, I won the immigration lottery! One of the questions is, do you want to include your spouse, and since we aren't divorced, I have the option to include you. Do you want me to include you?"

"Are you kidding? Of course I do!"

"We have a lot of paperwork to fill out, and we need to get medical exams."

We spent most of the summer having pictures taken, being x-rayed, and prodded. I had to list every place I had ever lived, which took two extra pages, not to mention three marriages and two divorces.

My personal life became more complicated. The search for the ideal woman of my long-ago dreams persisted. As a desperate move, I placed an ad in the singles section of the Nashville Banner newspaper. The first day that the ad ran, I received a call from a lady named Elaine. She told me that she lived out in the country near Murfreesboro, Tennessee. She agreed to meet me for lunch in Brentwood.

The most memorable event surrounding our date was that she stumbled and fell into the shrubs by the front door of the restaurant. I tried to catch her, but I was too late. The mishap did give me a chance to put my arms around her. Elaine was rather attractive, around thirty-five, with wandering eyes that seemed to dart around as though she was watching for someone.

"My husband is deceased," she said, peering down at the table.

"I'm so sorry. What happened to him, if you don't mind me asking?"

"Well, it was strange, really. He and my brother-in-law both died around the same time."

"Oh, God, that's terrible."

"Yes, it was. The cause of their deaths was never fully determined. We think it might have been food poisoning. It was an awful time."

"Really? I'm sure that it was a dreadful time for you," I said, as I placed my hand on hers.

"It was, and I miss him so much. I have had to take over the family business."

"Oh, what kind of business was he in?"

"He and my brother-in-law owned a jewelry store."

I imagined this poor, lonely, heartbroken, pretty lady out there in Murfreesboro trying to handle her late husband's business. I could at least console her. We finished lunch and agreed to meet again a few days later for drinks at happy hour, where there would be free food.

I met Elaine at the Music City Sheraton for happy hour and complimentary hors d'oeuvres. When we went back to her car, we kissed and generally smooched before saying good-bye but not before she issued a tempting invitation.

"Stan, I really like you. Why don't you come down and spend a few days with me in Murfreesboro at my farm?"

"Sure! I would love that."

I envisioned a weekend rolling in the hay. Real hay.

"Wonderful! Can you come up week after next, maybe Friday afternoon?"

"Sure, I can do that."

To supplement my paltry income, I had begun doing live Nashville news reports on a few radio stations around the country from my home phone. It meant getting up 6:00 a.m. and perusing the newspapers, trade magazines, and watching TV for any breaking star stories. It was Wednesday morning, two days before I was to visit Elaine on the farm in Murfreesboro.

It was a big news day but nothing that had anything to do with Music City. I screamed so loud that Kay came running to my room to see if I was okay.

"Holy shit! No!" I watched the story unfold on TV screen.

"Stan, what's wrong?" Kay asked from behind the closed door.

"I don't believe this! Kay, come in here!"

Kay and I watched a live news report from the front steps of the courthouse. A woman was being escorted in handcuffs up the steps by a robust policewoman. The reporter said that the woman had been charged with the murder of her husband and brother-in-law. It was Elaine, the girl I had kissed just two days earlier. The bodies were found buried on her farm property...the farm where I was supposed to spend the weekend. Maybe eternity.

"I guess this means that you won't be seeing her this weekend?" my smart-ass friend Bob said, as I told him the news on the phone.

*   *   *

"Hi, Stan, I listen to you every evening. I love your voice." She told me that her name was Sharon.

She was a regular caller whenever I was on the air. She told me that she worked in Nashville but lived in Hendersonville, north of Nashville.

"Stan, I'd love to meet you sometime to say hello and see you face-to-face."

"Hmm, I don't know if I that's a good idea."

I had been in radio long enough to know that the charm and sexiness of a voice is most often inversely proportional to the beauty. However, Sharon didn't sound like a lot of the nutcases that often call radio station request lines, so I broke the radio rule and agreed to meet her for a drink at a bar in Hendersonville.

She was waiting for me when I arrived. She was a bit overweight, perhaps thirty-five, and wore wire-rim glasses. We each had a Jack and Coke, and then I ordered up two more. That was all I could afford. She offered to buy a couple more. We got kind of loose and silly, and in a moment of temporary lunacy, I invited her to come back to my place. Kay was in Kentucky visiting her folks, so I had the place to myself.

We attacked each other, and in about the time that two people could light up a cigarette, which I didn't, she freaked me out.

"Stan, I'm sorry, I have to go. My husband is going to be wondering where I am."

"Your *husband?* You're *married?*" I whispered, as though he might be hiding in the closet.

"I thought I told you."

"No! I think I would have remembered that."

"Well, we don't get along, and he treats me like crap. He's a dyed-in-the-wool southern redneck."

I had an instant vision of an ugly guy with three brown teeth, driving a pickup truck with a loaded shotgun in a rifle rack in the back window. *Deliverance* played on the movie screen in my head.

"Absolutely, I think you had better go," I said, feeling a chill and a sense of urgency.

"Yes, he can get really angry if I'm out too late."

"Oh yeah, I'll bet, especially if you've been in bed screwing a radio DJ."

Sharon left in a hurry but suggested that she wanted to see me the next night. I didn't think that was a good idea. Then again, I had not had many good ideas in the recent past.

The next night, Sharon called and said that she desperately wanted to talk to me about something. Not having a reputation for smart decisions, I agreed. She came over to my place. No profound conversations ensued, just more of the previous night. I had to admit that I liked her, but truthfully, I liked every woman who liked me.

I carried on the forbidden affair with Sharon for a few weeks, even though my conscience insisted that it was very wrong, until one night, the situation elevated to code red. Sharon called me from home and explained that she just wanted to hear my voice. In mid-conversation, after some descriptive talk about bedtime manners, I detected a click on the phone as her volume dropped.

"Sharon...what was that?"

"I didn't hear anything."

"Do you have another phone somewhere else in the house?"

I was already jumpy.

"No. We don't have an extension. This is the only phone in the house."

"Are you sure your husband doesn't have a phone in the basement or in the gar—?"

"*You fucking son-of-a-bitch! I'm gonna blow your fucking head off! I know where you work, and I know where you live, and I will find you, and I will fucking kill you! You think you can fuck my wife and get away with it?"*

Click!

I assumed that that was a rhetorical question. I hung up and threw up.

Next!

For weeks, I slept under my desk in the office on 16th Avenue that I shared with David Shore, a partner in a satellite radio network project that I had been attempting to develop. After my on-air shift at the station and after scanning the horizon both ways, I sprinted from the studio door to my car to burn rubber out of the parking lot. I lived in fear of a brown pickup truck with a rifle rack in the back window and driven by a madman with a confederate flag baseball cap.

Just as I reached for the car door, a voice came out nowhere, causing me to yell."Fuck!"

"Hi, sweetie! Wanna go for a drink?" It was Sharon in a car next to mine.

"Damn! Are you nuts, Sharon? Are you trying to get us both killed?"

I leapt in behind the wheel of my car and rolled the window down, but just enough to deflect a bullet.

"Nah, don't worry about him. He's all talk."

"All talk? That's the kind of talk that scares me to death. Maybe, *literally* to death."

"Let's go to your place. I miss you."

"No! It's time we ended this. It was not only wrong from the start, but it's hazardous to our health."

"Please." She made a sexy, tempting face compelling me to choose between life, or illicit sex.

I paused and scrutinized the landscape for a sniper crouched behind the grassy knoll.

"Okay, let's get the hell out of here." I stomped on the accelerator.

I wondered if he was a good shot at a fast-moving target.

Following a rapid, racy rendezvous at my apartment, Kay stopped by my room on the way out the door.

"Stan, it's probably none of my business, but I want you to know that I think this isn't right, and Sharon, you need to go home to your husband, and if that's a problem, then file for divorce."

I agreed. "You're right, Kay."

Kay turned to Sharon. "Do you have a picture of your husband?"

"Yes, I do, right here." Sharon dug in her purse.

She pulled out a snapshot of herself with her husband and their kids. I had never seen him before. I experienced an epiphany.

I couldn't stop staring at his face. This was reality. I felt guilt in my gut and sadness for this man who was being betrayed by his wife and me. He didn't appear at all like the backwoods redneck that I had envisioned. Instead he appeared to be a gentle, simple man. In the picture he had his arms around his kids and his wife, Sharon. I felt tears well up.

I said good-bye to Sharon that day. I never wanted to see her again. If there were unhappy family secrets that caused her to crave something more, then I figured that she needed to solve them at home, not in my arms or in my bed. I realized that I should have applied the same model to my marriages.

* * *

During the spring of '87, I spent most of my time with my friends Kay, Charlene, Devon, and Bob and began to find some peace without a romantic or sexual connection to a woman. It wasn't easy. I still romanticized about that perfect woman. I had to find her and my birth mother. On a Friday afternoon in mid May the phone rang and re-routed my life again.

The voice was familiar and not entirely welcome. "Hi Stan, what are y'all doin'?"

"Sitting here talking to Kay. Why do you want to know?"

"Still mad at me are you?"

"No. Not really. I'm over it."

"Hey, what are y'all doin' tonight?" It was my former flame, Dixie.

I had to think fast. "Uh, I think Kay and I are going to see a movie."

"You lie! Don't be scared. I'm not invitin' y'all out on a date."

"That's probably good because I'm busy until Jesus comes back."

"I have someone I wancha ta meet. She's a good friend of mine, and I told her about y'all."

"Oh shit! What did you tell her?"

"I told her that you were a real stud!" She laughed out loud.

I wasn't laughing. "Oh, screw off! If I am such a stud, how come you needed to find a better one?"

"Oh, come on, Stan, don't y'all get pissy on me. Come on down to the Stockyard tonight for a drink and meet her. Her name is Susan."

"I don't think so. I have plans for..."

"Oh, bullshit, I know y'all were lyin' about you and Kay goin' to a movie."

I hesitated. "Okay, but only for one drink. I'm broke and I'm tired."

"Hey, Stan, you won't be sorry. She's a keeper."

"Right, just like all the rest...including you."

"I promise you, you will not be disappointed."

"Yeah, well, she better not be some old redneck broad, desperate and dateless."

"Stan baby, would I do that to you?"

"Yes."

"Nah, really, she's as cute as a button, she's blonde, five-foot-five with a pencil-thin waist. And, Stan, you will love this...big boobs!"

"I'm not impressed by big boobs."

"Whatever! See you at 7:00 at the Stockyard."

*   *   *

It had been months since I had spoken with Roddie or Mark. I called them. No one answered. Roddie had visited me in Nashville almost a year before. He had ridden all the way from Toronto on his motorcycle, so I was naturally worried about him riding and maybe drinking. Mark was always hard to find.

It had been what seemed like years since I had talked to Helen or Michael. I had all but given up trying to communicate with them. Barbara was the gatekeeper, and even though it had been ten years since we split, she still hated me just as fervently. Barbara reinforced my suspicions that Michael and Helen hated me too and had written me off as their Dad. They probably had a new Dad, a stepfather whom they loved and admired.

Nevertheless, I wrote a letter to Helen. I actually addressed it to Chrissy. I hoped that it would get past her mother, the censor. I told her that I still loved her and hoped that someday she would forgive me and that maybe sometime in the future I could tell her my side of the story, not that my side was without fault.

I also missed Mom and Pop back in Jamesville West. They had celebrated their fiftieth wedding anniversary two years earlier. I had driven alone from Nashville to Nova Scotia to help them celebrate, along with the whole parish. I knew that they hated the fact that I was so far away in Tennessee. I was anxious to get back to visit them and away from my crazy Nashville life. If they had only known how I was living. They thought that I was a big Nashville radio star.

*   *   *

At 6:45, I splashed on my favorite cheap cologne and slipped on my coolest shirt and headed to downtown Nashville to the sprawling Stockyard Restaurant on Second Avenue. Upon entering, one could still detect a smell of cow shit from the early days when it was a real stockyard. I was ready for more bullshit from Dixie. She sat at a high table at the back with an attractive, slender, blonde lady.

"Hey, Stan, you're lookin' good," she said in her best sales pitch.

"Hi Dixie."

"I'd like to introduce y'all to my friend Susan."

"Hi, Susan. Nice to meet you."

"Hi, Stan. Dixie told me all about you."

"Susan, don't believe anything she tells you."

We ordered drinks and told jokes, while Susan and I exchanged a bit of history. She was originally from a small town in Illinois. She seemed like a nice lady. She told me that she had a 12-year-old daughter, Natalie. After a couple of hours nursing drinks, I asked Susan if she would like to go with me to see a movie the next night. She agreed. It was refreshing to be able to date someone who wasn't married or had killed her husband. I finished my drink and excused myself, stating that I needed to get home because I had to work early on Saturday morning.

On Saturday evening, I picked Susan up at her place in the south end. We stopped and had a light dinner at O'Charley's. On the way out of the restaurant, she asked what I was doing on Independence Day.

"Oh, actually, I made plans with Veronica to go see a big band performance at Riverfront Park."

"You mean, with your ex-wife?"

I hesitated. "Uh, yes, well she's not my ex yet. We are separated, but we are friends. Veronica and I haven't lived together for over a year. It's not like it's an open marriage or anything. We are in the process of getting a divorce."

"That's crazy, going out with your estranged wife." Susan was clearly upset.

The rest of our date was a bit tense.

Susan and I continued to date for the rest of the summer of '87. My best friend and roommate Kay cautioned me that Susan was not right for me.

* * *

The pressure from creditors was alarming. As a result of the failed record business and the Cedar Creek management fiasco, I was indebted to a plethora of individuals and organizations. The bigger the business, the greater the intimidation became. Most friends and family were more understanding and aware that sometimes the loftiest of visions do not happen as planned, yet these were the very people that I cared most about. I had no money to pay anyone. I was frequently late with the rent to Kay and sometimes even pilfered food from her stash in the fridge when I had no money to buy my own.

In my next episode of temporary insanity, I had chosen to get married again. Marriage number four! Would this be the one, just as I had assumed that Sis, Barbara, and Veronica were the ones? After some disagreements, Susan and I agreed to a wedding date of October 20th, 1987, although Veronica and I were not yet officially divorced, and we had not yet been approved as legal permanent residents of the United States.

Susan was most often pleasant with a great sense of humor, but she was overly sensitive. I discovered early on that it was best to walk on eggshells by being cautious about what I said for fear that it would be perceived as a slight against her or a complaint. It was an acquired skill at which I was a slow learner. My failure to navigate the delicate minefield resulted in explosive verbal combat. I did develop a fleeting moment of clarity thanks to my roommate and best friend Kay.

"Stan, what are you doing marrying Susan? You guys always seem to be fighting. That doesn't sound like a solid, happy marriage ahead."

"Well, no, but I think we'll be okay after we get settled and she doesn't feel threatened by Veronica or concerned about my Green Card and a full-time job."

"Stan, there's another reason to not get married until you clean up that mess."

"Kay, I know that what you're saying makes sense. I think I will talk to Susan to see if we can put off the wedding until maybe early next year."

"Good idea, Stan. I care about you and would hate to see you get hurt again."

I believed that she did care about me. I began to realize how much Kay meant to me as a cherished friend. Maybe the right woman was right under my nose, but I viewed her as a caring sister, the sister that I never had. Maybe I did have a sister somewhere, but I doubted if I would ever find her.

Kay's advice should have been a warning, but for some reason, it wasn't. I also cared about Susan's daughter Natalie. I was three years away from being 50. I wanted to settle down and put an end to my rowdy, careless life. I wanted a family again, if I couldn't have my own back.

* * *

On Monday morning in mid August the phone rang. It was my boss, Greg Penner.

"Hey, Stan, can you come in to the station tomorrow morning to meet with the general manger, Bill Petersen."

"Oh, shit. What did I do now?"

"Nothing, man. As you know, the station was sold to a group in Houston, and we have a new consultant. I wasn't supposed to tell you this, but he is interested in hiring you full time for the afternoon drive."

"You're kidding!"

"No, I'm not, but the boss is looking at all his options."

I hung up and screamed. Then, I realized that I had a problem. Veronica and I had not yet received our Green Cards. I called her.

"What's the latest on our approval for Green Cards?"

"Oh, didn't I tell you? We have to go to the U.S. Consulate in Toronto on October 1st for an interview and then swearing in, if we are approved."

I spent the rest of the conversation telling Veronica that I was getting married again as soon as our divorce was final and I got my Green Card, if we were approved. I also had to be cleared on my medical exams. But I was worried about a potential problem.

"You're getting married again so soon? Are you crazy?"

"Yeah, probably. I hate to be alone."

"You're not alone. You are with Kay, and you have lots of friends here."

"That's not the same. I don't sleep with Kay."

"Is that all you need, someone to sleep with?

"No, but it helps."

"Apparently, you have had no problem finding women to sleep with, even married women," she said with a cynical laugh.

I didn't know she knew about that.

"It's not just about sex. I want intimacy and a normal settled-down life with a family before it's too late. Plus, Susan has a 12-year-old daughter, so I can be a dad again."

We made arrangements to drive to Toronto. I knew that traveling to Toronto alone with Veronica was not going to go over well with Susan.

As we got closer to the date with the U.S. Consulate in Toronto, I became more fearful of being rejected and sent back to Canada. Where would I work? I had never been granted much respect in radio in Canada, and if I returned from the States, I would be viewed as a failure. On the positive side, I would be geographically closer to my kids. I tried to calm my own fears, but I couldn't tell anyone about them, except Bob Van Dyke over a beer at the San Antonio Taco Company.

"Hey, man, you're going to have your Green Card in a few weeks."

"I hope so, but I'm really worried."

"Worried? About what?

"My medical exam, I said."

"Your medical exam? I'd be worried about my *mental* exam if I was you." Bob laughed.

"No, I'm serious. I'm freaking out. I'm terrified that I could have AIDS."

This was at the beginning of the AIDS epidemic.

"Stan, why would you think you have AIDS?

"Have you seen some of the women I've been with?" I suddenly dropped my voice level as the two Vanderbilt girls next to us looked our way. "I'm fucking terrified."

Bob got serious. "I'm sure you will be fine."

I wasn't so sure.

On Friday morning I drove to WSIX Radio & TV on Mufreesboro Road to meet with Greg, the program director, and Mr. Petersen to talk about a possible full-time job.

I was sick with a combination of fear and excitement. It could be a full-time gig, and yet I wasn't sure if I would be approved for a Green Card, and my L-1 visa was about to expire. This could be the beginning of a renewed radio career in the USA. Scotty Mason had been the afternoon drive guy but was leaving to launch his own business. I had heard that his salary was around thirty-five grand. That would be a huge improvement in my life and my self-respect.

Greg ushered me into his office. Petersen was nowhere in sight. The staff referred to him as *Mr. Cool* because of his expensive double-breasted black suits, his glossy black hair, the red hankie in his pocket, the flower on his lapel, and, of course, his red Jaguar convertible.

I assumed that Mr. Cool was too busy and maybe too cool to meet with a peon. After all, he had just closed a deal with a new morning show host from KLAC in Los Angeles for what was rumored to be one million dollars for a three-year contract. I had heard that the company had thrown in a new Jaguar for fun and had brought him to the station in a helicopter. I figured that since I was going to have the second best on-air gig, my salary might be pretty awesome. Hey, after all, the new station owners seemed to be throwing money around.

"Stan, Petersen asked me to meet with you and offer you the afternoon shift. You would begin in two weeks if you are able."

"Able? Damn right Greg!"

"Great. Petersen said that he will start you at twenty grand."

I stared at him. Was he joking?

"Twenty thousand? Like, twenty thousand dollars a year?"

Not that I was in his league, but the new morning guy was being paid more than that every *month!*

"Yes. Twenty thousand. Is that a problem, Stan?"

"Well, yes, it *is* a problem." I felt like I had fallen off the uphill side of a roller coaster.

"Well, I can go and ask Petersen if he can up it a bit."

"Yes, please do, Greg. That's not much more than minimum wage. The morning guy is getting a fucking million dollars." It occurred to me that the company had probably blown their budget already and that the rest of us got the peanut shells.

Greg came back from Petersen's office in less than a thirty-second commercial and said, "He'll go up to twenty-two thousand and that's it."

"Really? I understand that my predecessor, Scotty, was making thirty-five grand."

"Sorry, man. Petersen says take it or leave it because there are dozens of other guys who would be happy to work here."

I knew that Petersen was right. Most people in radio would die for an on-air job in Nashville, Music City, USA.

I realized that I had no choice. I desperately needed to earn a regular salary and also have health benefits. I had to get my Green Card quick. Maybe I could get a raise later if I proved myself.

I accepted begrudgingly, but the payback was coming.

I Swear

On Thursday, October 1, 1987, at 7:00 in the morning, Veronica and I lined up outside the United States Consulate in Toronto to receive our Permanent Resident cards. We had heard that there were no guarantees that approval was routine. I was especially tense. There were approximately one hundred other people in the line-up. The curt U.S. Immigration officers called out names. They processed several dozen people throughout the morning and then stopped for lunch. I was not hungry.

They came back at 1:30 and called more names. I pictured myself loading up my old Pontiac Grand Am and driving back to Canada. Fall was coming. I didn't want to see another Canadian winter. I saw myself lining up at the welfare office. It was a drab, depressing black and gray picture.

Time passed. The crowd thinned, and more names were called. Not ours. I felt ill and trembled, probably from hunger. The clock moved forward to 3:45, and yet our names were not called.

"What if they lost our paperwork?" I asked Veronica.

"I don't think that could happen." She was obviously not as jittery as I was.

"What if they left all the losers to the end?" I scanned the room for noticeable losers.

I wanted to tell Veronica that I was worried that I might have AIDS, but I didn't want to tell her why. We had been intimate a few times during our separation, which would mean—

"Campbell! Mataseejay!" someone shouted from down the hall.

It was almost 4:00.

"Oh, God! That's us! Say a prayer." I made a silent promise to God that I would behave from that moment on if He would open this door.

A stern-faced security officer ushered us into a drab room, where a graveyard-serious lady sat behind a desk.

"Please raise your right hand, and put your left hand on the bible, and repeat after me."

She read the oath slowly, and we repeated it. The only part of the oath I remember is that I would not become a burden on the United States of America.

I wanted to sing the oath! Following the oath, for the first time and only for a brief moment, I detected the slightest smile as she said, "Welcome to the United States of America."

I wanted to shout, *Thank God Almighty, I am free at last!*

Veronica and I had a drink together and celebrated like two old friends.

* * *

We arrived back in Nashville, where our divorce became final two weeks later. On October 20, 1987, I took another oath. I swore *until death do us part* for the fourth time, this time to Susan in front of a Davidson County Judge, accompanied by our closest friends and Susan's family. I had invited Mark and Roddie, but Nashville was a tough trip for both of them.

Smart ass Mark said later, "I'm sorry that I couldn't make it to your wedding, Dad. I'll get the next one."

On Monday following our wedding, I was back to work at WSIX, where I was told that the company could no longer keep me on unless I had a Green Card. What timing! I proudly showed off my new U.S. Green Card and social security number.

Several weeks later, while I was on the air, I received a phone call from Cincinnati from a former radio associate from Toronto, Glen Barrett. He was now a consultant at a new country radio station, WBVE in Cincinnati. He was on speakerphone with

WBVE's general manager, Neil Kearney. I hate those things because you never know who else is in the room.

"Stan, how would you like to come to Cincinnati?" Neil Kearney inquired.

"I don't know. I never thought about it. I love it here in Nashville."

Then Glen Barrett spoke. "Stan, I suggested to Neil that you might be a good choice to be our operations manager. It's a new station, and we are about to take on the country music giant in Cincinnati, WUBE. Interested?"

"Well, yes, I am interested."

I reckoned that this gig had to pay more than the paltry twenty-two thousand that WSIX was paying me, plus it was a management position.

"Can you fly up on Saturday?" Neil asked. "I'll send you an airline ticket."

"Saturday? Yeah, sure."

"I'll pick you up at the airport and show you around, and we can talk more about what we plan to do to kick WUBE's ass."

On Saturday, I caught a morning flight to Cincinnati, where tough, fast-talking Neil Kearney met me at the airport. He appeared to me to be the quintessential BMW-driving, assertive yuppie. We toured the studios and the offices downtown and discussed programming strategies. He suggested that I go back to Nashville to think about it and then fly back up the next weekend and bring my bride.

The following weekend Susan and I flew to Cincinnati. This time, we talked dollars and cents. He offered, and I accepted, more than double my WSIX salary. It was a done deal. We were moving, even though I had mixed feelings. I loved living in Nashville.

On Monday morning, I drove to WSIX early to see Greg, the program director. I handed him my written two weeks' notice. Greg understood that I could not turn down a promotion and the much higher salary. Mr. Cool was not as supportive. He would not tolerate a minion walking away from him and his kingdom. He gave a message to Greg to pass on to me.

"Mr. Peterson says he wants you to clean out your desk and get your shit out of here. His words not mine."

"Are you kidding? I gave him two weeks' notice. I am being more than fair."

"I'm sorry, man. He wants you out now."

"That fucking son of a bitch! Well, he still has to pay me my salary for two weeks."

Greg went down the hall and was back in thirty seconds.

"He says he won't pay you a cent." Greg was clearly embarrassed. "I'm sorry, man. It's not my call."

"Well, fuck Petersen. I'll sue the bastard," I said, loud enough for Mr. Cool to hear me down the hall.

I stormed out and called the Tennessee State Labor Standards office. The next day, Greg called to tell me that a paycheck was at the front desk. It was sweet revenge against a guy who had low-balled me on salary and then tried to screw me out of my last paycheck. I ran into Mr. Cool three years later in a men's room in Hollywood, California. He reached out to shake my hand. I shook his with my wet hand and walked out the door.

I started at WBVE in Cincinnati on November 16, 1987, and lived at the Holiday Inn until after Christmas. Until we could rent a house, I drove back to Nashville every other weekend to see Susan and Natalie. Natalie wasn't thrilled to see me. I was the one who had shown up and turned her life upside down.

When I went home at Christmas, thirty seconds after I stepped through the door, Susan and I were involved in another fight, which did nothing to engender affection from Natalie. By Christmas Day, the fight was over. I don't think either one of us knew what had initiated it.

It didn't take long for the bill collectors to find me. I had not even received my first paycheck in Cincinnati when calls from banks and collection agencies began. I tried to tell the insistent nasty callers that I had begun a new job, but they didn't care. They threatened to garnish my first paycheck. I knew that if that happened, I might be fired before I began. The collection people representing all the record company vendors and the banks who had supported me were now unrelenting and threatening.

To complicate matters even further, Veronica was pursuing me to pay her half of the business debts. I was furious. She had encouraged me to get into the record business and artist management business, and we had gone into it together.

I had to do something and do it promptly, or I would be sleeping in a car again...with a wife and a child. After Susan and Natalie arrived in Cincinnati, I hesitantly accepted a friend's advice and visited a bankruptcy attorney. I strode into his office feeling lower than the belly of a snake in a wagon track. I left, still feeling horribly guilty but with a huge burden lifted from my shoulders. I filed Chapter 7, claiming almost one hundred and thirty thousand dollars in debt.

Creditors warned me that filing for bankruptcy would ruin my credit. What credit? I had been sleeping in a car and on a floor with cockroaches. I had no hope of ever paying off such an enormous debt, and I would have been fired from my new job, leaving me with zero income.

Susan and I settled down to married bliss, with routine fights. Natalie was not happy. At 13, she had to begin life again at a new school.

The new job was fun, challenging, and exciting at times. I faked my way through the first few months but learned quickly. Neil was frequently a pain in the ass with his speakerphone, but somehow we got along and enjoyed mutual respect. I also had a great staff.

I enjoyed my position at WBVE, and I was back in radio and in the USA. I had never felt so accepted and successful in all my years on radio in Canada. I received media attention and felt as though I could potentially be even more successful. I hadn't dreamed quite as big as the job that had landed in my lap by accident.

I had been at WBVE for a year and a half when consultant Mike Cannon called to chat for a few minutes and then said good-bye in a hurry.

"Hey, man, gotta run. I have to give Bob Guerra, the ops manager at KLAC in Los Angeles, a call. He's searching for a program director."

My antenna went up. Could I actually throw my hat in the ring for that job, in biggest radio market in the USA?

"Oh, really?" I replied, trying to sound only mildly interested.

"Yeah, Bob is searching for a new program director and morning man."

"Okay, Mike, I better let you go."

KLAC was the biggest heritage country music station in the USA, based in Los Angeles. Did I dare dream that big? Could I seriously host a radio morning show in, of all places, Hollywood? Oddly enough, somewhere in my box of old photographs I had a picture of me taken in 1980 in front of KLAC, when Veronica and I had visited L.A.

Hooray For Hollywood!

I hung up the phone with Mike Cannon and called Gerry House at WSIX in Nashville. He knew people.

"Hey, Gerry, you worked at KLAC, so I assume that you are still on good terms with the people there?"

"Sure, Stan, what do you need?"

"I want to get the inside story on the operations manager, Bob Guerra. He's looking to hire a combination P.D. and morning host."

"You want to work in *L.A.?*" He made it sound like I wanted to move to North Korea.

"Hell, yeah! If you think I would have a shot at it."

"Stan, you want me to give Bobby a call and put in a good word for you?"

"Sure!" I did not expect that. "That would be great, Gerry. Thank You!"

Less than ten minutes later, Mr. Guerra called me.

"I hear you're interested in going after our morning show job?"

I tried to sound composed while my insides danced. "Yeah, Bob, I heard about it this morning, and I'm interested."

"Stan, I need you to send me an aircheck of your show tomorrow morning and your resume."

"Okay, I actually have an aircheck here that I can send you right away."

"No. I want to hear *tomorrow's* show. I don't want a greatest hits demo. Record tomorrow's show, and don't edit it. I want it raw and then overnight it to me along with your resume."

"Okay, Bob, I'll do it."

Bob was gone, wasting few words.

"Oh shit!" I said to myself.

Most radio on-air people have an aircheck (demo) tape, tightly edited over painstaking hours, which is usually a composite of some of their best moments on air, otherwise known as a greatest hits demo. This was different, and it was high anxiety, but I wanted this gig more than any other job I had ever wanted in my life. This was Hollywood baby! Hollywood!

I immediately began doing a ton of show prep and then tried to get a good night's sleep, but the more I needed to sleep, the more awake I was.

Susan warned me that I should not tell anyone about this dream job, but I couldn't help it. I told everyone and told them to tell no one. I have always had trouble keeping secrets. That's why it was so amusing that I was cleared to top secret while working on the DEW Line in the Arctic.

I slept sporadically but woke up in a great mood. I needed to be in a good frame of mind. Each day this was a challenge. A radio morning-show host has to present a different act each morning, whereas stand-up comedians perform the same act night after night, sometimes for years. On some mornings, thanks to a sleepless night, a hangover, or a bad mood, the show is a dud. Other days, everything runs like clockwork, and the timing and humor is on target.

It happened to be a good day. The morning team of *Proctor & Campbell* worked well. My sidekick Dave Proctor was excited for me and it showed. At 9:00 a.m. when we finished our show, we thought that we had kicked ass. I boxed up the un-edited tape and overnighted it to *L.A.* I waited for twenty-four interminable hours.

At noon the next day, the station receptionist Heather paged me. "Stan, a Bob Guerra is on line two for you."

"Oh shit! Already?"

"Hello, Bob," I answered, in my most self-assured voice.

"Stan, I got your aircheck. I thought I told you not to send your greatest hits tape?" He sounded a bit miffed.

"Pardon me?"

I felt a combination of disappointment that I had upset him and a simultaneous thrill that he thought my single-day unedited aircheck was a greatest hits tape.

"Bob, that was our show from yesterday morning only. It wasn't a greatest hits. It wasn't even edited."

"Really?" He sounded suspicious. "Well, I want you to do another one tomorrow morning. Same deal, and then overnight it to me again, okay?"

Obviously, he wasn't convinced.

"Sure, Bob."

He hung up and I panicked. Having a good day when everything clicks like clockwork is magical. But two days in a row? That almost never happens. For some reason, it did. Maybe it was the adrenalin, but again we somehow produced a fun and funny show. I packed up the tape and called FedEx for pickup.

I waited. Bob did not call back the next day, or the next day after that. I became depressed and then I felt stupid. Against Susan's advice, I had told friends and a few co-workers that I might be going off to do mornings and be the program director in Los Angeles. Hollywood! I was worried and embarrassed. What if the rumor got back to my boss, Neil Kearney? Forget *L.A.* I might end up with *no* job.

Neil and I had planned to go to Nashville in two weeks for the big Country Radio Seminar. I had been excited about going, but all of a sudden, not so much. I had dreams of Hollywood, Malibu, Beverly Hills, movie stars, and proving to my detractors in radio in Toronto that I was more than just a late-night jock.

Heather paged me. "It's Bob Guerra for you on line three."

My heart stopped. Could this be the *sorry, but we've found someone else* call? I had already gone though anguish for another dream job just months earlier. I had spent almost a full day in New York being dined and grilled for the prestigious position of director of programming for the ABC Radio Networks. I came in second to the program director from NBC, who had decided to cross the street. Thank God for unanswered prayers.

I said hello to Bob with the best upbeat attitude I could fake. I didn't want him to think that I was apprehensive, even though I could have been in the Guinness Book of World Records for time spent holding my breath.

"Hey, Stan, are you going to the Country Radio Seminar –in Nashville next week?" He always sounded like he was in a hurry.

"Yes, I am."

"Good. Our consultant Jim Wood and I will be there, and we can meet. Does that work for you?"

"Sure, that would be great!" I said, utilizing my best acting skills to cover my excitement, as I realized that I was still under consideration.

We set a time and a date to meet, and I was off the phone with my spirits high.

Ten days later, at the Opryland Hotel in Nashville at the appointed time, I wore my only black suit, a crisp white shirt, and a red power tie. I strolled down the hall and stood before Bob's door and knocked at exactly 11:00 a.m., as agreed.

"Hello, Stan, I'm Bob, and this is our consultant, Jim Wood," Bob said, turning away and waving his hand at a pale, stout man with gray hair.

Bob was dark skinned and medium height with black hair. After the introductions, the interrogation began.

"So Stan, give us a quick overview of your radio background," Bob said, as he raised his coffee cup.

I wanted to say, *didn't you read my résumé?*

I regaled them with my radio background, and they asked questions from time to time. After an hour of conversation, Bob stood and asked me if I would care for a Coke or coffee. As I rose from my chair, to go the bathroom, I realized that my pants zipper was wide open! Not just unzipped, but gaping. I looked up to see if they had noticed. They had.

Jim smirked and said, "Did you notice a draft?"

Bob chuckled. My guts were roiling. Would they really hire a guy who couldn't even zip up his pants?

When I returned to the room, Bob spent a few minutes warning me of the perils of L.A. and Hollywood and telling me that if I was hired, I would be in competition with some of the biggest names in the radio business, like Charlie Tuna, Robert W. Morgan, Jay Thomas and Rick Dees. He obviously tried to intimidate me by reminding me of the sheer size of greater Los Angeles and Orange County.

Finally, after two hours of grilling by Bob Guerra and Jim Wood, it ended.

"Jim and I will talk. We also have another candidate from South Carolina that we need to meet with and then, I have to fly back to L.A. this evening. I'll give you a call this afternoon before I leave."

"Okay, thank you gentlemen. I look forward to hearing from you," I said, with firm handshake and hoped that my competitor from South Carolina would show up drunk with his pants on backward...and his zipper undone.

I went back to my room to sit and literally watch the phone and the clock. It was 1:30. Then 3:00. Neil called and wanted to know what I was doing. I lied and told him that I wasn't feeling well. I wanted a drink bad. I opened a bottle of Jack Daniels from the mini-bar and drank it from the bottle to soothe my nerves. It didn't help. I opened one more. I waited for the phone to ring. I picked it up. No, it wasn't dead.

Finally, it was 4:00 p.m. I couldn't stand the waiting any longer. I called the hotel operator and asked for Bob Guerra's room.

"I'm sorry, sir, Mr. Guerra has checked out."

"Are you sure?" My heart sank to the floor in a floppy lump.

"Will there be anything else, sir?" she asked in her polite Tennessee drawl.

I tried to think of what was next, which was nothing.

"Sir?"

"Pardon me? Oh, thank you."

I panicked. I felt dizzy. I reached into the mini-bar, but Jack was gone. I popped open a Bud and swallowed it in two large gulps.

I called the hotel operator again.

"Would you ring Jim Wood's room, please?

"One moment, Sir."

I waited. My spirits lifted slightly, thanks to Jack and Bud and the fact she didn't say that he had checked out.

"Sir?"

"Yes?"

"We have no one by that name registered in the hotel. I'm sorry. Will there be anything else?"

"No, that's all, thanks." I hung up more dejected than before.

I assumed that they had left not wanting to break the news to me that I was not the chosen one. I swallowed another Bud. I changed into my jeans and casual shirt. I was going to get very drunk. It was a mission.

I consumed several more drinks in the Jack Daniels bar with an old music business friend from Canada. He introduced me to Andrew Bernstein from a radio syndication company from L.A. We all agreed to go to dinner together. I called Neil's room, but I didn't need to. As I looked up from our table in the atrium, I spotted him on his balcony with a sheet over his shoulders, apparently pretending to be the Pope. He was blessing everyone. I hoped that no one suspected that he was a member of the Ku Klux Klan.

At dinner, my memory began a fade to black, yet I was lucid enough to remember someone (I don't remember who) proposing a toast in front of Neil and a half dozen guys at the table.

"To Stan Campbell! Good luck in your new job in *L.A.*, my friend!"

My friends cheered, except my boss Neil, who was seated across from me. For a moment, I became sober. Neil gaped at me with a question mark on his face. Until then, he knew nothing of my job opportunity. I hoped that he wouldn't remember the toast.

I spent most of Saturday drunk or asleep. On Sunday, Neil and I drove back to Cincinnati with dueling hangovers. I had to tell him the truth. He was superbly gracious and wished me good luck. I wasn't entirely sure if he was being straight with me.

On Monday, I called KLAC and asked for Bob Guerra. He was on another line. I called later. This time he was in the production studio. I tried again. He was at lunch. I went home, downed half a dozen beers in rapid succession, and griped at Susan and Natalie for no particular reason. Susan did make sense through my haze. She told me to quit calling Bob Guerra. I was beginning to appear desperate. She was right. I was desperate.

* * *

On Wednesday, as I began to assume that I was never going to see Hollywood again, Heather came to my office door. She knew.

"Stan, the guy you've been waiting for is on the phone. Bob Guerra is on line two." She crossed her fingers for me.

I waited. He had made me wait. I waited ten seconds.

I delivered the words with faux-calm. "Hello, this Stan Campbell."

"Stan, Bob Guerra here. Jim and I think you are the guy we're looking for, but our general manager, Norm Epstein, wants to meet with you first. He has to have final approval. Can you fly out here on Sunday so that you can meet him on Monday morning? We'll overnight you a ticket."

"Absolutely!" I tried desperately not to laugh, cry, or babble incoherently.

"We'll put you up at the Universal Hilton in Studio City. You can rent a car at the airport, and we'll cover it."

I didn't care if I had to sleep under a bridge on the Hollywood Freeway. I hung up the phone and screamed. The station crew ran into my office. I had a great supportive staff. They genuinely congratulated me but also told me how they hated to see me leave. After they left my office, I realized that I had engaged in premature jubilation. What if Norm Epstein didn't like me?

* * *

I marveled at the tall palm trees along the San Diego Freeway on the way to the Universal Hilton. Bob had sent me *script*, which was a barter document to pay for my room, but there was a problem at the Hilton front desk.

"Sir, we'll need a major credit card to cover any additional room charges."

After the record company disaster and filing Chapter 7 bankruptcy, I had no credit card and would likely not get one for another five or six years. I was red-faced embarrassed.

"Uh, I'm sorry. I don't have a credit card."

The desk clerk became chilly. "Sir, we will need a five hundred dollar deposit to cover incidentals."

"Five hundred dollars? I don't have that kind of cash with me."

I didn't have five hundred dollars on me or anywhere else. I had gone through the same ordeal with the car rental people at the airport, but they were a bit more accommodating.

"I'm sorry, sir, we will not be able to give you the key to the mini-bar."

"Oh, that's okay, I don't drink." I laughed as I lied.

Thankfully, he gave me a room key, and I slithered to the elevator, humiliated. I threw my briefcase down on the bed and fell into the wingback chair in the corner. I picked up the phone to call Susan to let her know that I had arrived. I dialed 8 for a long distance call but got the front desk instead.

"I'm sorry, sir, but your phone is not operational because you did not place a deposit on the room."

"Oh, right. So, can I make a collect call?"

"No, sir, I'm afraid not, but you can use a payphone in the lobby."

My self-esteem was evaporating fast. I had to get my mojo working for the next morning. I had to get into a Hollywood attitude.

I checked myself in the mirror and headed downstairs to the parking garage and drove out onto the Hollywood Freeway north to Burbank. I figured that it would be a good idea to scope out the location of KLAC on West Alameda. The sun set as I drove with the windows open. I could smell California. No other place smelled like that. It was the heady combination of smog and bird of paradise flowers. The pencil-thin tall palm trees whizzed by, as I inhaled the aroma of Hollywood.

I found the radio station at 4000 West Alameda, a modern six-story black glass building. Warner Brother Studios was on the south side, and the Disney Channel building next door towered over the radio station. Up on the hill, I could see Universal Studios on the edge of the Hollywood Hills and Studio City. This was Hollywood!

I had to have this job! I had never wanted anything so desperately. I had never wanted to live anywhere as much as here, except maybe Nashville, a near second. I sensed what struggling actors felt when they came here for the first time. Okay, so maybe Burbank wasn't technically Hollywood, but Hollywood is a state of mind in the Southland.

I drove around for over two hours, exploring Burbank, Studio City, and down over the hill to Hollywood, through the famous intersection of Hollywood and Vine and then west past Mann's famous Chinese Theatre. For a moment, my thoughts returned to that wide spot in the road in Cape Breton and Mom and Pop. Hollywood was so far from home.

I finally realized that I needed to sleep, if I could. As I passed the front desk, I nodded to the same desk clerk. He looked away.

I slept uneasily, on and off through the night. I awoke at 5:30. My meeting was at 10:00 a.m. I got up, took a long shower, and went downstairs for a bagel and two cups of coffee. I had no appetite. I tried to calm my nerves, and coffee didn't help. I could have used a drink.

At 8:30, I drove out of the parking lot and onto the Hollywood Freeway, which was jammed. I panicked. I had to be at my meeting with Norm Epstein at 10:00. I prayed. My prayers were answered. I arrived at the station an hour early, so to kill time, I drove up and down West Alameda Avenue. I saw NBC and the studios where Johnny Carson did his show at 3000 West Alameda just down the street. I wanted this...badly.

At 9:45, I drove into the parking lot at KLAC. I checked my suit and tie to make sure that I hadn't dropped anything on them. I tugged at my pants zipper twice. I exited the elevator into the lobby on the sixth floor, where a rather distinguished older lady smiled at me. The place was quite fashionable.

"Hi, I'm here to see Norm Epstein." I choked.

I wasn't prepared for the squawk that came from my mouth.

"Your name?"

"Stan Campbell."

"Hi, Stan! Bob Guerra is expecting you. He will be right out. He wants to see you first."

"Oh, okay." I became even more nervous.

Maybe he changed his mind, or he was going to offer me a lesser job.

Bob Guerra stuck his head out the door and motioned to me to follow him down the long hallway. On the way, he gave me a tour of the studios. There were six modern studios in a row down the left side facing the Hollywood Hills. It was the most state-of-the-art radio station I had ever seen. I needed to be a part of this. The fact that Bob was showing me around was, I surmised, a good omen.

We strolled back down the long hallway to a corner office, where Mr. Epstein's secretary greeted us.

"Kim, I have Stan Campbell here to see Norm."

"Hello Mr. Campbell. Just a moment, Bob, I'll see if he's ready for you." She rose from her chair and knocked gently on his door.

"Come in!" A booming voice came from the other side.

Kim opened the door for us as Mr. Epstein rose from behind his massive oak desk. He looked like he could have been a retired football player.

Bob introduced me. "Norm, this is Stan Campbell, our new program director and morning guy that I've been telling you about."

"Hello, Stan. Welcome to L.A.!"

I responded as politely as possible. "Thank you, sir."

"Sir? It's Mr. Epstein to you."

"I'm sorry, Mr. Epstein." I felt stupid.

Norm let out a booming laugh. "I'm just kidding, Stan. Call me Norm."

I felt stupid again. "Okay, Norm."

I felt my face flush.

Norm went on to quiz me about where I came from, where I was born, and how much I knew about country music and if I thought I would feel comfortable in L.A. Throughout all of his questioning, I felt diminutive. I sat on a soft couch, where my butt was three inches from the floor, while Norm towered over me from behind his enormous oak desk. I saw a cartoon in my head, but it wasn't funny. Then, he threw a terrifying curveball at me.

"So, Stan, you want to do the morning show on KLAC?

"That's right, Norm. I am excited." I tried to sound self-assured.

"Okay good. So, say something funny."

I was dumbstruck. He wanted me to be *funny*? I suddenly froze. I felt a river running down from my armpits into my shoes. What do I do? I had to say *something*.

"Norm, I don't do jokes. That's not what I do. I consider myself more or less a humorist. I react to people and events."

It was the best that I could come up with, and frankly, it was true. If he didn't buy that claim, I was dead.

"So you don't have any funny jokes?"

"No, I'm afraid not." I tried to laugh it off. "Besides, Norm, it's not easy to be funny on command."

"Yes, I guess you're right." He wound up our interview after sharing some information about the station history. He ushered me out with a promise that he would discuss his thoughts with Bob Guerra.

I stopped by Bob's office to say good-bye. He also promised to get back to me in a couple of days. I left, feeling unsure. I wanted this.

I arrived back in Cincinnati that night, surviving an hour-long holding pattern over the airport waiting for the fog to clear. My head was also in a fog. I wanted that job, that city, that California lifestyle desperately, but on the other hand, I wasn't entirely confident that I was right for it. Hollywood was exciting but frightening.

Days went by with no communication from L.A. I finally called Bob Guerra. He said that he and Norm had not had a chance to talk. Damn! I needed an answer. Besides, my boss knew that I was going after the L.A. job. My employment was in jeopardy. A week went by with no answer. It became two weeks. Hope faded.

I called Mom and Pop back home in Cape Breton. My mother had never been happy with me living in the USA. She saw murders and violence on TV and believed that a slayer waited for me behind every tree. Pop was not well. He had suffered from heart problems for years, and now his ticker was acting up. He was displeased with the idea of my being even farther away. Cincinnati was far, but to him, California was on another planet. In a way, it was.

*   *   *

My secretary, Heather, instead of using the intercom, shouted down the hall loud enough for everyone to hear, "Stan, Bob Guerra from KLAC on line two!"

She was almost as excited as I was. I picked up the phone, waited a moment while I sucked in a long deep breath and then let out with a puff, before I pushed the button for line two.

"Hello, Bob, what's happening?"

"Stan, can you start in two weeks?" he asked, casually.

I was anything but casual.

I was hyperventilating and desperately trying to control myself. "Yes! Well, yes, I think so. Well, I mean I have to be fair with the company here."

"Okay, talk to your GM there, and let me know as soon as you can.

"Okay, I'll get back to you in an hour and—"

"Good. First we need to discuss salary."

"Oh, yeah, right."

I had almost forgotten about the money part. I wanted this so badly that I might have done it for minimum wage.

We tossed numbers back and forth. I didn't get what I asked for, but it was almost double my salary in Cincinnati. I would soon realize that in L.A., money doesn't go nearly as far as it does in Cincinnati or Nashville.

I called Neil Kearney, who congratulated me and agreed to let me leave in two weeks. He threw a going away party for me, at which I got falling-down drunk. My son Rod and his girlfriend, Jackie, came from Toronto. My partner and former news-lady, Bonna, and I shared the worm in the Tequila bottle.

Rod told me the next day that, as I left the party that Neil kindly threw for me, I turned to Neil and said, "Hey, Neil, did I ever tell you that you are a fucking asshole?"

I felt terrible about that smart-ass comment and apologized to Neil later. He wasn't a fucking asshole. He wasn't even a regular asshole.

Pop Dies And Mom Gets Tough

On Tuesday, April 4, 1989, with one hundred dollars cash in my pocket, I packed up my new '89 Dodge Daytona, kissed Susan and Natalie good-bye, and hit the road. Cincinnati to California. Susan and Natalie planned to stay in Cincinnati until Natalie finished school in June. Susan suggested that I should carry more cash, but I chose to withdraw money as I needed it along the way with my new ATM card.

After an overnight stay at a Red Roof Inn in Springfield, Missouri, I was on the road again at 8:00 a.m. with a plan to stop overnight in Amarillo, Texas. It was a sunny Thursday, and I enjoyed the drive, until I found out that my new ATM card wouldn't work in any bank machines in Texas. I ended up driving eight hundred and twenty-five miles to Albuquerque, arriving at 4:30 a.m. and broke. Thankfully my ATM card worked in New Mexico. My excessive alone-time gave me time to think and talk to myself.

I spent a few hundred miles devising a new plan to finally find out who my birth mother was. I knew that her name was Cecilia McNeil. Only her name appeared on my baptismal certificate. The father line was blank. She was 30 when I was born. That would make her 79 years old. Could she still be alive?

I wondered if she knew where I was. Did she keep tabs on me? Maybe she had gotten married after I was born and had other kids. If I ever found her, I imagined calling a brother or sister and introducing myself. Would they reject me? I was sure that my father, the sperm donor, likely didn't know that I existed. I suspected that he was a soldier or a navy guy passing through Cape Breton at the beginning of World War II. Damn! She knew I existed! Why had she never acknowledged me? This time, I would find her, dead or alive.

After another overnight stay in Kingman, Arizona, I arrived in L.A. on Friday at 1:10 in the afternoon to a genuine California welcome. It was a record 106 degrees and sunny...with a 4.7 magnitude earthquake. The real shaking would commence on Monday.

I was confident and thrilled about Hollywood while I was in Cincinnati, but as I arrived in California, and the realization hit me that I was there to stay, I was petrified. Los Angeles was hot, and the people were cold. No, make that detached. No one made eye contact. It wasn't like New York. The Big Apple wasn't cold, it was tough. To the lady in the office at the Oakwood Apartments in Toluca Hills, which was to be home for two months, I was invisible.

I moved my stuff into my apartment late Friday afternoon. I knew nobody in L.A., including the people at the station. I hadn't met them yet other than a brief hello when Bob showed me around. My apartment was modern with one bedroom, a large living room with a gas fireplace, and a kitchen. Maid service was included.

I felt out of place and lonely. I did what I usually do when I am alone and depressed. I found the nearest liquor store and bought a case of beer and a bottle of Southern Comfort. I hated Southern Comfort, but it gave me a buzz. I drove around to check out the neighborhood, including Studio City, Burbank, and Van Nuys. After I got tired of driving, I went back to my apartment to get a bigger buzz.

By dark, I was drunk but not any happier. Maybe I had reached too high. Maybe this high school dropout from Cape Breton wasn't ready for Los Angeles, Hollywood, Beverly Hills, and Malibu. What had Bob Guerra been thinking hiring me? Maybe, I wasn't L.A. material. If I failed here...then what?

Monday morning I arrived at the station ahead of time and met with Bob Guerra. I had been hired as the new program director for KLAC, a Southern California heritage country station, with a huge signal that covered an area from Santa Barbara down into Mexico and east to Arizona. Some of the greats of radio had worked at KLAC.

I had been hired to do double-duty not only as the program director but as the morning show host. Stoney Richards had been the acting P.D. and morning guy. I sensed that he was offended by being sent back to his mid-day show by a hick from Ohio. If only he had known that I was a bumpkin from a wide spot in the road in Cape Breton!

I spent the first week getting to know everyone, which was tough because there were over fifty people working at the station. I also had to become accustomed to the equipment in the studio where I would do my morning show. It didn't take me long to screw up and demonstrate my insecurity in Los Angeles. I felt as though the station staff, and especially my morning show gang, was judging me, and the verdict wasn't good. I imagined that Bob Guerra was second-guessing his decision to hire me. I had trouble sleeping, which further amplified my angst.

To add to my stress, Mom and Pop's best neighbors, the MacDougalls, called to tell me that Pop was not doing well. He was unhappy that I had moved so far away. I felt guilty that I could not be with him, and I was concerned that his illness placed an even heavier burden on Mom. I wished that I could have been there, but with the new job, there was no way to get away.

Over the next few months, I began to really like the KLAC people and most importantly, I gained their respect. I became more comfortable with my new environment in L.A. I even got my name on a billboard at Hollywood and Vine. I smiled when I remembered how anxious I had been when I had passed that famous intersection, just months prior.

On a personal level, the station covered the cost of two visits by Susan. She had her chance to see Los Angeles but wasn't thrilled about living in the Hollywood environment. I shopped around for a peaceful neighborhood. Someone suggested Agoura Hills in the far west end of the San Fernando Valley. I found a house to rent there that I liked, but the price tag was more than double what we had paid back in Cincinnati. I realized that the higher salary would be devoured by the insane cost of living.

Susan, Natalie, and I moved into the house on July 1, 1989, Canada Day. A day later, I received a call from home in Cape Breton that my father had been hospitalized for his heart condition again. With this new job, I wasn't sure if I should request time to go home to visit Pop. Besides, even though I was earning more money, we were still broke.

I had not recovered from the financial surprise that I had received during my second week on the job. I was warned that I had to join the union, or I would not be permitted to go on the air. I was compelled to cough up twelve hundred dollars for the AFTRA/SAG union initiation and dues. Embarrassed, I had to request a pay advance. The house rent was sixteen hundred dollars a month. The landlord demanded first month and last month up front plus a security deposit of an additional sixteen hundred. Mortified again, I had to request a pay advance.

Just three weeks after Susan and Natalie arrived, after I got off the air at 9:00 a.m. on Wednesday July 19th, I had a speedy meeting with Bob Guerra and went down the hall to my office. I needed to call the hospital in Baddeck, Nova Scotia, to check on Pop.

"Hello, this is Stan Campbell. May I speak to my father, Roddie Campbell"?"

"Just a moment, Mr. Campbell. Mrs. MacAuley will speak to you."

That was strange. Why didn't she just call my father's room?

"Mr. Campbell?"

"Yes, hello."

She switched to my first name, the one I was called as a kid. "Stanley, I'm so sorry to tell you this, but your father passed away less than twenty minutes ago. We were about to call you."

I felt like my own heart had stopped.

"No! No!"

I felt my throat close up.

Then she added the words that I will never forget. "Before he passed away, he asked for you."

At that, I fell apart. I despised myself for not being there. I tried to regain some composure. I managed to ask a couple of inane questions, of which I remember none. I hung up. I called Susan and sobbed the news to her. I then called my Mom and tried hard to sound composed. Because of her desperately poor hearing, the conversation was short, but she seemed to be much calmer than I was.

I hung up the phone and waited until I composed myself and wiped my face. I sat at my desk with my door closed and let it sink in. *My father is dead.* He asked for me. I let him down. I breathed in several gulps of air, cleared my throat, stood, and walked over to Bob Guerra's office. I felt as though I had regained my self-control. I peeked in. He was in a meeting with a man and woman, but he caught me peeking in.

"Is there something you need, Stan?"

"Bob, my father just died." As I spoke the words, I surprised myself as I began to weep.

I felt like a fool in front of Bob's guests. He got up and put his hands on my shoulders.

"You need to go home, Stan. Don't worry about anything. We'll take care of everything. Be with your family."

My father's viewing was in the Sacred Heart Mission Church a mile from our home next door to the old gray school, where my mushy brain developed from grade one to grade eight. My kids, Rod, Mark, Michael, and Helen, arrived, which gave me great comfort and pleased my mother. Mom appeared extremely tired and weak, but I knew that a part of her was relieved. She had struggled with Pop's illness for months, if not years. He was eighty-three when he died.

I had not been there to help, and I felt a great sense of guilt for that. I often wondered if I should have given up my career to go home and take care of both of them. My father was needy when he was ill and required my mom to wait on him every waking moment and many hours when she should have been sleeping. I was extremely concerned by her noticeable frailty. She could barely walk unassisted.

* * *

After the funeral service, we went back to the yellow house in Jamesville West where I had spent my teen years. I knew that decisions had to be made. I was sure that my Mom would not live alone in that house, so what was I to do?

Less than ten minutes after we had returned from the church, she made a shocking declaration. "I don't want to sleep here tonight. I will not stay in this house one more night. I will go to the MacDougalls."

Walter and Helen MacDougall and their children were my parents' next-door neighbors and best friends.

"Are you sure? Rod and Mark and I will be here."

She was adamant. "No, I don't want to live in this house one more day. I want to go to the Alderwood Retirement Home in Baddeck as soon as I can get in."

I was amazed and happy that she had made that decision on her own. Many elderly people view a retirement home as a prison. In spite of her wishes, I decided to make her an offer.

Even though I was sure that she would decline, I asked anyway. "Mom, would you like to come back to California with me? Susan would be happy to have you."

Susan adored her.

"No!" Apparently, I had made a ridiculous suggestion.

"Are you sure, Mom? It's a nice place with warm weather all the time, and we could take good care of—."

"No!" She was clearly annoyed by my offer. "I want to go to Alderwood. I have friends there."

California was out of the question. To Mom, Sydney, Nova Scotia, was big metropolis. The USA was a terrifying place in her mind. The decision was made. My mother *and* my father had decided.

* * *

When the phone rang, I figured that it was a bereavement call.
"Hello, who am I talking to?"
"This is Stan Campbell, Roddie's son."
"Stanley, this is Fisher Hudson. I am sorry for your troubles."
"Thank you." I figured that was it.
I knew of Mr. Hudson as a politician and a lawyer in Baddeck and my father's friend.
"Stanley, I am the Executor of your father's Will. I will need you to come to Baddeck for the reading of the Will. When can you come?"
"I can come tomorrow morning at 10:00, if that's okay."

My father's Will was a shocking surprise. He had written up the Will with Mr. Hudson's assistance on March 20, 1989. Through his Executor, my father decreed that fifteen hundred dollars be divided and given to three unrelated neighborhood children, whom I prefer not to name, with two hundred dollars to go to the Sacred Heart Mission Church. The remainder of his estate was to be divided, two thirds to me and one third to be divided between my sons Rod and Mark, whom my father referred to as nephews. My two younger children, Michael and Helen, were overlooked, and most shockingly, Mom was not mentioned in his Will.

Nowhere in the Will was there any indication of where the money would come from to bequeath to the three unrelated children and to the church. We subsequently discovered that he had approximately two hundred and fifty dollars saved in the St. Columba Credit Union, but that wasn't nearly enough to cover his promises.

I was advised by Mr. Hudson that the house would have to be sold. There was no choice in this matter. He also advised me that Pop had made it clear to him that my mother would go to the Alderwood Retirement Home in Baddeck immediately following his death. I tried to determine if that was my father's decision or my mom's?

I contacted a Baddeck realtor to list the house. It was on two acres of land. I expected that we could sell it for thirty-five thousand. In retrospect, I would have preferred to have sold the house to a friend for one dollar and then bought it back. My son Rod wanted to keep the house in the family as well. However, at the time, none of us could afford to cover the financial terms of the Will and the taxes. We had no choice. Several months later, the property sold for the ridiculous sum of eighteen thousand dollars.

I had been granted a week away from work to attend the funeral and decide what to do about my mother. She continued to sleep at the MacDougalls next door and alternately at her friend Margaret McClusky's place. Mom had been close to the McClusky family long before she had met my father, first, with her older friend, Catharine, and later with Catharine's daughter, Margaret. Seventeen years later, Catharine's granddaughter, Georgina, would open a door to the biggest surprise of my life.

My son Michael and I attempted to get Mom into the Alderwood Retirement Home, but it was fully booked. Finally, she agreed to go to a new retirement home in Port Hawkesbury, fifty miles away, with the promise that as soon as a room opened up at Alderwood, she could move there. However, she couldn't get into Port Hawkesbury right away, either.

An angel came to our rescue. Angela MacDougall agreed to have my Mom stay with her for a month or so until she could get into the Port Hawkesbury Retirement Home. Angela had been our former next-door neighbor, but she lived in Antigonish, a Nova Scotia college town. Angela was a loving angel of mercy.

My time at home passed quickly, so we had to get everything handled in a hurry. Because Mom was extremely frail, I took her to see her family doctor in Baddeck. Immediately, he checked her into the hospital. She was unable to walk unassisted up the steps of the hospital, so Michael and I each held an arm and practically carried her up to the door.

It broke my heart to see her like that, and I felt miserable that I had to leave her, but I was confident that I was leaving her in good hands with Angela. I feared that I might have to return home soon to attend another funeral.

* * *

A surprise awaited me in LA. Norm Epstein had initiated a unique sales and marketing strategy targeting the tourism industry. One of the first tourism clients was Hong Kong Tourism. A live broadcast was part of the plan, so the station sent me to Hong Kong for a week, along with a production crew, to broadcast my morning show live back to L.A. It was a fun and exciting trip, especially when Jackie Chan joined me on the air. Not long after I returned from Hong Kong, Norm sent me to Montréal to repeat the campaign, this time for Tourisme Québec. Over the next few years, I also broadcast my show from Scottsdale, Calgary, London, and Jerusalem.

While I was on the air one morning in Jerusalem, broadcasting live to L.A., my producer, Eric Redd, back in the studio in Los Angeles whispered into my headphones. "Hey, Stan, you have a visitor here to see you."

"A visitor? Don't they know that I'm not in the studio?"

"Apparently not. It's Shania Twain"

"Shania! You're kidding."

I was thrilled that my old friend had stopped by. She had morphed from Eilleen to Shania.

"Yeah, she didn't know that you weren't here, but she is leaving her new CD and a picture with a note for you"

"Oh, man, I am so sorry I missed her. Please tell her hello and give her a big hug for me."

Eric told me later that he did and that it was enjoyable!

When I returned from Jerusalem, there was indeed a CD and a picture waiting on my desk. She had written a note on the photo. *Stan, I sure wish you were here during my visit to KZLA and KLAC. Hope to see you soon old friend. Love, Shania Twain*

On her CD she had written, *Can't wait to see you again. Love, Shania Twain*

Apparently she *could* wait to see me again. My efforts over the years to communicate with her resulted in applications being sent to me from her fan club. Since writing those notes to me in 1993, she had reached the pinnacle of super-stardom. When that happens, the definition of *friend* apparently changes.

The Beverly Hillbilly

Almost every weekend I was assigned to make personal appearances and some nights introduce country stars at venues like the Universal Amphitheatre or the Greek Theatre in Hollywood. Occasionally, celebrities spent mornings with me on air, including Dolly Parton, Garth Brooks, Randy Travis, Johnny and June Carter Cash, Dick Van Patten, and one of my favorite morning guests of all time, Steve Allen. I spent an afternoon with Jaclyn Smith at a fundraiser at Anaheim Stadium and an evening in the outdoor backstage lounge area with Chuck Norris. Both Jaclyn and Chuck left me with embarrassing memories.

Jaclyn Smith naturally gathered fans everywhere she went. At an afternoon event at Anaheim Stadium, a crew from a local cable TV station was present in the outdoor backstage area. The producer approached me and suggested that because I was a radio personality, would I agree to interview Jaclyn Smith for him. I politely told him that I would rather not since I didn't follow the careers of Hollywood stars. I tried to convince him that I wasn't the best choice as an interviewer. He insisted. I relented. He handed me a mic.

"Hi, Jaclyn. It's nice to be with you this afternoon for a worthwhile cause."

"Thanks, Stan, I'm happy to help out."

It was then that foot-in-mouth struck.

"Jaclyn, tell me about your time on the *Police Woman* series."

An exceptionally long pause was accompanied by a stare straight into my eyes, apparently to determine if I was trying to be funny. I wasn't. Susan stood behind the camera. Her eyes exploded to twice their normal size. The cameraman gazed skyward, presumably to a drifting cloud.

"I wasn't on *Police Woman*. That was Angie Dickinson."

Her facial expression and body language implied *you poor sap, you don't have a clue, do you*?

I switched gears and asked a couple of safe questions about the fundraiser. After the brief interview, I apologized profusely to Jaclyn. She was charming in spite of my unmitigated ignorance.

My assignment one Friday night was to introduce Willie Nelson, Kris Kristofferson, and Randy Travis at the Universal Amphitheatre, which is a magnificent theatre complex with a large backstage courtyard and bar where celebrities, managers, record company people, and radio guys like me can hang out and dine on hors d'oeuvres before or after going on stage. I endeavored to be Hollywood country cool, so I wore my Stetson hat and my ostrich-leg western boots for the occasion. Chuck Norris, one of Randy Travis's good friends, was backstage.

I donned my cowboy hat in the dimly lit area behind the backdrop. On cue, the lights went up, and I stepped out onto the stage to introduce myself, do a plug for KLAC Radio, and then introduce the opening act, Kris Kristofferson.

As I usually did, I raced back and forth on the stage attempting to pump up the crowd. On either side of the stage were two giant Jumbotron big screens. The audience didn't want to see *me*. The folks were waiting for the big act. I thought I detected scattered chuckling. In my most forceful radio voice, I introduced the opening act.

"Ladies and gentlemen, please welcome to the Universal Amphitheatre, Kris Kristofferson!"

I didn't wait to see Kris, since I wasn't a fan of his on-stage political ranting, so I strolled back out to the courtyard to join Randy Travis and Chuck Norris for a drink. I was thinking, *Wow, I'm sitting here with Chuck Norris!*

Chuck turned to me as a smirk lit up his face. "I guess no one told you that your hat is on backwards."

I ripped the hat off of my head, and yes, the wide part was in the front. Randy and Chuck laughed. Crawling under the table was out of the question. I was the rube from a wide spot in the road in Cape Breton, pretending to be a cool cowboy in Hollywood.

I might have been laughing at work, but at home there was nothing funny. Susan and I had been married for almost three years. She was unhappy in California. I wasn't happy, but I wasn't tempted to initiate an affair, as I had been in the past when things at home got rough. I did revisit an old addiction.

I usually arrived home at 2:00 in the afternoon with a bottle of Tequila, my new favorite blues chaser. I twisted open the bottle, grabbed a saltshaker and few limes off of the tree in the backyard, and headed for the hot tub on the patio. I didn't sit in the hot tub like most people. I picked up an air mattress and placed it on the water, then laid on it and rotated with help from the hot tub jets. On every other slow rotisserie 360-degree turn, I downed another shot of Tequila. By 5:00, my lights went dim. I got a great tan, but the one-man Tequila party added more fuel to the fire of fights.

On the way home from work, especially on down days, I called Kay in Nashville. She wasn't simply a former roommate. She was a treasured platonic friend. I moaned the blues to her about my marriage woes. She remarked that she didn't want to say I told you so, but she did.

In spite of our bickering and sometime screaming fights, Susan and I did go through good periods too. She disliked California and its people. I began to identify with her loathing for the materialistic side of California. Then, the L.A. riots struck, followed by an earthquake which was followed by fires that came much too close to our home. After four years with KLAC, I began to explore opportunities elsewhere...someplace peaceful, and maybe somewhere a bit closer to Mom, who was doing much better, finally living in Alderwood.

There was a new country station in Toronto. I was tentatively offered the morning show gig. However, I did not want to return to Canada, so I demanded an outrageous salary, more than twice my L.A. salary. I didn't want to go to Toronto or New York or Chicago. I had changed. I wanted to live in a quiet, small city or town where, unlike Los Angeles, I could meet my neighbors. I also saw the writing on the wall at KLAC. It was an AM station, so its days as a music station were numbered. I knew the end was coming. It did.

Northern Exposure

"How would you like to go to Traverse City, Michigan?" It was Jim Wood, the former KLAC consultant on the phone.

He had become an independent broadcast consultant.

I laughed out loud. "Michigan?" I had visions of Detroit riots and rusty Saginaw.

"Yes, Traverse City, Michigan."

"Traverse City? I have heard of it but know nothing about it."

"The owners are in the process of buying a second station, so they're searching for an operations manager. If you are interested, I can put you in touch with the president, Richard Dills."

"Yeah, I guess. But, *Michigan*? Shit!"

"Stan, it's *Northern* Michigan. It's magnificent up there. Driving up along the coast of Lake Michigan is like the California Pacific Coast Highway."

"Really Jim? In *Michigan*?"

"Yes! Humor me. Check it out."

"Okay. I'll give him a call."

Jim gave me Richard's number in Grand Rapids. I hesitated, focused for a few minutes, and called.

"Richard Dills!"

His rather brusque style put me off balance. I hesitated.

"Hello, Richard. Jim Wood suggested that I call you about the ops manager job in Traverse City." I attempted to be as aggressive as he sounded.

"Petoskey!"

"Pardon me?"

"Petoskey! The station is in Petoskey."

"Petoskey? Where the hell is Petoskey?"

"Pretty town, an hour north of Traverse City. It's a tourist area with million dollar summer cottages on the beach."

I had hoped to go to a small city or town somewhere in the USA but not to a place that sounded like a hamlet.

"Send me your resume and aircheck, and I'll get back to you."

"I'll do it today, Richard."

"I'll call you when I get it."

I wondered if I wanted to work for this guy. He sounded like an asshole, but I figured that it couldn't hurt to send him my resume and tape.

A few days later, I heard from Richard.

"Okay, I got your tape and resume. It's good. Let's talk money."

I assumed that this deal could be done quickly. I knew that I was going to have to take a significant cut in pay to go from L.A. to, where? Oh, yeah, Petoskey.

Richard made his pay pitch. My response was rapid.

"Holy shit, Richard!"

I had not intended to go *that* low. It was less than half of what I was earning at KLAC. However, I guessed that the cost of living would be far less than in Los Angeles.

We tentatively agreed on a salary, benefits, and perks, but I had to discuss it with Susan first. Richard agreed to fly us to Traverse City to see the area and drive up to Petoskey. I anticipated a sleepy lumber town, like in the TV show *Northern Exposure*.

In reality, Traverse City was a beautiful, tidy city of fifteen thousand that blew up to three times that size in the summer. It boasted gorgeous, wide, sandy beaches framed with fashionable resorts. Petoskey and neighboring Harbor Springs was a picturesque perfect small community somewhere between

Norman Rockwell and Robert Redford, with mansion-style summer homes on the beach.

Susan and I shopped around and made an offer on a house in the wooded community between Harbor Springs and Petoskey. It felt so damn peaceful. Unlike Californians, Petoskey people made eye contact and often smiled. Kids still wore their baseball caps with the peak in the front. How quaint!

The company had just bought the station, WAIR, and I was to be the station manager. The music format was oldies. I was also the new morning host. It was fun re-launching the station. Richard and I got along well. His bite was not nearly as bad as his bark. He visited Traverse City and Petoskey once a week from Grand Rapids, which meant brain-storming, planning, chit-chat –radio gossip, and lunch.

Susan found a job, the first time that she had felt comfortable in a job since Cincinnati. She wanted something to do since Natalie, at 17, had stayed behind in California. Besides, we needed the extra income.

It didn't take long for the tension to build. She found her job stressful. The tension spilled over to home. I worked long hours, often from 5:00 a.m. until 4:00 p.m. I began to drink alone again. By the time Susan arrived home from work, I was bombed. She was in a bad mood, and I was not in a mood to listen to her complaints about work. The more she complained, the more I felt somehow that it was my fault. Susan was oversensitive, which meant that an ugly yelling match could ensue with just a raised eyebrow and then, silence, with each of us retreating as far from each other as possible in the same house.

Natalie eventually moved from California to Petoskey to live with us. So, when Susan and I scrapped, she naturally defended her mom. The fights became three-way matches, and on one occasion evolved into a shoving bout.

After that ugly event, Susan left for an extended period to visit her sister in Cincinnati, and Natalie moved in with her boyfriend, Jerry. I assumed that this was it. I had been warned seven years earlier. A shouting argument on our first date was probably a harbinger of more bad times ahead. I could not go through life walking on eggshells. Two weeks later when Susan came back we gradually returned to our routine.

I spent two or three afternoons a week with my Mexican friend, José Cuervo. I could finish most of a twenty-six ounce bottle in an afternoon. No help needed. Drinking alone felt good. Actually, I didn't drink entirely alone. I had a telephone.

After six shots of Tequila, I regularly developed *telephonitis*. I acquired the urge to pick up the phone and call every old friend and acquaintance that I ever had known. The next day, I couldn't remember what we talked about. I know I confused many of them.

Occasionally someone called me back the next day and asked, "What the hell were you talking about yesterday?"

I didn't know.

I was married, had kids, a few friends, but I felt lonely almost all the time. I missed something or somebody. Truthfully, I had felt that way for most of my life. I romanticized about the perfect girl...the idyllic love of my life. Did she really exist? Somewhere? The dreamy vision never left my imagination for long.

Alcohol not only fueled the fire for fights but my fantasies too. As I grew older, the dream of finding the love of my life began to wither, along with my hair. I was angry. I had no blood connection to a real father, a mother, or siblings. I had run into roadblock after roadblock in a futile attempt to find out who I was.

I was a failure in matrimony...again. It looked like the end of marriage number four. I was in my late fifties, and I still didn't know who Cecelia McNeil was. A piece of paper indicated that she was my mother. What had happened to her? I talked to her when I was alone. *Do you know anything about me? Do you still live in New Waterford? Did you ever marry? Are you alive, or are you a spirit now, watching me?*

If she was alive, she would be almost 90. How could a woman go through life and never try to make some kind of contact with a child that she had given up for adoption? I vacillated between anger and despondency. With each request for information from the Nova Scotia government, I had received the same infuriating response. *Identifying information about persons involved in an adoption can only be given when there is mutual consent among the parties.* I considered it a stupid policy, which meant that I would likely die never knowing anything about my origin.

Fatal Attraction

"What do you think about changing formats, dropping oldies and switching to country?"

Whenever Richard called, there were no greetings, no pleasantries. He got right to the point.

"You want to flip the station from oldies to country?"

"Yeah, let's go after WTCM."

WTCM was the number one country station in Northern Michigan, which had huge ratings.

"What do you think, Stan?"

He valued my opinion, a fact that appeared to rankle the rank and file at the station's head office in Traverse City. They seemed threatened by the fact that I had come from the big market of Los Angeles. Their attitude was, *oh, you think you're hot shit because you came from L.A.? Well, we'll show you. We have our own way of doing things here.* I didn't view myself as superior to them, in spite of the fact that I was older and had outstanding broadcasting experience. I agreed with the plan to make the format switch and move the Petoskey studios to the head office in Traverse City. In December 1998, Susan and I planned to sell our house and move from Petoskey to Traverse City. Richard and I agreed that I would give up my position as program director at WAIR and concentrate on hosting the morning show on the re-born station known as WBYB, *The Bee*. Richard had hired a new program director, B.D. Remington.

At a lunch meeting with Richard and B.D., Richard announced a policy that was to be clear to all. Even though B.D. was the program director, my morning show was off limits to him. It was my show, and as Bob Guerra had told me several years previously in Los Angeles, *we bought the show.* It was to be treated as though it was a syndicated show. I perceived from the disagreeable expression on B.D.'s face that this policy did not sit well with him.

My first morning on the air was on January 2, 1999, on the new *Bee.* The WAIR oldies fans were furious that we had taken away their rock 'n' roll oldies. I had fun with them and aired their calls live on the air. Some cried and others ranted. One lady was so incensed that she wanted to remind us that her husband owned a gun. We were off and running with our new country station.

Every radio station studio has a *hotline* phone, a private number that only a handful of inside management people know. It rang at 7:35 a.m.

B.D. Remingston was on the line and he was clearly not happy. "Stan, I want you to cease airing those phone calls immediately."

"Come on B.D., they're fun, and it gives the WAIR fans a chance to air their beefs." I was miffed that B.D. was already defying Richard's hands-off policy.

"No! I want them off the air, right now."

"B.D., I want to remind you that it's my show, and you agreed to not get involved."

"Well, I am the program director here and responsible for this station."

My pulse went into double-time, and I felt my face catch fire. "B.D., we will discuss this after I get off the air."

"Indeed we will," he replied, attempting to use his most intimidating tone.

"I have to go, my stopset is coming up. Good-bye."

I slammed the phone down. It is a monumental test of one's acting ability to sound calm and friendly on the air when one is in a flaming fury.

After the show, I stormed out of the station and called Richard and the general manager, John Dew, followed by our consultant Jim Wood, in Nashville, breathless with anger. I also realized that I had made a colossal mistake by agreeing to give up the program director position.

When I returned to the station at noon, I received an invitation.

B.D. stood in his office doorway. "Stan, I want to see you in my office."

Okay, it wasn't exactly an invitation. It was apparent that B.D. had been contacted following my angry phone calls. I sauntered into his office and shut the door behind me. I expected shouting. My expectations were correct.

"You want my job, Stan? If you want my job, go ahead and let Richard know."

"I don't want your job, B.D., I want you to honor your agreement with Richard and leave my show alone."

Actually, I wasn't being totally honest. I had had his job and had been happy to relinquish it, never expecting to open the door to a control freak.

"Well, unless something changes here, I am the program director and therefore responsible for everything that airs on this station."

"Except my show, B.D."

"Your show is on my station and under my authority."

"B.D., unless Richard changes his policy, it is not your responsibility."

I could see that this was going to be a long-term problem. After ten minutes, the shouting diminished, and I left his office with no resolution. The next day I was back on the morning show, but the atmosphere had been poisoned.

The air was further polluted when the office staff and junior management began taking sides in the Stan versus B.D. war. B.D. was successful in swaying most of the ladies in the office by pampering them with gifts and taking them out to lunch. I became increasingly frustrated and angry. I recalled how I had earned and enjoyed respect and support in Cincinnati, Nashville, and Los Angeles, yet I was viewed with contempt in a small town in Northern Michigan.

I left the station around 2:00 each afternoon and stopped off to befriend José Cuervo. If I was drinking and driving, I chose Peppermint Schnapps to give me that fresh minty breath, in case I got pulled over. I was drunk or pleasantly wasted most nights and sounded like *Lurch* from the Adams Family on the air the next morning, as a result of a colossal hangover.

Every radio personality has fans, but some devotees are more admiring. Maybe my husky hangover voice attracted Allison. She had been calling me on the request lines regularly for a couple of years at the oldies station, WAIR. She often dropped by the station to say hello or showed up at one of my live broadcasts. I couldn't tell for sure if she was simply a station fan or if she was flirting with me. The staff at WAIR was convinced that she had a *thing* for me.

Allison was a tall brunette with big eyes and...a husband. Not just any husband down at the factory. He was a county sheriff. I did not flirt back. I wisely assumed that it was not prudent to trifle with a woman whose husband carries a gun to work. Since we had switched to country music, I didn't expect her to call or visit anymore. I was wrong.

"Hi, Stan, what are you doing for lunch?"

"I was planning a brown-bag lunch in my car, anywhere but here in the station with the Ice-Queens. They're liable to poison my tuna fish sandwich."

"Let me buy you lunch." Allison sounded unusually serious.

"Nah, I don't think that's a good idea." I imagined gunfire.

"I won't bite, Stan. I need to talk to you. Actually I want to apologize."

"Apologize for...?"

"I want to apologize for harassing you for the past year or so. I know that it was wrong."

I wasn't convinced but I relented, and I lied. "Okay, but I have to get back to work at 2:00."

"Deal! Meet you at Schelde's."

I needed any excuse to get out of the sub-zero atmosphere at the station. I was angry and depressed, and I needed a drink.

* * *

Allison sat in a booth at the back. She already sipped on a large draft beer. The server brought me a beer without asking.

"Stan, how's it going at work?"

"Lousy! I hate it. I should have moved downstate or back to L.A., or gotten a job washing cars."

"It will get better."

"No, it won't. One of us will get fired."

I took a long swallow of beer, wiping the foam from my upper lip. I didn't want to talk about that hell-hole anymore.

"Alison, what were you talking about on the phone? You said something about an apology?"

"Yes, Stan. I know that I've been annoying you by following you everywhere, and I wanted to apologize to you in person. I'm so sorry, Stan." Allison said, touching the back of my hand.

"I appreciate that Allison." I gave the waiter a hand signal for a jug of draft.

We finished the jug of draft as we talked about her husband, Jack the Sheriff. She told me that they were separating and that she was moving into an apartment. The waiter came back to the table and asked if we wanted another jug of draft. I was about to say no.

Allison shot me a wicked smile. "Sure, one more."

"Allison, I can't. I have to get back to work. I have an unfinished production project, and B.D. is on the lookout for any excuse to drop me in shit."

It was too late. We started in on our third round of bucket-sized jugs of beer. I was beginning to forget my troubles and get happy. We talked about her home situation and mine.

I had to go pee, and as I walked to the men's room, I thought that maybe my balance was off. When I arrived back at the table, there was yet another fresh jug of beer on the table. I noticed that Allison's big eyes weren't quite as big. She wore a stupid smile.

"Holy shit, Allison, I can't go back to the station like this." I realized that if I returned this late I was in trouble, but if I showed up drunk, I would be in great danger.

"Oh, screw them! You deserve a break, right?"

I stared across the table at her. It was a Mickey Gilley moment. His big hit song was, *Don't the Girls All Get Prettier at Closing Time.* I triggered another change in the course of my life.

Me And Bill Clinton

Iwas angry, frustrated, lonely, depressed, and slightly out of my mind. It was 4:00 in the afternoon. The lunch crowd had all gone home, and Schelde's Grille and Spirits had only two customers, Allison and me, and we were drunk.

I rose forward from my seat and kissed her, full on the lips. I sat back down feeling rather proud of my audacity. She stared at me with a gaze that said, *have you lost your mind?* I had.

We drank two smaller glasses of beer and decided that we had better get out of there before someone kicked us out. Besides, after having imbibed a gallon or two of adult beverages, we wanted to finish what we had started in a more private environment, namely my hotel room. The Cherry Hill Hotel was home until the house in Harbor Springs was sold, at which time Susan would move to Traverse City.

Once again, two consenting adults had committed adultery. She might have been separated or on the road to separation, and for me, I knew that my drunken betrayal was the nail in the coffin of my marriage to Susan. Susan and I had had a rocky marriage over our twelve years. I had grown angrier with her over the years for her mood swings and what I termed verbal abuse, but Susan did not deserve this. We had enjoyed some good times too.

I chose the coward's selfish way out of a marriage just as I had done on three other occasions. I did expect my one-night affair with Allison to be just that, one night. After all, we were both drunk. That was my pathetic excuse, but I wanted to end my marriage with Susan in the most civil and least hurtful manner possible.

Allison and I both tried to end it but we kept returning to cry on each other's shoulders. She would show up but then walk away, tearfully vowing no more flings. Later, it would be my turn to rebuff her. Yet, a virtual elastic band tied us together.

Susan and I sold the house in Harbor Springs and bought a house in Traverse City. In spite of buying a house and moving, the on and off affair with Allison continued...on and off.

One day Allison espoused a religious rationale, pointing out that what we were doing was sinful, but the next day we sinned. I was 59 and grew doubtful if I could ever be faithful to any woman.

I had seen President Clinton admit to an affair with Monica Lewinsky. He had allegedly been involved a string of affairs in the past. His ardent supporters claimed that he suffered from sexual addiction. I didn't buy that excuse originally but then I began to consider that maybe it was a real disease like alcoholism. I also began to believe that maybe I was an alcoholic too. For the first time in my life, I felt like I needed help for my obsessive behavior before one or both of the addictions killed me, or someone else.

The beginning of the end came one evening in March of 1999, when Susan made it clear that she suspected that I had been unfaithful and no longer loved her. I could not lie. I had lied far too much already. Susan had been hurt throughout her life. She did not deserve the pain that I inflicted. It was an awful night and a horrible few months. I hurt her deeply and for that I will be eternally sorry.

I continued to live at home, and we tried to pretend that we were okay. On April 10, 1999, I arrived home early from the station. To my surprise, Susan met me at the door. She had tears in her eyes. It was different this time, especially when she hugged me.

"Stan, I received a phone call a few minutes ago. I'm so sorry, but your Mom died this afternoon." We held each other and cried.

She loved my Mom. Most people did.

I flew home alone the next morning, and together with Michael and Helen, we buried my lovable, gentle mother Tena on the hill next to my father, as a lone piper played her favorite tune, *Flowers of the Forest*. Her passing was as she had lived for the previous ten years, peaceful. At the home where she had insisted on living, Alderwood Retirement Home, she simply sat down after dinner and went to sleep. I loved her. Yes, I wanted to find the identity of my birth mother, but Tena was the only Mom that I had ever known and loved.

Back in Michigan, Susan and I tried to fix our broken marriage by visiting a marriage counselor. Our sessions usually ended in an argument, with Susan convinced that the counselor was on my side. She opted out of counseling.

I knew that I needed to fix whatever was wrong with *me*. I needed to know how and why I had arrived at this place with divorce number four looming. I also had to stop drinking. Maybe I wasn't a classic alcoholic, but I was, as author Pete Hamill described himself in his book *A Drinking Life*, a drinker. Nevertheless, I needed support from somewhere. I had wanted to go to Alcoholics Anonymous years earlier. I knew that I needed help. I made a decision to go to AA, but it may have been too late. Changes were in the wind, including a near-death experience and a career-ending meeting.

Miracle On Munson Avenue

The end of the world was coming. Chaos was about to erupt around the world. We would starve in the dark. It was Y2K.

Nothing happened...except to me.

On January 1, 2000, I moved out of the house that Susan and I had bought only ten months earlier on Lamp Post Lane in Traverse City. Maybe it was an omen of coming events, but the Lamp Post Lane neighborhood was the coldest community I had ever lived in, apart from California. Maybe my drunken philandering reputation had spread.

Cyndi Husted was a sales associate at the radio station and had been searching for a roommate to share an apartment. She found the right guy right under her nose. We shopped around for an apartment and found exactly what we were looking for on La Casita Avenue. The Spanish street name was perhaps a clue to coming events.

I continued to host the morning show at the *Bee* as the hallways grew colder while B.D. continued his covert campaign to alienate me from almost everyone on staff. The chill grew even colder when someone in accounting leaked my salary to the entire staff. Because I had been hired from L.A., and because of my considerable experience, I was paid somewhat more than other employees. The staff then groused that I didn't require or deserve my own office, which was probably true, so Richard, in an attempt to appease the staff, assigned me to a desk in a corner of the production studio.

There was one ray of sunshine. One evening, after most of my enemies had gone home, I found general manager John Dew still working at his desk. Maybe he felt the pall in the hall too. I was suffering through an especially down evening.

"How are you doing, Stan? Is everything okay?" John apparently noticed my gloomy mood.

I lied. "Well...yeah, I'm fine."

I felt a lump form in my throat.

I was moved that someone in the station seemed to give a damn about me.

"You sure, Stan?"

"Not really. I am persona non grata around here, and on top of that, Susan and I are going through a divorce."

Lately, I had focused more and more on my questionable birthright. I had never felt more like an orphan. I had no roots, no father, no mother, no sisters, no brothers, and now, few friends. I was drowning in self-pity and booze. I felt intense guilt for hurting Susan as I had. I knew that Natalie hated me for what I had done to her mom.

I didn't care if I lived or died. I wasn't about to take my own life, though. My Catholic upbringing had taught me that people who commit suicide go to hell. I didn't completely buy into that philosophy, but I wasn't about to test it, just in case.

"You need to get your mind off all of that trouble. Why don't you come down and audition at the Old Town Playhouse for a part in *Annie*. The director is casting right now, and she needs to fill a few more parts."

"No, I don't think so. I don't think that would be too much fun with my bad attitude."

"No, Stan. That is exactly what you need. You would be perfect for the part of Bert Healy, the radio announcer. Come on. Give it a shot. They are all great people."

"I dunno..."

"Rehearsals are tonight at 8:00, so come on. It will do you a world of good."

"Okay, I will." I began to think that maybe he was right.

"Don't back out, Stan."

"No, I promise. I'll be there." I wasn't so sure.

I wanted a drink. I desperately wanted to get unconscious, but I kept my promise to John.

I crept into the rehearsal room, where around thirty people sat watching the auditions. I was immediately fearful. I saw other people try out. A few were really good. When the director called my name to come up front to audition, I wanted to run out the door.

In my radio and television career, I had been on-air live from coast to coast all over the United States and Canada with millions of listeners and on national TV every week for two years. I had performed as an emcee before fifty thousand people at outdoor concerts, but this was different. I was way out of my comfort zone.

The director beckoned me to the piano. "Stan, we would like you to sing something."

"Sing? I can't sing." I backed away from the director.

I felt stupid. I didn't know that singing was part of the deal. John sat in the front row smiling. *Damn! Why had I let him talk me into this? I know he's enjoying seeing me sweat.*

"Sure you can. Everyone can sing, at least a little."

The elderly piano player lady asked, "What songs do you know?"

"None." I was painfully aware of the crowd behind me.

"Oh, you must know at least one song. How about, Happy Birthday?"

"Happy Birthday?" I laughed.

Fuck! I look like an idiot. I wish I could get out of here and throw down a double-shot of Tequila.

"Okay, how about this one?" The director reached for a music sheet.

She shoved the music and lyrics to *Edelweiss* in front of me as the piano lady pounded the keys on the upright piano. I managed to mumble my way through the chorus. I felt foolish. Scattered applause echoed through the room, probably thankful that the pain had ceased.

The next day I got the word. I was in but not as Bert Healey. The director gave me three parts, Bundles the Laundryman, FDR's assistant Louis Howe, and a Hooverville bum. The second embarrassing moment came when the director told me that I had to dance. My dancing was worse than my singing.

But John was right. *Annie* was a wonderful uplifting experience. I enjoyed the rehearsals and the show that ran three nights a week for six weeks. The sweet, young girl who played the part of *Annie* was Chelsee Oaks. She received standing ovations every night. (A decade later she was a contestant on American Idol, making it through Hollywood week.)

As a result of my involvement in *Annie,* I gained a circle of friends in Traverse City, who have remained some of my most cherished friends. I am indebted to John Dew.

*   *   *

Back at the station on Hastings Street, it appeared that an internal cold war was being waged against older, experienced people. First, the general sales manager, Bob Scott, was fired, followed by my *Annie* mentor, John Dew. They were the two oldest, most accomplished people in the company. I personally felt that it was a violation of age discrimination and harassment laws. I figured that my days were numbered. I didn't care. I hated going to work. Radio wasn't fun anymore. My only friends at work were my morning partners, Sylvia Stahl and Jen Donnelly, and station engineer, Dennis Murray.

The radio road to freedom began in September when Richard, in an apparent effort to get me out of B.D.'s hair, suggested that I move over to the sister rock station WKLT with Dean Berry. The alleged idea was to revive the winning morning show team of *Stan & Dean* from the WAIR oldies days. I had a funny feeling that a disaster was about to develop.

I knew almost nothing about contemporary rock music, therefore, my ignorance would be obvious on the air. Rock fans are probably the world's most hostile music snobs. By contrast, Dean was a virtual rock encyclopedia and viewed ignorance of rock artists and their music as a capital offense, punishable by death. It didn't help that WKLT's program director, Terri Ray, disliked me.

The team lasted less than two weeks, when Dean bounced off the wall during the morning show in an uncontrolled, tearful temper tantrum because I mispronounced the name of a rock artist. He bellowed up and down the station hallway pounding on the walls just as the office staff arrived for work. Fortuitously, the microphone was off. It was the beginning of the end. I guessed that Richard had known what would happen and this latest event was possibly part of the master plan.

Richard called a meeting on Wednesday October 18th in the conference room. In attendance were Richard, Terri Ray, Dean, and me. I imagined how a condemned prisoner felt in medieval days when a jovial crowd showed up to cheer on a beheading.

Richard spoke first. "I don't think the Stan and Dean team is going to work."

"No shit!" I said, as I stared Dean down.

Richard spoke directly to me. "Well, what am I to do? You can't go back to the *Bee,* and it's not working on WKLT. Where do I put you?"

"It's obvious that there is no place for me here, Richard."

Terri Ray couldn't contain a thin smile.

"Maybe I should just leave."

"That might be the only option, Stan. Maybe our consultant Jim Wood can find you a position at one of his stations."

"Yeah, maybe." I was doubtful.

It was then that Richard made an offer that could not be refused. "I have to fire you, but at least you will get severance pay for twelve or thirteen weeks."

A severance package had been part of my contract. Terri's and Dean's eyes bugged out. Apparently, it was not exactly what they wanted to hear.

"I guess that's the best option, Richard. It will give me time to find another job."

"Okay, it's a deal." Richard, wasting no time, rose to leave.

I was unemployed but at least financially safe through Christmas. Most of all, I was relieved to be out of the angry, toxic environment. It was ironic. I had been a program director and morning host in the second largest radio market in the USA, and in a few short years I had been reduced to a reviled outcast by an insecure, vengeful horde. Luckily, I escaped before they showed up with pitchforks and fiery torches at my door!

I knew that I could count on a regular paycheck until the New Year, and I did have some money in a 401k plan. I needed to get off my ass and find work. I did. It took one week to decide that my radio days were over. I was going to fly solo.

*   *   *

I continued my on-again, off-again relationship with Allison. One positive result of our bond was that she invited me to the New Hope Community Church. I found it friendly and motivational, unlike the Catholic Church, which felt robotic, usually with priests that lulled the assembled masses to sleep with mechanical sermons. At the New Hope Church I felt closer to God and simply more spiritual. But it didn't cure my boozing binges.

There were days when I wished that I had a stiff drink to settle my nerves, like the day I encountered Allison's husband, the sheriff. Allison had moved to an apartment but had not yet moved most of her dishes and some furnishings from their house. She pleaded with me to help her move. I was not delighted with the plan to go to the sheriff's house to remove *stuff*, but I agreed, reluctantly. Besides, she promised that he would be at work.

We rented a U-Haul truck and drove to her house on the outskirts of town. She loaded up dishes and pots and pans, then the microwave and all the small kitchen appliances. Then she went for all the table lamps. It seemed that the longer we were there, the more stuff she packed into the truck. I grew more nervous by the minute. When she decided that she wanted to take her husband's coveted big-screen TV, that was where I drew the line.

"Allison, I am not taking his TV. I've heard how much he loves sports."

"He can get another one!"

"No! If he comes home while I'm loading that TV on the truck, I'm a dead man."

"Nah, he won't be home, so unhook it and take it."

His big-screen TV was not like the thin plasma and LCD televisions of today. It was a rear-projection monster, and it was upstairs in the loft.

"How the hell am I supposed to get that thing down the stairs?" I complained, hoping that she would change her mind.

"Just drag it."

"Oh, sure! Do you know how heavy this behemoth is?"

"I'll help you around the corner at the bottom of the stairs."

The stairs had a right-hand turn just before the last four steps. Maneuvering that giant without smashing it to smithereens against the wall at the corner would be tricky, especially when trying to make a 90-degree turn three-quarters of the way down the stairs, but I reckoned that I better get at it before Sheriff Jack came home from work at 5:00.

I unplugged the cables and dragged the beast across the carpet to the edge of the stairs. Then, I gingerly tipped it down over the edge and began gradually sliding it downward. It was a tight fit but, if I carefully held my shoulder against it, it might make it okay. I arrived to within a few feet of the right turn in the stairs. As I stopped to consider how I was going to turn it without crashing it against the wall at the corner, I heard the unmistakable sound of wheels in gravel in the driveway.

"Shit!" I screamed to Allison. "Is that him?"

"Yes, it's him, but don't worry, I'll take care of it."

"Don't worry?! Are you fucking insane? When he sees his favorite TV halfway down the stairs, he'll take care of *me!*"

As I waved my arms wildly at Allison, I unwittingly released my hold on the two-ton TV. Like a slow-moving avalanche, it gave way and slid down, pinning me against the wall at the right turn. It hurt, but not as much as I figured a bullet would. The sheriff ambled into the house in full uniform. My eyes darted immediately to the Glock pistol on his belt.

"What the fuck are you doing with my TV?"

I said nothing as I gawked at him. *Please God, don't let me die pinned behind an ugly TV.*

Allison yelled, "It's my TV, and I'm taking it!"

I wanted to plead with her. *For God's sake, don't argue with him!*

A screaming match ensued while I stood squashed like a dead cockroach between the titanic TV and the wall. Thankfully, he never spoke to me but focused his attention on his out-going wife and his out-going stuff. After an intense argument that ended in the driveway, he sprayed gravel against the house and was gone. While they were outside bellowing, I had squirmed my way out from behind the TV, but as it hit the wall, it created a horizontal hole in the drywall. *Great! Something else to piss him off.*

We loaded up and roared out of the driveway. I'll bet that the U-Haul people were not aware that their trucks could go that fast. I felt sorry for the sheriff. He seemed like a nice guy ordinarily, when he wasn't shooting anyone.

* * *

At AA meetings, I felt welcomed by four hardened old guys who had been there for ages. When we held hands and recited the Lord's Prayer, I wept. I'm not sure why. I had seen those TV sitcoms where people in an AA meeting say, *Hello, my name is Ralph, and I'm an alcoholic.* When my turn came around to say it, I was terrified, except that I didn't say that my name was Ralph. I didn't say that my name was Stan, either. Instead, I used my first name, Alex. I left feeling good.

I went to several AA meetings and enjoyed the repartee, but it didn't seem to help derail my drinking much. Besides, I kept forgetting my name. *Hello, my name is Stan...uh, I mean, Alex.* They assumed that I wasn't Stan *or* Alex, but then that's why it's called Alcoholics *Anonymous*."

After leaving the radio station, I bought a professional quality microphone and an audio mixer and began offering my services as a voiceover talent. In the first week, I scored a new client who needed a dozen or so new radio commercials every month. It didn't bring in a lot of money but the income paid the rent and groceries.

I had not spoken to Allison in a few weeks. We were growing further apart, but on Friday night November 17th, she called me.

"Stan, what are you doing tomorrow?"

"I don't know. I have nothing planned really."

"My friend Bob Johnson, a police officer from Saginaw, is coming up with his wife to visit. They are staying in a suite at a bayside resort on Munson Avenue for the weekend. We're going to get together for dinner and drinks. You want to come along?"

It was a gray, dreary November, as Novembers in the north always are, so I was up for anything to kill the blues. I was depressed and hung over again and busy analyzing my miserable life. I was 60 years old, living in one room sharing an apartment. Most men my age enjoyed a reasonably happy home that had been paid off years earlier and cruised off on vacations to Bora Bora, spent their winters in Boca Raton and summer weekends with their kids and grandkids. I talked to my kids from time to time. They were adults, had their own lives, and were, for the most part, doing well. Rod and Helen were happily married, and both had kids...my grandkids.

Allison and I met Bob Johnson and his wife at the Cherry Capital Inn on Munson Avenue. In their suite, I spied a table covered with more varieties of liquor, wine, and liqueurs than I had ever seen outside a liquor store. Bob and I each downed a shot of tequila followed by sambuca and chased by a beer. Then we left for dinner. At dinner, we consumed a couple of bottles of wine.

By the time we returned to the suite, I was already getting drunk. We continued sampling the myriad intoxicating potions. My lights went out not long afterward, so the anecdote of the evening was hearsay.

Apparently, I became unintelligible, followed by unconscious, followed by violent projectile vomiting throughout the nicely appointed suite, but especially in the bathroom, where I attempted to pray to the porcelain god but mistook the bathtub for the commode. My hosts were apparently not amused. At least that is what I was told.

Being thoroughly drunk out of my brain wasn't enough. After hurling uncontrollably, according to the somewhat less plastered people in my midst, I consumed a few more drinks in a pathetic attempt to settle my stomach. Not surprisingly, I passed out. I displayed no noticeable injuries, so I can safely assume that my unconscious state was self-inflicted. Eventually, our hosts suggested that it might be a good idea if I got to hell out of their vomit-reeking suite. I learned later that they had called the front desk and asked to be moved from their room, as far from the vapors as possible, likely to the next county.

I hereby apologize to the hard-working ladies in housekeeping. Imagine the foul-smelling air when they strolled into that room, a stench only surpassed by a week-old corpse on a hot August night.

Because I have no memory of that night, the following is Allison's recollection, which she kindly agreed to share in writing.

Bob had to carry you out of the bathroom to a bed. Then he proceeded to clean up all of the vomit in the bathroom. You lay on the bed, and we made sure you were on your side, so you didn't choke when you threw up in the waste basket. Bob got you to my car, and I brought you to my apartment because I was afraid to leave you alone. It was another miracle from God that I was able to get you up two flights of stairs, especially when you wanted to just lay down on the steps.

I spent the night next to you in the living room listening to you breathe and sometimes stop breathing. I shook you to make you breathe again. You also had a gurgling in your chest that I had never heard with anyone before. I was so afraid you would die. Stan, I literally prayed for you all night long! I prayed for God to spare your life and perform a healing in you. I was so scared for you, Stan!

When you started to become coherent the next morning, I got you to drink some fluids...of course that made you sick again, but at least some type of liquid got into your system. Eventually, you were able to just take one swallow at a time, wait a bit, and take one more swallow. Actually you were still drunk when you started to come around. I continued the sips of liquid until you were able to take in enough fluid and sit up. When you were strong enough to get up by yourself, I took you home and stayed with you at your house until I knew you were okay.

Allison's description shocked me to the core. There is little doubt that I came close to death that night. It was the beginning of metamorphosis number one.

Tripping Over The Twelve Steps

I had flirted with death by drinking rubbing alcohol on my high school non-graduation night. I drove drunk at more than one hundred miles an hour in Tennessee, flew through the air over a fence in my Gran Torino, and jogged drunk across the tundra in the Arctic clad in a T-shirt and jeans in 60-degree-below-zero weather to wine and seduce a rather attractive Inuit lady. And then there was the latest flirtation with the long sleep. But, something miraculous happened the night that alcohol almost killed me in Traverse City, Michigan.

I was done. No more drinking. Yes, I know, people say that, especially after a dinosaur's hangover, but I was damn sure. The latest drunken night was jarringly different. Maybe I did die briefly. Maybe Allison's prayers saved me. Alcoholics Anonymous was interesting but not helpful other than making me aware of the Twelve Steps.

I did admit that I was powerless over the alcohol monster. As for Step 2, I believe that God did restore me to sanity. I stopped drinking, but unlike most alcoholics, I was honestly blessed with a loss of interest in drinking. I no longer struggled with the desire or need to drink and get drunk. For the first time, I had an out-of-body experience. Not the kind where you float up to the ceiling and see yourself having your tonsils snipped out. I stood outside myself and hated what I saw. I did not like that drunken Stan Campbell guy. When he drank, he was an angry, rude slob. Would this enlightened feeling last?

With my new sobriety, my fiery arguments with Allison decreased as our shaky liaison dissolved. We saw less of each other. The bleak days of late fall segued into Christmas. I'm not a commercial Christmas fan, but I knew that I didn't want to be in Traverse City alone. My friends Tracee, Barry, and Gail wouldn't see me spend Christmas alone, but I really wanted to be around family.

I was barely making it financially with my new voiceover and production business. Luckily, I had acquired a long-term contract to voice and produce radio commercials for a chain of casinos based in Sault Ste. Marie, Michigan. Occasional clients paid poorly and slowly.

Just before Christmas in 2000, a video and movie production company in Traverse City hired me to voice a movie trailer. I thought that this might be my big break. However, it was a low-budget film. The company paid me with a chicken. Well, it was fresh and unfrozen.

Even though money was tight I still had credit cards. I flew to Halifax, Nova Scotia, to spend Christmas with my son Michael and his girlfriend, Sara. My daughter Helen agreed to come from Sydney to Michael's right after Christmas. It was a joyous week and cheered me up to be able to spend time with my two youngest kids.

Back in Traverse City in January, business was slow, the skies were still dark, it snowed every day, and I was alone with no one in my life. That was generally okay. For the first time, I was learning to live with me.

With help from therapist Dr. Kerri Schroder, I began to comprehend some of the scattered idiotic antics of my life and view the wreckage in a new sober light. I was adopted when I was two and a half years old. Even at that age, I might have felt abandoned, hence the fear of being alone.

I was more determined than at any time in my life. I had to find my birth mother! I doubted that I would find her alive, but I needed to make one more desperate attempt to identify her, and thus identify me. I also had to get off the matrimonial merry-go-round.

During one session, Dr. Kerri asked me a question that I could not answer, at least with any clarity.

"What kind of woman do you want in your life?"

"Uh, I don't know. Attractive, nice personality, uh..." I wasn't sure what to say.

"Describe her."

"Describe her? Uh, well, I guess I'll know her when I meet her."

"You don't know?"

"Yes, well, no, I guess not."

I went on to talk about that elusive perfect girl of my dreams. I couldn't see her in my mind, but I had always felt that she was out there, somewhere. I somehow felt that if I could find the ethereal girl that I had been dreaming about, I would love her forever, and we would have peace and joy in our lives.

"Stan, here's an assignment for the next couple of weeks. I want you to go home and make a list of all of the qualities of the perfect woman for you. Take your time, and give it a lot of thought."

I was hesitant. It sounded like a test.

"I also want you to tell me what you cannot tolerate. Every time you think of something, maybe from your past relationships that bothered you, write it down, and bring it back for our next session."

Back home I embarked on a new project apart from describing the perfect girl. This time I would find my mother. Besides, I was in no hurry for another relationship or marriage. For the first time in my life, I was less apprehensive about being alone. I had my great friends, Barry and Tracee and Gail. Gail was going through an ugly divorce. She and I became close friends and yet maintained a warm platonic relationship. I still saw Allison from time to time. She assisted me with my new old project, searching in earnest for my mother, while I assisted her with a weighty project.

Allison was completing her degree at a local college, and the deadline for her thesis was coming up fast. She wasn't ready. She wasn't even close. She was working two jobs and as a result, couldn't seem to find enough time. I offered to help. My assistance expanded into a full-time project. I wrote her thesis for her and handed it in within an hour of the deadline. Weeks later, she received an A. I desperately wanted to brag because I was the guy who hadn't graduated from high school, but I could not divulge the topic or my contribution without the fear that the college would revoke her degree.

Allison and I found several Cecelia MacNeils in Cape Breton all closely matching my mother's age, if she was still alive, which was doubtful. She would be 90. We needed to be sensitive. You cannot call an elderly woman and say, *did you have a kid out of wedlock sixty years ago?*

One lady laughed and said that she had never been in New Waterford, where I was born. The second woman was evasive and sounded guarded. We also spoke to the sons and daughters of women named Cecelia McNeil. Most of them hung up on us. The one suspicious Cecelia needed more homework.

Three weeks later, I went back to Dr. Kerri Schroder's office with a list two pages long describing my perfect woman. The good qualities covered half a page, and the negatives filled the second page. I never again wanted to hear, *what's that supposed to mean?* I had no more patience for the infamous silent treatment. If I ever became involved in another relationship with a woman, it had to be a true partnership, not a competition.

Dr. Schroder seemed impressed with the depth of my list. I was too! I had never given much thought as to what type of personality fit my life and my needs. It was more than liking the same kind of music and movies. Previously, I had seized the first girl who liked me, and marriage was a sure-fire method of keeping her attached to me. Dr. Schroder encouraged me to keep adding to the list.

I was learning to live alone, in my own skin. Well, *Mama* and me. *Mama* was my 10-year-old gray cat. She was no fun to invite out to dinner, and she wasn't allowed in a movie theatre.

Even though I didn't feel the need to be united in matrimony or in a committed relationship, I was lonely and going through a somewhat sex-deprived interlude. I didn't have a buddy to hang out with. I had never gotten into hanging out with the boys, especially as I grew older. I was not a major-league sports fan, and sitting around drinking beer on a Saturday with a bunch of jocks didn't interest me.

I enjoyed an hour of one-on-one lunches with a male friend to discuss politics, work, or life in general, but I preferred the company of women. I sometimes wondered if I might be gay, but given my sexual fixation with women, it wasn't likely. The thought of intimacy with a male gave me a chill.

I looked forward to the end of the dull days of the winter of 2001. On an especially boring evening, I searched the Internet for dating websites. I wanted a site that wasn't only about sex and marriage. Of course, if sex was involved, that would be an additional benefit.

I browsed the typical singles websites. Most were cheesy and focused on kinky sex or immediate marriage. I was over both of those things...well, one of them. I searched for Christian or conservative sites in an attempt to weed out the cheese. I found more cheese of a different flavor until I stumbled onto a site called *Singles with Scruples*. The focus was on a slightly older and more conventional crowd. I paid nine dollars and ninety-five cents for a month-long membership and logged on as Alex in a thin attempt to avoid detection by friends and relatives. After all, Alexander is my first name.

I reasoned that I should keep my search local in Northern Michigan so that if I found someone, we could meet for dinner, a movie, or a drive in the country...or rowdy, reckless sex in the Northern Michigan woods! I narrowed my search to ages 45 to 60.

Most women in Northern Michigan were pictured in army fatigues or a plaid shirt standing by a pickup truck, rifle in hand,

and a deer hanging head down on the front porch. That might work for some people. I widened my search to include all of Michigan. I found an attractive professional lady in Farmington Hills in suburban Detroit. She claimed that she was an entertainment attorney. I sent her a message.

Where are you? The lawyer lady asked.

I'm in Traverse City.

Where is Traverse City?

I was bewildered. She had allegedly passed the bar exam but evidently flunked geography. She lived in the same state.

Hey, I know where Farmington Hills is. How come you don't know where Traverse City is?

The conversation was over. That issue was on my list. My perfect woman must possess some knowledge of the world around her.

I widened my search, realizing that whomever I might meet would be a pen-pal due to the probable geographic separation.

The search went on for two weeks until Saturday, April 7, 2001, when I found a pretty lady standing on a sand dune with her hair blowing in the wind. Her nickname was *La Boheme*. I read her short profile, and something about it caught my interest. She said that the person she most admired was her father. I liked that. She wrote that she spoke English and French as well as her native Spanish. I assumed that we would never meet, but we could write back and forth, if she would only respond. I sent her a message.

On Sunday morning, my roommate Cyndi announced that she was moving out in two weeks to an apartment in Elk Rapids, just north of Traverse City. I had the place to myself...Mama and me. Cyndi was a good friend, but I was pleased to have the apartment to myself, even if it was tough to pay the rent alone. I would convert her bedroom into a studio and stop using my bedroom closet as a sound booth. If I did find a lady who enjoyed sharing a night of lust, I wouldn't have to worry about our noise.

On Sunday afternoon, I logged onto the dating site. There was a pleasant note from La Boheme. She wanted to know more about me. I surmised that this might be a short conversation.

Four?

La Boheme started out with the usual banter, and the conversation evolved into personal questions about height, weight, and age. I lied. Just a little. In La Boheme's profile, she indicated that she was interested in someone between 45 and 58. I was over the limit. I had just turned 60 but in my profile, I said that I was 58. After a couple of days of e-mailing each other, I finally felt comfortable enough to tell her my real age.

Alex, you don't look like you are 60 in your pictures.

Thank you. I take good care of myself.

I didn't mention that only six months earlier I had almost died of alcohol poisoning.

How old are those pictures? She inquired, demonstrating her distrust, now that I had admitted lying about my age.

The first picture that I had sent to La Boheme was a Glamour Shot from five years earlier. Not a huge deal, but my candid pictures looked different.

I liked La Boheme. She was charming with a quick sense of humor. However, I didn't break any ice with my less-than-perfect honesty. She was more forthcoming, or so it seemed. She divulged her real name, Marta Ramirez. Her family called her Martica, which in Spanish means little Marta. I suspected that she might be a poor Latin lady seeking an easy path to the USA.

However, she claimed that she came from a successful and artistic family. She said that her father had owned a business for almost sixty years and that she and her family had traveled throughout the world. She claimed that she had been educated in Europe.

I wanted to ask why she was on a dating website. After all, she was attractive (unless her picture was twenty years old, or it wasn't her picture) and part of a seemingly secure, creative family. She alleged that her mother was a renowned painter, and she had a brother who was an opera singer in Milan. That wasn't all. She told me that a brother-in-law was a senior member of the Colombian government, rubbing shoulders with the country's president.

I, on the other hand, was a 60-year-old man sharing an apartment with a 10-year-old gray cat and struggling to make a living in a bedroom closet with my voice-over business. I had little to offer, and I had admitted to lying about my age and sending an old Glamour Shot. I decided that from this moment forward, I was going to be completely honest and up front. My truth-in-advertising timing couldn't have been worse.

Alex, in your profile, you said that you are divorced?

Oh, no! This was going to be the beginning of the end. *Yes, that's right.*

Maybe I should simply say good-bye and sign off.

Just once, right?

No...

Twice? Her font size increased to maybe a 14.

No, I'm afraid not. I was more than afraid.

Alex! Three times? The font blew up to a 20 bold.

No...

I thought I heard a countdown like when the space shuttle is about to take off.

It took what seemed like two hours for the response to come back to me on Yahoo Messenger.

I waited.

Across the width of the screen, huge bold red letters jumped out at me.

FOUR TIMES?

I hesitated and finally wrote *yes* in the tiniest font I could find.

I waited. I stared unblinking at a blinking cursor. Had La Boheme logged off for the last time? My heart sank. I liked her. Okay, so I hadn't actually met her yet, but from what I could tell during our several days of conversation, she seemed like a gentle soul. She was also educated and creative, and to my surprise, she loved country music, or was she toying with me in an attempt to get closer? Maybe she was a talented actress? Maybe hens were pecking their way through her adobe casa and a mule was tied up out back.

How could I know for sure? Well, she did have a computer. I knew that the dating sites were rife with women in foreign countries who were clever at duping North American men to gain a fast track to citizenship or their money. The money part wasn't an issue for me. I didn't have any.

FOUR TIMES? Alex, you've been married four times? The words blazed across my screen, still in red. At least she was still talking to me.

I typed another tiny *yes* in my reply space. I wanted to lie and tell her that my ex-wives were all drug-crazed, serial-killer psychopaths. I waited. Maybe she needed to confirm that shocker before she said good-bye. At least I hoped that she would say good-bye and not simply disconnect. Again, I waited. I could not take my eyes off the screen. I didn't blink. I feared that I would see, *La Boheme has logged out.*

Alex, are you divorced now? She was back in black type.

Yes, six months ago.

Then the question came that exonerated me. *How long did your marriages last?*

The first one was seven years, the second one was also seven years, the third was five years, and the last one to Susan was thirteen years.

You were serious about the last one. You stayed together for thirteen years.

We continued talking and talking and talking...for three weeks. One Sunday we chatted online for seven hours non-stop. Well, we weren't talking. We were typing. In 2001, Internet voice communication around the world was erratic.

I thought that I should surprise her. One evening in late April, I called her on the phone. We both laughed with embarrassment at finally hearing each other's voices. I did my best to impress her with my richest radio voice. It was then that she dropped an ultimatum.

"Alex, we have chatted on Yahoo Messenger as much as we can. If we are to go any further, we need to meet. Why don't you come here to Colombia and meet my family and my friends?"

"Uh, why don't you come here?" I countered.

I instantly recalled stories of murder, kidnapping guerrillas, drug lords, and Pablo Escobar while visualizing sinister pictures in my head when I heard the city name, Bogotá. It almost sounded like boogieman.

"No, I think that since you are the man, you should come here first. Besides, you will love my country."

"But you have family in St. Louis and Montana."

I was also aware that a flight to Colombia would be expensive. I could barely pay the rent with the money from my one-man business.

"No, I can't come there right now. I cannot leave my father's company, and my daughter Natalia needs me here while she is finishing University."

I relented. "Okay. I will think about it tonight."

"Good! You won't be disappointed," she whispered with her sexy Latin accent.

That did it. I would find a way. I had to check my one and only credit card balance. Did I really have the courage to travel all the way to South America...to see a woman? What about the violence? What if she was a front for the Marxist guerillas or the drug lords? I had heard about women who entice a guy into a trap in a foreign country, and then he is never heard from again. Then again, I had been honest with her. I had told her that I was living a frugal life with barely enough money coming in to pay the rent and buy groceries. Maybe after our conversations about working in L.A. and Nashville and rubbing shoulders with big stars, she might have thought that I was really rolling in dough and that *I* was the one playing the game, pretending that I was a poor boy.

I was torn. Should I go? What if I didn't go? I would have to say good-bye to this seemingly adorable lady. I slept on it. I told Cyndi. She didn't mince words. She told me that I had lost my mind. However, I was 60 years old. I had lived an unruly, foolish life up to that point. What did I have to lose?

Only my life.

Kidnapped

I signed my Will. I was prepared to die. I boarded my flight from Traverse City, Michigan, to Bogotá, Colombia, with a stop in Miami. I was excited and fearful.

The A320 lined up to land on the runway at El Dorado International Airport in Bogotá. I had read that about eight million people lived in this sprawling city on the highest plateau in the Andes.

My fear rose as the wheels touched the tarmac. What the hell was I doing? My ex-boss Richard was right. I might die here. Cyndi told me that I was crazy. Maybe. It was too late to turn back. The flight attendants opened the cabin door.

Passengers from my flight filed out into the airport. Everyone around me spoke Spanish. I knew *hola, como estas?,* and the most important phrase, *donde esta el baño?,* in case I needed a quick escape to the men's room.

I picked up my one bag and got into the long line for Colombian Immigration. I spotted two intimidating men in uniform with what looked like AK-47s at the ready. I assumed that they were there to protect us, but the fact that they required that kind of weaponry didn't exactly make me feel warm and fuzzy.

I was next. I handed the immigration guy behind the glass my Canadian passport. He said nothing, examined my picture, and flipped through several pages and then ran it under a scanner. I was afraid that he might ask me a question in Spanish, and I would have to give him the dumb look.

"Sir, what is the purpose of your visit to Colombia?" he asked in surprisingly good English.

I think that is when the unsettling reality struck me that I was actually in Colombia, South America, notorious for violent drug lords and guerillas.

I spoke softly, hoping that the American couple behind me wouldn't hear me. "Uh, I'm here to meet a woman."

"Sir, you will have to speak up."

"I am here to meet a lady."

"What is the lady's name, Señor?"

"Marta Lucia Ramirez," I answered, this time a bit louder, trying to show off how well I could pronounce *Ramirez* with a Spanish accent.

He didn't seem impressed.

"How do you know this woman?"

"We met on the Internet." I whispered again.

He paused scanning his computer screen.

He smiled ever so slightly. "Go ahead, Señor. Enjoy your time in Colombia." He handed me my passport.

I was relieved that I was not escorted to a dirty concrete room by menacing men with AK-47s and rubber gloves for an in-depth interrogation.

I was about to meet her face-to-face. I suddenly felt more fearful of this encounter than of a kidnapping. Then again, this *could* be a kidnapping. Maybe her amigos waited out there in the shadowy city? Nevertheless, I was there, and I was ready for whatever fate awaited. Almost. I was also dressed for the occasion, as directed.

*   *   *

A week before my flight, Martica had made a request.

"Do you have a black suit?" she asked.

"Yes, I have a double-breasted black suit."

"What about a pink shirt?"

"A pink shirt? Are you kidding? No!"

"I want you to wear a pink shirt and tie."

"A pink shirt *and* a pink tie?"

"Yes, please."

"Okay...I will have to go buy one. I hope nobody I know sees me."

I found a pink dress shirt, and to balance it a bit I found a cool Jerry Garcia tie with some pink in it. I even found a pink handkerchief.

One other issue came up in our many conversations over our six weeks of chatting. We had talked about family, ex-spouses, friends, work, philosophy, and our spiritual and religious beliefs. I rarely attended Mass anymore but instead, spent more time at the New Hope Community Church, which was essentially non-denominational Christian. In a discussion about our beliefs, I described myself as Christian. Martica seemed uneasy with that. Her encounters with Christians in Colombia had been unpleasant. They were apparently the extreme fundamental variety that condemned all forms of fun, including television, movies, music, sex, and dancing. You do not tell Latinos to stop dancing!

That Christian label came close to being a deal-breaker when I exited the secure area and out into the main Bogotá terminal to search the waiting crowd for a sign with my name *Alex* on it. An imposter almost changed my life.

Martica stood behind the glass in the main terminal with the assembled masses waiting to greet loved ones and business associates. She held her *Alex* sign aloft. She scanned the crowd exiting the baggage claim area searching for a man in a black suit, pink shirt, and pink tie. She waited. Hundreds exited. There were black suits but no pink ties, until she spotted a short, rotund man in a black suit and a pink shirt. He appeared angry. Then she noticed that the grouchy man in the black suit and pink tie sported an enormous cross around his neck, extending down to his midsection. He looked like he could be an anti-dancer if ever there was one! She swiftly yanked the *Alex* sign down out of sight. Dejected at first, she watched him as he passed by her. He seemed to know exactly where he was going. He met with an equally crabby friend.

Relieved, she raised her sign again in time to see another black suit, pink tie, and pink handkerchief. This guy was not quite as short or as round. She smiled. I smiled, kind of the way that a baby does when he poops in his diaper. I was relieved and terrified.

I stopped. I thought she appeared different from her picture. She was pretty but taller than I expected. We hugged uncomfortably, stopped, and looked at each other again and exited out into the forbidding Colombian world.

She had a car with a driver waiting outside. Martica and I slid into the backseat. As we left the airport and drove out into the surprisingly dark streets of Bogotá, I wondered if the quiet man driving was really a driver, or an *accomplice*. Now that I had met Martica in person, she was unusually silent. So was I. It was as if we had never engaged in those long, intimate conversations just days earlier.

Martica had arranged a hotel room for me. Before I left home, I suggested that maybe I could stay at her place. That idea was flatly rejected. As we drove on and on, I hoped that we were on our way to a hotel, and not to a shallow grave on the mountain above Bogotá. As we drove through dimly lit streets and neighborhoods I noticed that every house and business was protected by heavy bars on the windows and doors.

I felt more relaxed when we reached a brightly lit neighborhood with a large shopping mall on the right and fashionable apartments and condos on the other side, and my hotel. We pulled into the underground parking at the La Fontana hotel. I breathed a sigh of relief, until a man with an automatic weapon stepped out of the shadows. For a heart-stopping moment, I thought that was it! He was in fact a hotel security guard, who politely motioned us to a parking spot. No one holding an AK-47 had ever smiled at me before.

Our driver unloaded my bag. I relaxed as I watched him drive away. Checking in was easy with Martica's help. We walked up to the second floor to my room, which was a nicely-appointed suite overlooking a courtyard with a tiny white domed mission church in the middle. I sat on a couch. Martica sat across from me in a wingback chair. A massive coffee table separated us. We stared at each other. Now what?

Once More With Fear

After Martica left, I barred the door with a table and a chair to prevent the bad guys from crashing through and robbing me of my Timex watch, a maxed out credit card, and fifty thousand pesos, which amounted to twenty dollars. I felt nervous. I heard noises in the hallway. I suspected that it was *them* preparing to blast through my door.

Martica and I had spent three hours seated, facing each other across the room, engaged in conversation about every mundane subject we could fabricate. We didn't kiss. We didn't hug or even hold hands. No romantic talk. Our nervous conduct contrasted with our highly intimate online conversations. We had both already uttered the *love* word online. There was no love apparent in room 223 at La Fontana that night.

We laughed nervously and told stories, but we acted like friends who had lived next door to each other many years earlier. We engaged in an unromantic kiss and a hug as we said good-night. As soon as she was out the door, I fortified my room and brushed my teeth with bottled water. I slept fitfully with the window slightly open.

"*En el nombre del padre, del hijo y del espiritu santo...*"

Oh, my God! Had I died and gone to heaven? I awoke to voices reciting what sounded like the rosary in Spanish. I felt my face. Yes, I was still alive. I could still hear women's voices, and I heard the words *Ave Maria*. It sounded familiar like *Hail Mary*, which my mother had taught me.

I jumped out of bed and ran to the window and peered into the entrance of the white mission-style chapel in the courtyard, where a group of ladies kneeled in prayer. Instead of fear, I felt moved. It was a beautiful scene, interrupted by the phone.

A lady asked in broken English, "Señor, would you like your breakfast now?"

I had forgotten about that part. Room service was included, and not only delivery.

"Oh, yes, please give me ten minutes while I get dressed."

The ladies reciting the rosary put me at ease, if only a bit. It took me back to my childhood in Cape Breton, yet this was a long way from Jamesville West.

Ten minutes later, there was a knock at my door. I cautiously glanced through the peephole to see a pretty lady holding a tray. I opened the door cautiously, still wary.

"Buenos dias, Señor Campbell! Did you sleep well?"

"Buenos dias, Señora! Si...yes," I answered, switching to English in case she might switch to Spanish.

She made coffee in the room, cooked eggs, set the table, and served breakfast. I could get used to this. Someone knocked at the door again. My heart stopped. I peeked through the peephole expecting to see a gang of armed banditos. It was Martica, grinning from ear to ear, ready to show me around Bogotá.

After a shower and breakfast, Martica and I set out. We walked and walked. I had an important mission. I needed to visit the Canadian Embassy. I was told back home that I should register with my Embassy, just in case I was killed or kidnapped. I rode the elevator up to the 14th floor in a modern building on Carrera Septima while Martica sat outside in the sun. A security guard stopped me at the door and scanned me for God knows what.

"No pistola?" He laughed.

"Huh? No! No pistola." I chuckled with him.

He was obviously Colombian and friendly. That is where the friendly zone ended. Legally, I was in Canada. A picture of Prime Minister Jean Chrétien hung on the wall along with a prominent

Canadian flag and a picture of a red canoe. It felt like home until I introduced myself.

"Excuse me. I need to register as a visitor in Colombia."

I expected a smile and a welcome to Colombia. Instead, a scowling lady tossed me a paper through a slot in the glass.

"Fill in the form and bring it back here," she said curtly.

"Thank you." I expected a response.

There was none.

I answered the questions on the form and handed it back with a smile.

"Is that all?" I asked.

"Yes." She didn't look up

I offered a friendly, "Bye."

She turned her back to me.

Canadians like to boast of their friendliness. It was not evident at the Canadian Embassy.

For the next few days, Martica and I walked, flagged down taxis, and rode in her car through gridlock Bogotá traffic, where stopping at stop signs and red lights is simply a suggestion.

On a personal level, Martica and I became closer and then, much closer. I adored this Latin lady with the positive, fun attitude. The feeling was obviously mutual, but the stress level suddenly intensified when it was time to meet her mom, and under nerve-racking circumstances.

Before I had left Traverse City, Martica convinced me that I should show off my culinary talents by preparing dinner at her place. Not solely for her but for her entire family. It was my fault for bragging about my kitchen talents, which in reality were mediocre to good but lacking in consistency.

We scheduled the big dinner with la familia on Saturday night with Mom and Dad, brother Juan, two sisters, Pilar and Amparo, with their husbands, and Natalia, Martica's youngest daughter. The general consensus was that if Natalia didn't like me, I was toast.

On the day of the dinner, the first vote came in. Mama voted me down. She made it clear that she would not endorse this shoddy, quickie relationship and therefore would not attend. She was not aware that we had met on the Internet. Martica had fibbed, telling her that we had met through a mutual business acquaintance. Papa, otherwise known lovingly to the family as *Tato*, agreed to come. I had heard that he was a likable man.

I chose a menu that I assumed would be novel to them...a mix of Indian and Thai dishes. It was an unwise decision. I discovered too late that they had traveled throughout the world, so I was not about to impress them with my exotic menu. As I arrived at Martica's apartment, I met her 22-year-old daughter Natalia for the first time. She was beautiful and adorable like her mom. We seemed to connect.

My bill of fare consisted of tandoori chicken, saffron rice, and something I called a New Delhi deli salad. Dinner was set for 7:00 p.m. At 6:50 the intercom buzzed. The family was downstairs with a surprise. Mama was with them. Holy crap! This was going to be a nail-biter. Her imposing reputation preceded her. A minute later, there was a knock at the door. I hid in the kitchen.

Sisters Pilar and Amparo strolled into the kitchen with their husbands. They were gracious. Then Tato entered the room. He could have floated in. He radiated an aura of tranquility. I liked him immediately. It was obvious that he was highly respected and loved. Then she walked in. Bertha, Martica's mother. She was fashionably attired. I felt as though I was in the presence of royalty as I shook her hand.

Twenty minutes later, after drinks, we served dinner. The family approved of my culinary efforts. Everyone beamed and declared how delicious it was. I found out later that they had not been completely truthful. Apparently, they burped cardamom for a week! It was not an ideal introduction to the family.

During dinner, I was under observation. I got along well with Martica's brother Juan. He had lived in the USA for several years, so we were able to connect easily. He displayed a zany, dark sense of humor. Most significantly, the family noticed that Natalia and I enjoyed each other's company.

The family left around midnight, but the jury was out. Had I won anyone's heart? More importantly, what did Mama think? We would have to wait. Martica drove me back to my hotel. Sleeping overnight at her house was forbidden, especially with her daughter living at home. There wasn't much sleeping back at the hotel, either. I tossed and turned, belching cardamom.

The phone woke me out of bad dream about a disastrous radio show. I had a lot of those.

"You're not going to believe this!"

I was in fog but woke up at once.

"What happened?" I asked.

Martica sounded like she might have good news.

"My mom called this morning."

"Oh, crap!" Maybe it wasn't good news after all.

"She has never done this!"

At 60 years of age, I felt like a teenager on my first date. It was as though I needed her parents' blessing before I could date their daughter, but as Martica had expressed in her profile, she admired and respected her father and mother.

"Well, first of all, my father really likes you," she said, as she apparently braced me for the rest of the news.

"I also like him, but I don't think your mom likes me very much, or she doesn't approve of me."

"Well she called this morning and asked if I thought that you might care to come to lunch at her place tomorrow."

We were both thrilled, but I then had something new to worry about. It was just lunch, but I had a feeling that I was going to be grilled.

I was wrong. It was a somewhat formal but pleasant lunch at which Martica's mom served her home-made soup, *Ajiaco*. It was delicious and contained no cardamom. Juan came to lunch too, which made me feel more comfortable.

My time in Colombia was ending, but I could not end my relationship with Martica. I had fallen in love with her and was not about to let her go. I could not leave without a commitment, yet, here I was, scarcely six months out of a divorce, and I was doing it again! Again! I asked myself if I had ever felt like this before. Something told me that this was out of the ordinary. Besides, this time it wasn't because I was afraid to be alone. I was much more comfortable in my own skin. I asked Martica if she would move to the USA with me so that we could simply live together. The idea of another marriage terrified me. She rejected the proposal but offered an option.

"Why don't I come and visit you and meet your family and friends, and I can see how you live?"

Her reasoning was based on the maxim, *show me who your friends are, and I'll tell you who you are.*

"Okay, deal! Let's buy your ticket right now."

I was unwilling to let this opportunity slip away. I called my travel agent friend in Michigan. I bought a ticket for Martica to visit me in Traverse City for ten days in July. It was done. So was my credit card.

On June 5th, I said a gloomy good-bye to Martica at the El Dorado International Airport and farewell to a country that I had begun to love. It was not as scary as I had been led to believe. Colombia and Marta Ramirez were in my heart. I arrived back in Traverse City on Tuesday night, missing Martica immensely and yet hopeful.

I became particularly irritating to all my friends, including Tracee, Barry, Gail, and Chelsee, nattering non-stop about Martica and Colombia. I played Latin music at home and in my car incessantly with the sun-roof and windows wide open. I played it for my friends, over and over, and expected them to love it as much as I did.

I was in love, and I wanted to flaunt my new Latin love. Martica and I burned up the phone lines and Internet discussing our plans. I wanted to take her to visit Canada, my home and native land. Therein began my second bad experience with the Canadian Embassy in Bogotá.

Colombians require a visa to visit the USA and Canada. She already had a U.S. visa. That was easy. However, obtaining an approval to visit Canada was a long, exasperating process dealing with exceptionally rude Canadian immigration personnel in Colombia. I was compelled to send the Embassy my bank records, my birth certificate, rent receipts, police records, and a picture of the birthmark on my butt. (Okay, that last one was an exaggeration). The paperwork requirement was as frustrating as their rudeness was infuriating. As a Canadian, I was ashamed that these people represented Canada abroad.

Martica arrived at the Detroit airport on Tuesday, July 17th. I booked a hotel room in Windsor, Ontario, across the border from Detroit. The next day we drove to Montréal for a few days and returned through Ottawa, North Bay, and on through Sault Ste. Marie to Traverse City. The weather was perfect, and I was blissfully happy with Martica by my side. What could go wrong?

When we arrived at my apartment in Traverse City, there was a message from Martica's older, married daughter Penelope in Missoula, Montana. Although Natalia was carefree and fun-loving, Penelope was much more serious. She wanted to fly to Traverse City to visit her mom. I knew that this wasn't only an opportunity to see Mom, but she wanted to check out the dubious new boyfriend that her mother had met on the Internet. I'm sure she thought that her mother had lost her mind, especially when she found that that I had been married four times previously.

When Penelope arrived, I was sure that she was going to attempt to talk her mom out of this foolish Internet relationship. I sensed her analyzing my every move and phrase. To her, my previous marriages were troublesome, as they should have been. After several days, Penelope returned to Montana, and Martica packed. I was not going to let her go away from me without planning the next step, so I did something that I had never done before. I got down on bended knee and asked her to marry me. She tearfully said yes.

We set a date. I loved her madly, and yet I was apprehensive about getting married again...and so soon. I had no choice. I was not about to let this angel fly away. Martica was equally determined that she was not going to go through the rest of her life alone. She had been divorced eleven years earlier and had seriously dated only one man during that time, until she caught him in bed with another woman. She needed to know that I would never do that to her.

Could I truly do this? My history was appallingly stained with affairs in my previous marriages, yet there was something exceptionally different about this woman apart from the obvious. Or, was it just my imagination? Hadn't I been sure before?

I felt in my heart and soul that she was *the one*. I felt more convinced than at any time in my life that no other woman could entice me. I made a promise to myself and to her that I would never lie to her about anything, no matter how trivial. We made a plan, one that was swift and dramatic.

Upon Martica's arrival back in Colombia, she would sell or rent her condo immediately and come back to me in the USA for good. We set our wedding date for October 27, 2001, only three months hence. It was a colossal leap of faith on her part. For me, the idea of wedding number five was frightening and truthfully, embarrassing. I knew that my family and friends would either laugh or groan with derision.

Martica had never been away from home for an extended period, other than when she attended University in Europe for a year. She was about to leave her mom and dad, her sisters, a brother, devoted friends, and most of all, her daughter Natalia, who was still attending University in Bogotá. The enormity of her life-changing decision did not impact me until I began to write this book. For her, it was an enormous leap of courage, faith, hope, and above all, love.

Almost immediately, she found a renter for her condo. She sold or gave away most of her possessions (another heartbreaking choice) and bought a ticket to fly to Detroit, Michigan, on September 12, 2001. Fate would intervene.

9/11

My former wife, Susan, called. "Can you help me install a ceiling fan?"

Following our divorce, Susan and I remained cordial, and sometimes she asked for handyman help around her new house. Martica was okay with that. It was one of the many attributes that I loved about her.

"Sure, I'll come over tomorrow morning around 9:00."

I was in a great mood. Martica was due to arrive in just over forty-eight hours. I felt that it was best to not share that information with Susan, though.

Tuesday morning arrived, and I showered, dressed, had my morning cereal, and hopped in the car for the ten-minute drive to Susan's place. Being a radio guy, I scanned the dial in the car listening to different radio stations. I picked up a weak signal from the news-talk station WJR in Detroit. A man and a woman talked about how an airplane, apparently a commercial jetliner, had crashed into one of the World Trade Center towers in New York. I was shocked. How could such an accident happen?

As I arrived in Susan's driveway, the announcer shouted, "Another airplane has just crashed into the second tower!"

Like everyone else in the world, I was stunned. I ran to Susan's door and rang the doorbell and knocked simultaneously.

"Susan, turn on the TV!" I shouted, as I barged in the door.

She had already heard the news. "It's already on. My God, this is horrible."

Susan and I watched the terror unfold and cried as the towers fell. I felt like I would throw up. The world seemed like it was coming to an end. This was Armageddon. My joy of a few hours earlier had dissolved to despair. All incoming flights to and from and within the USA were cancelled until further notice. All flights already in the air had to land immediately. What was happening to the world? Would this be the beginning of World War III?

After several hours and a hastily installed ceiling fan, I drove home, still listening to the radio. I felt like the world had suddenly changed. Martica would not be coming tomorrow. I developed an intense feeling of dread. I grieved for the innocent people who had perished in front of the entire world that day and the pain of their distraught families.

For me personally, I couldn't help feeling that I would never see Martica again. I called her at her father's office and spoke to her brother Juan. He, like everyone else, was shocked beyond belief. Martica wasn't there. I felt even more desperate.

My oldest son Rod called from the road in Alberta. "Dad, are you okay?"

"Yes, yes, I'm fine."

"Dad, I was worried. I know how often you travel. I wanted to be sure that you weren't on one of those planes."

"No, thank God." I was touched by his call.

We talked a bit more about the horror of the day and how we needed to get together soon. Family seemed to mean so much more than usual on that day.

Later in the afternoon I finally got to talk to Martica at home. We were both in mourning for the innocent people who had died that day. Of course, her flight was in doubt. If and when she did fly, I was terrified that more of these insane terrorists might bring down more planes...including hers!

For three nights, I did not sleep except to doze off to a quick nightmare. I was convinced that I had found the woman that I had dreamed of since childhood. Now, I imagined that because of the sins of my life, God was about to take her away from me as punishment for my immoral deeds. I had already stopped drinking, and I was determined to get my act together, once and for all. I just needed one more chance.

On Friday evening Martica called. "I'm on standby for tomorrow morning. The planes are flying again. I have to be at the airport at 3:00 a.m. The flight leaves at 6:00, stopping in Atlanta."

Martica had sold almost everything she owned and rented out her condo. Natalia moved in with her Dad, Ruben. I was awestruck by Martica's faith in our six-month-old relationship.

I didn't sleep on Friday night. I got up early on Saturday morning and began the four-hour drive from Traverse City to the Detroit Metro Airport. This time, the airport was like a fortress, with military and security guards with automatic weapons slung over their shoulders.

A war was underway in my stomach. Martica called me on my cell phone from Atlanta. I was at least relieved that she was in North America. Her flight was one of the first to arrive in Atlanta since September 11th. I asked God to guide her plane safely to Detroit.

At 5:50 p.m., her flight touched down in Detroit. At 6:30 there was no sign of her. I scanned peoples' gloomy faces as they passed me dragging their luggage behind them. I witnessed loved ones hugging each other. Many wept. It had been a highly emotional week. I waited. I became almost panic-stricken until...I thought I saw her far down the long hallway wearing a heavy winter coat dragging her carry-on bag.

It was her! She was, as always, smiling. She was here! I was never going to let her out of my sight again. She was here...for good.

I booked a room at the Hampton Inn in Madison Heights, where we could spend the night before our drive north to Traverse City. After all, it had been a stressful day. We were finally together, forever.

I made one embarrassing gaffe. As people regularly do when dragging luggage into a hotel room, I had turned the deadbolt lock out so the door wouldn't close all the way. In our excitement, I forgot and left the door, more or less, open. Later that evening we discovered why the kids across the hall giggled outside our door.

The next day, we drove to Traverse City to begin our lives together. It was September 16th. We planned to get married on October 27th in Toronto or Montréal. We determined that there was a ton of red tape in getting licenses and approvals in Canada, so we were forced to change the location to Traverse City. In addition, the Canadian Embassy in Bogotá, in its customary inflexible manner, refused to grant Natalia a Canadian visa, yet she had a U.S. visa, which she had easily obtained several years earlier.

On October 27, 2001, Martica and I were married, with her daughter Natalia as bridesmaid and my friend Dale Oaks as my best man, at our Harbour Ridge Community Clubhouse in Traverse City, Michigan. The ceremony was conducted by Reverend Judy Wise from the Unitarian Church. I had been married three times previously by judges. This time, I wanted God to be included.

My best true blue friends in Traverse City attended. Sadly my kids couldn't attend. Rod had planned to come, but when we moved the wedding to Michigan, he couldn't come. Martica wanted her father and mother to attend, but Tato had serious leg problems and could not make the trip. Instead, Martica's brother Jaime drove from St. Louis to give her away. He was unsure about me. A part of me wasn't sure either.

I loved Martica very much. She was the sweetest, most gentle lady I had ever known. She was witty, bright, talented, and educated, and I knew that she loved me, but I was uneasy. I had promised myself and Dr. Kerri Schroder that I was not going to rush into another marriage.

A part of me felt like a fool. What were my family and friends thinking? There I was getting married *again*...for the fifth time, and this time I had been divorced for less than a year. I prayed that I was right this time. I was sure that I was, but hadn't I been sure at least two or three other times? I convinced myself that I had never been *this* sure. Or was I fooling myself?

Martica and I settled into married life in the apartment that I had shared with Cyndi. I worked as a freelancer, voicing and producing commercials and working part-time on-air at WTCM Radio. I liked WTCM. Unlike at my previous radio station, the management and staff treated me with respect.

Martica and I loved Traverse City and enjoyed spending time with our treasured friends there, but we wanted to be closer to the action. We both loved the culture, the history, and the style of Montréal. Well I *thought* I did. We decided to move. After all, I was a Canadian citizen, and I was self-employed. I could move there with no problem.

This time, back in Canada, I would formulate a final no-holds-barred goal to uncover my birth parents' identity, dead or alive. This time, with Martica's help, I would put that ghost behind me. This time, I would not stop until I knew where I had come from.

Mom's Note From The Other Side

During radio broadcasts back to L.A. from Montréal ten years earlier, I had thought of Montréal as European chic. What I had not considered was the fact that I was viewed as a mini-celebrity from Hollywood back then. Martica was thrilled. She remarked that Montréal felt Latin. It was a new life together in a new place. However, it was 2002, and I was no celebrity.

On the first night in Montréal...or what we had thought was Montréal, everything changed. The apartment was actually in Laval, across the river north of Montréal. Over the course of one evening, I hated it. We hadn't noticed when we checked the place out and signed the lease that this modern, new 24-story building on the edge of the river was filled with cranky, rude seniors, much older than us. I spoke almost no French, but Martica had studied in Europe and spoke fluent French. Because her French was not Québécois French, she was snubbed, as was I with my English and minimal French.

On a positive note, Martica and I grew closer. More and more I became convinced that I had finally made the right decision. We began the process for Martica to obtain Landed Immigrant status, the equivalent of a U.S. Green Card. Within a year, she was accepted. We celebrated, but she missed her daughter Natalia. We applied for Natalia to also immigrate to Canada. I was nervous because she had been denied a visitor visa by the obnoxious Canadian Embassy people in Bogotá.

I began again, as I had done so many times, to attempt to find out who my natural mother was. I could not understand why my adoptive parents had been so hush-hush about my origin. In fact, our neighbors and friends in Cape Breton seemed to whisper behind closed doors about my roots. They changed the subject or ran away when I broached the topic. *I am going to get to the bottom of this. Who am I? Why the mystery? What if I have a half-brother or half-sister?* I needed to find out. I would not give up this time.

While in Traverse City, I had applied to become an American citizen. I had been living and working in the USA for almost twenty years. I loved living in the United States and began to feel more American than Canadian. I felt accepted. I had moved to the USA in 1984, and within a year, following a disastrous five years in the record business, I was back in radio. The first day on the job, I had received praise from co-workers, management, and the industry in general. In a few months, I had received a promotion, then a bigger job offer in Cincinnati, followed by a huge job offer in Los Angeles. I was invited to host coast-to-coast radio shows live from Hollywood and Nashville.

I had achieved more success in my first seven years in the USA than in my previous 44 years in Canada. As a result, I wanted to be a part of the United States of America, the land of opportunity. I also felt in my heart that I wanted to be one with the American people after the tragedy on September 11th, 2001. There are elements of both countries of which I am proud.

Back in Canada, make that Québec, we loaded up a U-Haul again and moved from the Tower of Cranky Old Farts in Laval to a friendly apartment complex in Pointe Claire on what is referred to as the West Island. It's not actually a separate island. Montréal is an island, and Pointe Claire is on the west end.

At home, I became convinced that I had gotten it right. We *both* had. This wasn't just another in my long line of mistaken loves. I loved Martica more with each passing day. We had been married for eighteen months, and neither of us had raised our voices to the other. There was never a moment or a day of moody silence.

We were deeply in love, but financially, we were deeply in trouble. Martica had a tough time finding work until she landed a huge graphic design contract for a team of doctors and pharmacists in the U.S. I was hired for small jobs by regular U.S. clients but none from Canada. Overnight, Martica's big new client went broke, owing her thousands of dollars. For months, we scraped nickels, dimes, and quarters together simply to buy groceries. We went through a financially tough couple of years.

A happy event occurred when Citizenship and Immigration Canada approved Natalia's application to become a Canadian Permanent Resident. It was a joyful day to see mother and daughter meet again, this time in Canada. A part of me felt envious. Martica had a large, close-knit family, including aunts, uncles, and cousins all over the world whom she loved and who loved her.

For my side, it angered me that I was in my sixties and still didn't know if I was Scottish, Italian, Jewish, or Vulcan. I thought that if I could only see my father for sixty seconds, I'd kick his ass, and if I could talk to the woman who had brought me into this world, I would give her hell, not for simply abandoning me but for never giving anyone a clue that I existed.

At times, when I was alone, I shouted at her, "Why did you dump me without a trace?"

Did she ever wonder what became of me? Did she know?

In February of 2003, Martica and I were unpacking after our move to Pointe Claire. I opened a box that had been sealed since our move from Traverse City a year earlier. Among file folders and other bric-a-brac, I found my old Franklin Planner. I hadn't used it for several years. Because it was an expensive leather-bound planner and money was tight, I thought that I might try to sell it on e-Bay. As I cleaned it out, I came across a tiny scrap of paper on which appeared a hand-written name and a phone number. The name was Georgina Muise. For a moment, I couldn't place the name. Then it came to me.

Four years earlier in 1999, when Tena, the only mom I had ever known, died, a lady had approached me at the luncheon following the funeral and handed me a note.

"Hello, Stanley, do you remember Georgina McClusky?"

"Yes, of course I remember Georgina," I said.

Georgina was the daughter of my mom's best friend, Margaret McClusky. When Mom and Pop were having another one of their fights, my mom spent a few days or even weeks with Margaret and took me along. Georgina and I played together, even though she was a few years younger than I was. I had not seen her in over thirty-five years.

"Georgina wants you to give her a call. She lives in Dartmouth, Nova Scotia," the lady said, as she handed me the note with Georgina's name and phone number on it.

"Thank you. I'll definitely call her when I get back to Michigan."

Back in Michigan, a few days later, I called the number written next to Georgina's name. It rang and continued to ring with no answer. There was no answering machine or voice mail. A few days later, I tried again with the same result. I assumed that it might be a wrong number. I slipped the paper into my leather Franklin Planner. Not long afterward, I decided that leather-bound paper planners were of no use anymore, so I stored the planner in a box in the basement and forgot about it, until Martica and I were unpacking in February 2003. There, inside a pocket in the Franklin-Planner, was that mysterious slip of paper again with a phone number and the name *Georgina* on it.

I stared at the number for a few minutes. After all, it had been four years. I told Martica how I had tried to call this old friend, but there was never an answer.

"Why don't you try it one more time before you throw the note away?"

"If it didn't work then, why would it work now?" I asked, more or less questioning myself.

"You never know, mi amor."

"Okay, I'll give it a try."

It rang three times. A woman answered. I had no idea that she would open a door with shocking surprises.

The Letter

"**O**h, my God! Stanley Campbell!"

"Georgina! It's been how many years?'

"Too many. Stanley, tell me, where are you, how are you, what are you doing?"

Georgina sounded as I remembered her when she was 16. We exchanged life stories for almost two hours and then agreed to talk again soon. Georgina had been almost like family. My Mom considered her family, especially Georgina's grandmother, Catherine McClusky, and later, Catherine's daughter, Margaret. Catherine's house was her place of refuge in troubled times, and I was in tow with her when Mom sought shelter from the storm at home.

Georgina and I talked at length almost every week. Eventually, the conversation came around to my origin. We spent hours guessing who my mother might be. I had always assumed that Cecelia McNeil was someone close to home in Iona parish. I complained to Georgina about the near misses and countless dead ends that I had encountered over the years. I felt so damn frustrated. The dead end searches angered me. I became irritated all over again as I talked about it.

"Wait a minute," Georgina said, pausing. "I know someone at the Nova Scotia Adoption Registry."

"Yeah, I've talked to people there before several times, but they keep telling me that they can't release any identifying information."

"Well, the laws have changed over the past few years."

"Not that much."

"I know a lady there. Do you mind if I call her?"

"Sure, whatever you think." I was sure that it would be another waste of time.

"Okay, I'll call you back."

I had talked to so many people who claimed that they had an inside scoop on the adoption process, but it always fizzled out. I had no positive expectations. Two minutes later, the phone rang.

"Stanley, call Irene at the Adoption Registry. I just spoke to her." Georgina commanded me with a degree of urgency, as if the information might vanish by dinner time.

She read out the phone number to me carefully.

"Stanley, call that number right now. She's waiting for your call."

"Thanks, Georgina, but do you really believe that she will have any new information?"

"Well, call her, anyway. It won't hurt to try."

"Okay, I'll call her." I tried to hide my cynicism.

I dialled the number and asked for Irene. Surprisingly, Irene answered the phone. I was further surprised that she had my name on file from previous searches. She couldn't promise anything but requested that I send all my personal information and any details that I might already know about my adoption, including my birth mother's name, my adoptive parents' names and address, and so on. *Here I go again.* I had done this so many times over the years, but I agreed to write it all out and send it...again.

Point Claire was a vast improvement over Laval, but I became increasingly incensed by Québec politics and the feeling of not belonging. Montréal did not turn out to be the place of my dreams. As a visiting Los Angeles radio personality years earlier, I had been corrupted by limos, five-star dining, and penthouse hotel suites.

In 2006, I convinced Martica to agree to move to Toronto. We wanted to be close but not in Toronto. We chose St. Catharines,

Ontario, an hour from Toronto on the Niagara peninsula. Besides, one of my best friends, a fellow radio broadcaster, Tim Denis, lived there. I had produced an album with Tim in 1984, the one where he sang a duet with Eilleen Twain.

Again, I must confess to my blind self-indulgence. I was improving but not completely cured. I wanted to be closer to the USA, Anglos, and my friends in Ontario, but in doing so, I took the woman I loved away from her daughter Natalia in Montréal. I guess I convinced myself that she wanted to move as much as I did. She didn't. She agreed because it was what I wanted.

We found a condo on the edge of Lake Ontario and made new friends and renewed some old friendships. In addition, we were closer to Michigan, a place that will always be in my heart, where I had treasured friends and where my former step-daughter Natalie lived.

I abhor using the title *step-daughter* but *ex-step-daughter* is even more distasteful, yet I could not refer to her as my daughter, even though we have grown closer over the years since her mom and I divorced. I sincerely thank Susan for our relationship. Unlike most ex-spouses, Susan chose to not drive a wedge between her daughter and me.

Two years passed. I forgot or maybe gave up on hearing from Irene at the Adoption Registry in Halifax. I had planned to go to Nova Scotia and spend a week searching and snooping around on my own when a letter arrived that floored me. It was detailed and shocking. I read it over and over, struggling to digest the story. The letter from Nova Scotia Community Services, dated August 9, 2005, read:

Your birth mother was born in 1911 and was living in Nova Scotia. She was of Scottish heritage and was unmarried. She was described as being 5 feet, 3 inches tall, weighing 124 pounds, with blue eyes and dark brown hair. She attended a country school to grade V.

Your birth mother's parents died when she was about 14 years of age. Apparently her father died of exhaustion and hunger at age 70 years. Her mother was said to be in an asylum at one time and said to be simple. Their home had been in a terrible state – windows out, holes in the floor, bed made of boughs, children ragged with few clothes. One child was said to have perished during the winter.

Your sister was born in 1939. My sister? A sister! I have a sister? *After her birth, your birth mother was at a loss to know what to do as she was without home or money. Your sister's birth father lived alone at the time and invited your birth mother to his house with the child. She kept house for him and his two little children, as his wife had left him. She became pregnant with you, apparently by the same individual. His religion was Protestant and he worked in a primary industry. Because her situation was deemed unsatisfactory by community people, your birth mother left and employed herself in domestic services, leaving the children with your birth father. With the effort of the Children's Aid Society, she then placed your sister with Little Flower Institute and you were brought to Mercy Hospital. Your birth mother signed consent for you to be placed for adoption. It appears that you were placed for adoption with the Campbell family in February of 1941. It was later reported that your birth mother's brother and his wife adopted your sister when she was approximately five years of age.*

At the time of your adoption, you were said to be a very attractive little boy, with big blue eyes and a fair complexion. You wore a little blue suit. The worker reported that when you first saw the car, you began to cry, afraid that they were going to take you away. You were afraid of cars and trains.

I trust that this is helpful.

Helpful? I'm not sure that *helpful* was the appropriate word. It was overwhelming! I had a sister! The more I learned, the more I needed to know. *Where is my sister? Is she alive? If so, where does she live? What is her name? Does she look like me? Does she have a family? Does she know that I exist? What about my mother Cecelia?* The anger that I had felt for so many years toward my birth mother swiftly evaporated. Instead, I felt sadness for her and her plight and especially furious with the so-called community people who had found her situation unsatisfactory.

Irene and her staff had uncovered amazing and heartbreaking information about my natural family. In short, they confirmed my mother's name, Cecelia Catherine MacNeil.

I had factual information to use to dig deeper, or was this it? I had speculated, guessed, and at times become angry that I had been adopted by people who apparently knew my origin and even taunted me with that knowledge but never divulged it. My adoptive mother Tena, whom I adored, became tense and angry when I pressed her for information, but she was never forthcoming. It was apparent that my past was something of which she felt ashamed and believed that I should never be permitted to find out my true origin. My father Roddie, after a few too many hooters, goaded me with *we know who your people are*, but when pressed, would not divulge any information.

I begged Irene for more information but ran into familiar brick walls. She assured me that she and her people were still digging, but so far, nothing else had turned up. A year went by. I called again. Still nothing.

Christmas of 2006 was only two weeks away. Martica and I were living blissfully in the Niagara area. We began our Christmas shopping. Financially, our lives were improving. Then, on December 11th, the gift of a lifetime arrived by telephone.

The Ugly One In The Middle

It was a wonderful Christmas at our new home in Niagara with Martica and my son Rod with his wife Jackie, my grandkids, Roddie, Kaylah, and Michael, and my son Michael, but I could hardly wait for Christmas to be over. I had received a shocking phone call two and half weeks earlier. As a result of that call, Martica and I were to return to Montréal on December 27, 2006, for what would likely be the most exciting and intimidating moment of my life. We weren't sure what to expect. Neither were the people in Montreal.

It was bitterly cold as we arrived at 5:00 p.m. in Pierrefonds, Québec, two miles from where we had lived in Pointe Claire. My heart galloped. I was nervous. Martica was anxious. We parked in front of a low-rise apartment building on Boulevard Gouin. Martica and I stepped out of the car and ran into the lobby to avoid the frigid air. I stood for a moment, hesitated, and then pressed the intercom button for apartment 303. We waited.

Click!

"Stan?" A woman spoke through the squawky intercom.

"That's me." I chuckled nervously.

"Come on up!"

The door lock buzzed. We entered the elevator and pressed button number three. It was the slowest elevator ride I had ever taken. When we reached the third floor, my heart raced as the doors opened. We exited and peered down the hallway to the left and then to the right. We strolled hand in hand toward apartment

303 where a lady stepped out into the hallway. She had blonde hair and a slight build, about five-foot-five.

"Come on! I'm down here," she shouted down the hall.

"We're coming," Martica and I said together.

I felt my eyes moisten and my throat dry up as we approached her. Martica squeezed my hand. I stopped and stood in front of her and gazed into her rather familiar face. She stared back at an equally familiar face, yet we had not met before.

"Hello, Sis!"

"Hello, Brother!"

We hugged.

My sister. Audrey. Audrey Jewer. I had trouble saying the word *sister*. After all, I had never in my 66 years uttered the phrase, *my sister*. Yet, there she was. There was no doubt. We looked alike.

I have to admit that I was more uncomfortable than she was. I was tongue-tied, but she made up for my lack of conversation. I soon learned that she liked to talk and enjoy a beer and a laugh. My sister. *I am Alex Stan Campbell, and I have a sister!*

After half an hour of chit-chat, Martica, Audrey, and I dressed for the freezing weather and hurried out to our car. It was a short drive, only four blocks, through a residential neighborhood to a house on Rue de Savoie. We pulled into the driveway. I noticed a man and a woman in the window. My heart raced again. Audrey rang the doorbell. I felt my knees wobble. The door swung open wide. Martica began to weep. So did the lady who answered the door. They both gazed at two men who looked remarkably like each other.

He spoke first. "Oh, my God, it's our father!"

Audrey agreed. "Yes, he does resemble him, doesn't he?"

He said, "Stan, welcome to our home. This is my wife, Gail."

It was a surreal moment as I stood next to my brother. He was apparently looking at the face of my father.

My brother, Ben.

He could have been my twin. The feeling was indescribable. As Ben and I walked and talked, Gail, Audrey and Martica noticed that our mannerisms were similar. We were the same height, had the same body shape with slightly high foreheads, the same nose, the same eyes, and the same laugh.

I had just met my sister Audrey and now my brother Ben. Not half siblings but sharing the same mother *and* father. Cecelia and Percy Jewer. The story of their lives was heartrending and scandalous at times. I acquired an insight into the traits that I had inherited. My father was a colorful character, and my mother went down a road that she had never intended. I also found out why my mother Tena seemed to know my origin but refused to discuss it.

This was a joyous occasion and the greatest Christmas gift, but the elation in our meeting was muted. The glad news was that I had found my sister and my brother, a near-twin and a genuinely nice guy but someone who had led a life quite different than mine. He had been married to the same wonderful woman, Gail, for forty-two years and raised four kids with whom he had a loving, close relationship. He was a hero dad. I was not.

I was still overcome from finding a full brother and sister after all these years. What was most astonishing was that they lived less than two miles away from where Martica and I had lived in Pointe Claire only one year earlier. We might have crossed paths on the street or at the mall. Ben, Audrey, and our parents Cecelia and Percy had lived in Montréal almost all of their lives. There was another surprise. I had a half-brother and three half-sisters from my father's first marriage, Gordon, Beulah, Irene, and Dorothy.

After fifty years of searching, beginning at age 16 until age 66, I had finally found out who my real parents were. Ben and Audrey shared story after story of their upbringing in the rough St. Laurent neighborhood of suburban Montréal. My mother and father, Cecelia and Percy, were poor. Percy was a binge drinker and a scrapper, which was almost amusing considering his diminutive size, five-foot-four. My mother Cecelia was more often than not the breadwinner for the family. They fought a lot, but they loved each other.

Percy Jewer had been a coal miner in New Waterford, Nova Scotia. He was separated from his wife, Jesse, and for some reason, he had custody of their children. It didn't take long for him to meet the attractive but poor Cecelia MacNeil. She was essentially homeless but dreamed of becoming a nun. Percy was a smooth talker and a snappy dresser. He had a way with women. He invited destitute Cecelia to live with him to act as a live-in nanny.

The inevitable didn't take long. My sister Audrey was born in 1939. Gossip spread around New Waterford. A poor Catholic girl was living with a married Protestant man, and then a child was born out of wedlock. A year later, the situation escalated. I came along. That was it! The community would not tolerate such a wicked, sinful relationship.

With the help of the Catholic Church, Cecelia was forced out of Percy's home with two babies. She became destitute again and truly homeless. Her only option was to immediately offer the two babies for adoption. Audrey was placed in the Little Flower Institute. I was taken to Mercy Hospital, where I became ill with a temperature of 104.

Audrey was not at the Little Flower Institute for long. Cecelia's brother Benny and his wife took her in with the intention of adopting her. I was left with the nuns at Mercy Hospital with the hope that I would be adopted by a nice family.

In the meantime, Percy and Cecelia plotted a reunion. She had been treated as a pariah and common whore by the community and the church. My adoptive mother Tena had grown up nearby and apparently knew of Cecelia's scandalous reputation, which is why she refused to tell me anything about my origin.

In another example of the church's despicable influence, Cecelia was compelled to undergo a venereal disease test, but when the test was proven negative, she was sent to work cleaning hospital wards.

It didn't take long for Cecelia and Percy to get out of town. They packed up and moved three hundred miles away to much larger Halifax, far away from the gossip and judgmental people of New Waterford.

In 1941, my brother, Ben was born in Halifax. And coincidentally in 1941, I went to live with Roddie and Tena Campbell in Jamesville West, in Iona Parish as part of a deal with the parish priest, Father Rankin. It was a test run. I was officially adopted a year later. I was not to know of my brother and sister for another 64 years.

Percy and Cecelia moved to Montreal in 1950. Even after Percy and Cecelia had been living together for ten years, his estranged wife, Jesse, refused to consent to a divorce. When Jesse died in 1960, there was a subdued celebration. Percy and Cecelia were married immediately afterward. Ten years later they died within months of each other.

Martica and I visited their graves three years ago. I cleared the weeds and grass away from their grave markers and read the names, *Percy Jewer* and *Cecelia Jewer*. I was not moved as much as I was intrigued. I imagined the romance and the struggles that they must have had when they met and the three children they created, yet one child was a secret. Neither Ben nor Audrey could remember either of our parents mentioning another child. Given the fact that my father Percy was prone to inebriation, it's surprising that he didn't let the secret slip out.

There are countless stories of locating a sibling or several brothers and sisters only to be spurned by them. At first, Ben was not open to meeting me when he was told of my existence. He assumed that it was a scam, until he saw my picture. He e-mailed it to his four kids with a simple note, *who is this*?

The responses were predictable. *What do you mean, Dad? It's you.*

Ben answered, *No, it's your Uncle Stan.*

Who? You're joking right? We don't have an Uncle Stan!

You do now!

For the next fifteen months, Ben and I spoke often on the phone, e-mailed each other, and I visited him several times in Montréal. We shared stories of our lives. I also visited Audrey, and we shared different stories and had a beer or two together, but Ben was so much like me that it was like watching myself. His wife, Gail, surmised that the birthdates had gotten messed up and thought that maybe we were twins. We did have our differences. Politics and religion. We debated but never argued. Life was too short for that...much too short. Ben died on March 23, 2008, of kidney cancer.

Martica and I drove to Montréal for my brother Ben one last time. If there was anything remotely funny, it was at the viewing. Most of his huge circle of friends, colleagues, and distant family did not know of my existence. As Martica and I walked into the funeral home, I seriously spooked several of his friends. For a moment, they thought that they had seen Ben's ghost!

I had only known my brother Ben for slightly over a year. Yet, I miss him. A few friends and family members have expressed how heartbreaking it was that I had just met my brother and then he died. I embrace a positive viewpoint. It was a miracle that I found him before he died.

Audrey put it candidly when she said, "I'm losing one brother and gaining another."

What a shame it would have been had I met my family after his passing, only to hear them say, *I wish that you had known Ben. He was such a great man with a wonderful sense of humor, and he looked just like you.*

Ben's sense of humor was evident even on the day he died, when he heard a musical chime ring in the hospital hallway, obviously paging a nurse.

He opened his eyes and said, "Avon calling!"

He could also hand out a zinger. One afternoon, several weeks before he died, Ben and I were engaged in one of our long phone conversations. The subject got around to the most talked about issues in our lives, his upbringing, our parents, and how my existence could have been kept so hush-hush. Yet, there we were, so many years later, after five decades of searching. I had finally found out who my parents were and found an incredibly magnificent bonus in a brother and a sister and a new family of nieces and nephews and cousins. I had asked Ben the same question several times, yet aware that neither of us had the answer. One day, just weeks before he died, Ben offered a different response.

I said, "Ben, there is one thing I'll never understand. You are a year younger than me, Audrey is a year older, yet I was put up for adoption. I was the one in the middle. Why *me*?"

Ben didn't miss a beat. "Because you were the ugly one"

We both laughed.

THE END
(not really)

EPILOGUE

Dire predictions preceded the new millennium. For me, miracles began to happen, miracles that I felt I did not deserve, given the careless, immoral, self-absorbed life that I had led.

My mother, Tena, the only mother I had known and loved, died in 1999. Not long after her passing, positive changes began to occur in my life. I sometimes imagine that in her new world, she pulled some strings and influenced my life. After all, she was about as saintly a woman as I had ever known.

First, I quit abusing alcohol forever. Okay, I didn't just quit. I lost the *desire* to get drunk or derive a buzz. Unlike most alcoholics, I don't fight a yearning to drink. Now, almost like astral traveling, I stand outside myself and see the ugly person that I became when I drank. I don't like him. I can now enjoy a glass of wine or a beer on a hot summer day and yet not struggle with a desire to have another and another, as in the past.

Second, I spent a lifetime fantasizing about my perfect, enchanting woman. Even throughout my four marriages, I envisioned her as I lay next to my wife-of-the-decade. I pictured her, not overtly in a sexual way, but as a loving friend. Was I a hopeless romantic? Maybe. Throughout most of my life, I have been unquestionably a hapless romantic.

I found my angel on another continent. Martica and I have been married for twelve years, and unlike any previous marriage or relationship, our marriage grows stronger every day. I love her more every day. We have never had a fight. Really! Sure, we've had disagreements and arguments, but never a yelling, angry fight or moments or hours of not speaking. We have each found peace. I believe that our encounter was spirit-guided and influenced by my mother, Tena. After all, the positive changes in my life began immediately after Mom died.

Finally, after fifty years of searching, guessing, and frustration, I discovered the identity of my birth mother Cecelia and my natural father Percy. As a huge added bonus, I found a brother and a sister and an extended family of nieces, nephews, and cousins.

I have a warm relationship with my sister Audrey, even though she lives hundreds of miles away. We visit a few times a year and talk on the phone. I still have trouble saying *sister*, *brother*, and *niece* and *nephew*. When we call each other, I say *hey sis* and she says *hey bro*, and we chuckle happily at that appellation.

Martica and I have maintained a warm relationship with Ben's adorable wife, Gail. I don't think that she will ever get used to seeing me because I resemble her husband of those many years.

My life has been a mosaic of bad times, good times, and egregious self-indulgence to the detriment of my children and the unfortunate women to whom I made promises that I didn't keep.

Together, Martica and I have partially mended what was once a cold and sometimes non-existent relationship with my children, mostly caused by an ugly divorce from Barbara, where my kids were negatively influenced and used as pawns in an endless war between my ex-wife and me. Sometimes ghosts from the past jump out and send us back to the days of the family cold war.

My oldest son Rod and his wife Jackie and kids, Kaylah and Michael, live in Huntsville, Ontario. Unfortunately, we don't speak often.

My second oldest son, Mark, and his partner, Kim, live and work in Newmarket, a suburb of Toronto. When we do speak, Mark and I enjoy long conversations and share stories from his childhood. He always ends a phone conversation with, *I love you Dad.* That means the world to me.

My youngest son, Michael, lives and works in Dubai. He has been there for five years and has been dating an attractive and bright lady, Sagari, for the past five years. I miss him. We have a superb relationship, which feels more like a close friendship.

My daughter Helen lives in Sydney, Nova Scotia. She is married to a great guy, Val MacDougall. They have three bright kids, Katie, Gregor, and Meggie. She owns her own business. Our relationship has gone from chilly to a renewed loving bond. I will always miss my *Chrissy*.

* * *

Sadly, it takes a tragedy to bring a family together. On October 16, 2007, I received the most shocking, horrible call of my life.

My son Rod's sobbing words still echo in my ears. "Dad, Roddie is dead!"

My heart stopped. My heart broke. It broke at the sound of my oldest son weeping. There is nothing more painful than hearing a man who is a tough Harley-ridin', truck-drivin', heavy-metal rocker weeping.

My handsome 16-year-old grandson Roddie was dead. He had lost control of his mom's car and ended up in a river in Huntsville, Ontario. He drowned with his dog, Russell. My three other children, Mark, Michael, and Helen came from across the country for the funeral and to support Rod and his wife Jackie and Kaylah and Michael. It was the first time that all of my kids had been together in fifteen years.

* * *

I am proud of my relationship with Susan's daughter, Natalie, and her husband and kids. I simply refer to her as my daughter, because it's too complicated to use any other title.

I enjoy a loving bond with Martica's daughter's Natalia and Penelope and their husbands, as I do with all of Martica's Ramirez family. I love them all, and I have never felt so loved.

* * *

As Martica and I celebrate our thirteenth year together in 2014, I often wonder why I deserve this angel by my side as my wife, best friend, lover, confidant, soul-mate, and eternal partner. She is *the one* who starred in my dreams and fantasies all those years. We remain completely in love and hope that God will allow us to spend an eternity together.

Finally, I found out who I am. I'm still not sure *why* I am here, but I am The *Ugly One in the Middle.*

ADDENDUM

(Because inquiring minds may want to know more.)

Eilleen Twain – She is known publically now as Shania Twain. In her autobiography, *From This Moment On*, she does not mention the association she had with me from ages 14 to 19 or her first recording session in Nashville with me in 1984. In her autobiography, she refers to a *Henry* character (which she says is not his real name), whom she claims made sexual advances toward her. Some friends and former associates speculated that the *Henry* character was me because he was a manager or producer, and the event occurred around the time that I worked with her. I was notorious for my philandering ways, but I never flirted with or made advances toward Eilleen, a claim that I feel confident that she would confirm. Frequent efforts to contact her for this book resulted in no response.

Kay Birdsong – While writing this book, I searched for Kay, my former roommate in Nashville. She always held a special place in my heart as a dear friend. After several years of searching, I found her...in a cemetery in her home town in Kentucky. She died of breast cancer at age 42. God bless my dear friend Kay.

Singles With Scruples – Since 2001 this dating website has changed, disappeared, was reborn, and as of this writing, is not the site that it was 2001.

Tato – In April 2007, Tato collapsed and died at his home at age 86, as he was preparing to go to his office. I have rarely known a man as beloved by his family and friends.

Bertha – Martica's mom became ill in early May of 2013. She passed away on May 27, 2013. She and I grew close over the years, since she first intimidated me in 2001.

A few other people from my book deserve a mention. **Howard** was my best friend growing in Cape Breton. We both moved to Ontario, but when I relocated to the USA in 1984, I lost touch with him. He had moved and so did I. My friend Georgina not only helped me find my family but my old friend Howard. Sadly, when I found him, he had contracted lung cancer. Even after a doctor told him that he had two months to live, he beat it and lived for another five years before it took him in 2010. I miss my zany friend.

Georgina lives in Dartmouth, Nova Scotia, with her husband Clarence. We speak regularly. She is more like a sister than a family friend.

Deanna, my first wife, lives near Halifax, Nova Scotia, and spends her winters in Florida. We speak occasionally and are generally on good terms. Her second husband, Ed passed away several years ago.

Barbara, my second wife, is re-married and living in Sydney, Nova Scotia. We never speak. Never.

Veronica, my third ex-wife, lives in Las Vegas. We rarely communicate.

Susan, my fourth former wife lives in Petoskey, Michigan, near her daughter Natalie. We speak occasionally and are on good terms. I regard her very highly for her unwillingness to create a gulf between Natalie and me.

Dixie Lee (not her real name) was the only other woman with whom I had a live-in relationship. To the best of my knowledge, she spent some time in prison. I have not been able to contact her.

Allison, the sheriff's wife, who witnessed my near-death alcohol event, is re-married and living in Northern Michigan.

Oh, and two more people. **Martica** and **Me**. We own a voiceover and radio production recording studio in Niagara Falls, Canada. I am a professional voice actor providing services for clients throughout the world, and I also host a syndicated radio show. Martica is a graphic designer and a professional Spanish voice talent with clients in New York, L.A., Buenos Aires, and Bern, among other centers.

Photographs of the characters in this book can be viewed on the book website at: www.theuglyoneinthemiddle.com

CPSIA information can be obtained at www.ICGtesting.com
Printed in the USA
LVOW06s1954181015

458697LV00002B/58/P